750
30

Explore
The Word!

Henry M. Morris, III

D0684041

CLP

**CREATION·LIFE
PUBLISHERS**

San Diego, California

EXPLORE THE WORD!
Copyright © 1978
CREATION-LIFE PUBLISHERS, INC.
P. O. Box 15666
San Diego, California 92115

Library of Congress Catalog Card
  Number 78-55611
ISBN 0-89051-047-4

Library of Congress Cataloging in Publication Data
Morris, Henry Madison, 1942-
  Explore the word.
  1. Bible—Study. I. Title.
BS600.M76   220.07   78-55611
ISBN 0-89051-047-4

Printed in United States of America

Printed by
El Camino Press
La Verne, California

PREFACE

No one writes a book without help. This book has been given input from many people over its two-year incubation period, and it would be impossible to give credit to them all. However, permit me to recognize a few.

The first real encouragement to start working on the book came while teaching Christian laymen how to use the Strong's Concordance in the home of Andy and Shirley Anderson. Cecil King, a member of that group insisted that I put the essence of that study course in outline form. Gene Ocetnik, a good friend and hard worker in the Sunday School class I teach, consistently disagreed with me when I was sure that no one would care to read such a book.

Then there was the encouraging response from a volunteer "Pastor's Class" at Christian Heritage College. Those young men and several interested young ladies wanted to learn how to research the Scriptures—so much so that they gave up prime time to meet with me for an entire school year. Later on, some people at Scott Memorial Baptist Church, the parent organization of the college, requested that I give a series on study methods on Wednesday evenings. The response to that was exciting! Many families began to develop their own personal study habits and became more concerned for accuracy in their doctrine.

Christian Heritage College formally asked me to prepare a regular three-unit course for our Bible majors for the Fall of 1977. So, I researched the libraries and course offerings of many colleges and seminaries but was unable to find anything that presented an adequate mechanic for Bible research. There seemed to be no end to the books providing a system of Bible reading and a good quantity of excellent works on hermeneutics—the science of interpretation. But, I could find nothing that gave instruction on how to use a concordance to mine the Scriptures for their treasures. Having agreed to teach the course, I was obligated to write a text.

Over the years of my pastoral ministry, I had used the skills learned from my father, Dr. Henry Morris. From my earliest memories, I recall him researching the Scriptures hours on end and using a concordance. I thought everybody did that. But I was surprised to find few of God's people were aware of the existence of such a tool, let alone possessing the skill to use it. Fortunately, the man with whom the Lord allowed me to serve as co-pastor, Willard Ramsey, had been given a gift for careful analysis of the Scriptures which he painfully gave to me. It was the combination of these two lives that began to congeal as I started to write this book.

As the writing of this book progressed, I drew on my father's expertise as an author. He counseled, comforted, encouraged and motivated me during the intensive writing agonies. My precious wife, Jan, loved and babied me when I came home despondent over the various difficulties on the project and tenderly reminded me of reality when I began to dream of worldwide acceptance.

Charlotte Herzog put up with the original job of typing the manuscript and setting the camera-ready copy for a limited edition. Pat Ennis, Chairman of the Home Economics Department at Christian Heritage College, read through the manuscript, offering many valuable suggestions for structure and format.

Then, when the first edition was printed, I gave that text to the first students who were to take the new course in Biblical Research Methods. I received a chapter-by-chapter critique of the book, along with their evaluation of the skills taught. They were most honest! Many of their reactions were used to help structure the book more specifically and develop some more clarity in the difficult sections. Generally, the students were positive. So much so, in fact, that I was convinced that the book met a definite need.

I have not written the book to be a quick answer to Christian knowledge. There is no such answer. Nor have

I written the book to show some "easy" method of Bible study. There is no such method. I have, however, set down step-by-step procedures that can be used effectively to discover significant information from the Scriptures without dependence upon the commentaries of men. These procedures are such that the layman can use them to open up the Scripture far beyond the ordinary "norm." And the pastor will find his own ministry enriched and made more effective using these basic approaches to God's Word. It is my prayer that God will use this book in your life to bring a love for His Word, an increasing encouragement from your life to others, and great glory to His matchless Name.

ABOUT THE AUTHOR

Henry M. Morris, III

Dr. Henry M. Morris, III is Administrative Vice President of Christian Heritage College and Professor of Apologetics and Bible. Dr. Morris is a frequent and popular speaker in church services and Bible classes. He is rapidly becoming known for his down-to-earth messages on tape. He holds the M.Div. and D.Min. degrees from Luther Rice Seminary and the B.A. in Ministerial Training, Summa Cum Laude, from Christian Heritage College.

TABLE OF CONTENTS

Chapter   **Page**

The additional skill of researching the Scriptures by
means of the concordance listings is treated in detail.
The student is taken through each step in the
development of the same study passage outlined in
chapter nine. Careful attention is given to the basics
as well as the problems.

Each potential piece of information must be examined for its application to the study passage. This
chapter details the procedure and skills required to
insure accurate information gathering from the
pages of the Scriptures.

Since the skills involved in this step are more complex, this chapter provides an overview of the
remaining work to be done. The student is brought
through a review of the preceding work to an awareness of the final product.

This chapter begins the step-by-step organization of
all the data collected through the process described
in earlier chapters. The same Scripture study passage
is expanded on the worksheets that have been
developed thus far.

Further refining and organization is necessary
before a final outline of information can be made.
This chapter discusses the technique for relating the
various categories and their many sub-points.

A discussion of the concepts is undertaken in this
chapter before the working example is detailed. All

of the information is funneled into a working sentence outline from which the student is able to critique the knowledge gained, as well as use for whatever external opportunities are available.

This chapter gives a complete outline of the entire procedure for Biblical thought analysis. Each point is covered briefly so that the student can use this single chapter both as a review and as a teaching outline for others.

Conceptual study is more demanding and time consuming than passage analysis. This chapter discusses the overall approach to such studies. It follows the Biblical guidelines already amplified in this book and provides a good perspective with which to view the detailed study ahead.

This form of analysis, while similar to the skills already discussed, is more complex. It involves the research of all terms applicable to the study concept, an analysis of the Hebrew and Greek, and an understanding of the language parallels.

Worksheet development is the main thrust of this chapter. The student is shown how to research every potential verse relating to the teaching under study. The subject begun in chapter eighteen is kept and expanded through the remainder of the book.

Chapter

Attentive Bible Study

Every
word
of God
is pure...

Proverbs 30:5

1

IMPORTANCE OF PERSONAL BIBLE STUDY

The Bible contains over 250 passages in the Old Testament and about 55 in the New Testament that require us to be obedient to everything that the Lord has commanded. That much emphasis is surely not incidental. Therefore, it is well worth our while to try to understand precisely what the Lord expects us to do. Most sincere Christian men and women make an effort to study their Bibles, but it is usually difficult to find either the time or the direction to gain real depth from study. Almost every city offers a dozen or so Bible study groups, most of which are enjoyable to attend. Yet, it seems that these groups tend to share only what they "think" the Bible says, rather than making a serious effort to "know" what the Bible says. As a matter of fact, if one listens carefully, the words "I think. . ." occur fairly frequently in most of the discussion groups, Sunday school lessons, and sermons that we attend. Well. . .so what?

The best way to answer that question is to spot-check various sections of the Old and New Testaments which provide a perspective from which to view the more detailed applications of this dilemma. When Moses was delivering his last sermon, he told the children of Israel what kind of people the Lord wanted for service to Him. "Oh, that there were such an heart in them that they would fear me, and keep all my commandments always, that it might be well with them, and with their children forever!" (Deut. 5:29). That plea from God Himself desires a heart that would stand in awe of Him, that would keep every one of His commandments all of the time, so that God could bless that heart forever! Moses later reminded his hearers that the Lord had offered ". . . blessing and a curse: a blessing if ye obey the commandments of the Lord your God, which I command you this day: and a curse, if ye will not obey the commandments of the Lord your God, but turn aside out of the way which I command you this day, to go after other gods, which ye have not known" (Deut. 11:26-28). That instruction makes it clear that obedience is never optional; when we are determined to disobey, the Lord promises to produce the result of disobedience: a curse.

It is possible that some people may not feel much personal involvement with the Old Testament, since the bulk of it seems to have been written about a different kind of people and a different set of circumstances. Other people might feel that the "obedience" to which the Lord referred only applies to the "sacrifices" and "ordinances," though the Lord did tell us by His prophet Samuel that He would prefer obedience over "burnt offerings and sacrifices" (I Sam. 17:22). Even so, it does seem like the Old Testament is "old" and stern. After all, is not this the "age of Grace"? Certainly! And, since it is, we must know what emphasis the New Testament gives regarding the validity and significance of the Old Testament.

During the early part of the Lord's Galilean ministry, a woman who had observed some of His miracles and

4

heard His marvelous teaching, was moved to shout out loud, "Blessed is the womb that bore thee, and the paps which thou has sucked." She was no doubt thinking what a wonderful blessing it was for Mary to be chosen to have such a close part in the incarnation of God in the flesh and was praising God for what He had done. However, the Lord Jesus knew that men could be easily sidetracked to "personages" or "ministries" if they were unusually dynamic or magnificent, so He said, "Yea, rather, blessed are they that hear the Word of God, and keep it" (Luke 11:27-28).

Later, during His last passover observance, the Lord took the disciples aside privately to encourage them to practice and preach what He had taught them. During those quiet hours with His inner circle of key men, the Lord told them, "If ye love me, keep my commandments" (John 14:15). For all practical purposes, this is the same appeal made to the children of Israel in Deuteronomy 5:29. The Lord is not "softening" His appeal in this "age of Grace," but He is making it very clear that to "love" Him is to obey Him. "He that hath my commandments, and keepeth them, he it is that loveth me" (John 14:21).

Much later, the Apostle John, who had heard these words directly, wrote letters to those churches that were under his ministry, recalling the emphasis that the Lord had made that night at the Last Supper. In one letter, he set down a very clear definition of love: "For this is the love of God, that we keep his commandments: and his commandments are not grievous" (I John 5:3).

This definition puts a real limit on the way that we are to "love" God. The word "love" seems to give the impression that we should "feel" something, that we should be emotionally motivated or stirred. Yet the emphasis in this verse is an active, joyful obedience to the written Word of God. As a matter of fact, the Scripture stresses again and again that we should be obedient to *every* word! Deuteronomy 4:2 demands that we not change the words one bit!

Ye shall not add unto the word that I command
you, neither shall ye diminish ought from it, that
ye may keep the commandments of the Lord your
God which I command you.

The Lord told Joshua that he was required to study and
reflect on the Scriptures constantly.

This book of the law shall not depart out of thy
mouth; but thou shalt meditate therein day and
night, that thou mayest observe to do according
to all that is written therein: for then thou shalt
make thy way prosperous, and then thou shalt
have good success (Joshua 1:8).

Later, the Lord revealed to the prophet Isaiah the magnificent nature of His Being and the importance of His
judgment. God clearly stated that each person must listen
carefully to the words He had revealed, since no man is
capable of thinking as God thinks.

For as the heavens are higher than the earth, so
are my ways higher than your ways, and my
thoughts than your thoughts. For as the rain com-
eth down, and the snow from heaven, and return-
eth not thither, but watereth the earth and maketh
it bring forth and bud, that it may give seed to the
sower, and bread to the eater; so shall my word be
that goeth forth out of my mouth: it shall not
return unto me void, but it shall accomplish that
which I please, and it shall prosper in the thing
whereunto I sent it (Isaiah 55:9-11).

In the "hymnbook" of the Old Testament, the Psalms,
David noted that his praise to the Lord had a basic root
in the magnificence of God's Word.

I will worship toward thy holy temple, and
praise thy name for thy lovingkindness and for
thy truth: for thou has magnified thy word above
all thy name (Psalm 138:2).

Psalm 119, one of the most majestic poems in all literature, uses nearly every one of its 176 verses to teach the
necessity of obedience to and love for the words of God:

Blessed are the undefiled in the way, who walk in

the law of the Lord. Blessed are they that keep his testimonies, and that seek him with the whole heart (vs. 1-2).

Wherewithal shall a young man cleanse his way? by taking heed thereto according to thy word. With my whole heart have I sought thee; O let me not wander from thy commandments. Thy word have I hid in my heart, that I might not sin against thee (vs. 9-11).

On and on, section after section, book after book, the Lord makes sure that we get the message: My word is important, treat every word as absolutely true. "Every word of God is pure: he is a shield unto them that put their trust in him. Add thou not unto his words lest he reprove thee, and thou be found a liar" (Proverbs 30:5-6).

Most Christians "believe" that the Bible is God's Word and have great respect for what it says. But few Christians really know how much emphasis is given to the absolute authority that has been placed by the Lord in the words of Scripture. An exposure to these teachings in the New Testament will be profitable, especially since it expands and applies the Old Testament directly to us.

One of the more familiar sections of the ministry of the Lord Jesus is His encounter with Satan in the wilderness of Judaea following the Lord's baptism by John the Baptist (Matthew 4:1-11). At that time, Satan tried to gain control over the authority that Jesus had by "tempting" the Lord to perform special feats or use different methods to position Himself as the King. Our Lord was quick to respond to the clever arguments of Satan in a way that has set the pattern for us: each time Jesus was approached with "temptation," He countered and resisted successfully by quoting directly from the Scriptures.

Jesus had been out in the desert for forty days. During that time He was "fasting" and had become quite hungry! Christ's body required food to keep going, and the Devil knew it. So he said, "If you are really the Son of God, then use your godly power to turn these rocks into bread." Well, why not? Jesus was there for good purpose; He had the power to do it; no one was around to know if He used His power for Himself. Why could He not do it? Because, He was not in the world to promote Himself. He had not been given any instructions by the Father to use His godly ability to satisfy His human needs. He had been instructed to "seek and to save that which is lost" and to speak only those things that the Heavenly Father had told Him to say (John 12:49). So, the Lord responded to Satan by quoting from Scripture: "Man shall not live by bread alone, but by every word that proceedeth out of the mouth of God."

That "memory verse" was quoted from Deuteronomy 8:3. Deuteronomy is the last book of the five books written by Moses and is a long sermon delivered by Moses to the children of Israel prior to their move into the promised land. In the passage quoted by the Lord, Moses is reminding God's chosen people how they had been tested by the Lord "to know what was in thine heart, whether thou wouldest keep his commandments, or not. And he humbled thee, and suffered thee to hunger, and fed thee with manna, which thou knewest not, neither did thy fathers know; *that* he might make thee know that man doth not live by bread only, but by every word that proceedeth out of the mouth of the Lord doth man live." In other words, God sometimes tests us to see if we are willing to be obedient to what He has told us to do, in spite of the "needs" of our situation.

The Lord Jesus undoubtedly remembered why the Children of Israel needed to be reminded of the necessity of being obedient to *every* word that God had given to them. Those ornery people had fussed at the Lord for bringing them out of slavery, they had complained about the lack of comfort, and they had circulated a petition to demand "their rights." All of that was done in spite of having just seen the marvelous power of God during the ten terrible plagues of Egypt, walking through the

8

Red Sea, and watching water flow from solid rock! In spite of their complaining, God told them that He would provide food for them each day, in the form of "what is it?". . .the "manna"of God. However, each person was to gather only enough for himself. If they took too much, the "what is it?" would rot and produce worms.

Needless to say, some of the people refused to believe "every word" of God, and picked up a little extra manna for emergency purposes. Perhaps they reasoned that they might have some friends drop in unexpectedly, and God would not want them turned away without some refreshments. However, God had said not to take *any* more than was necessary for one day's ration for each person in the household, and God meant *every* word. Those who did not believe *every* word of God's message, disobeyed and gathered more than they needed. The manna rotted, stank, and produced worms—just as God said it would, and the disobedient went hungry unnecessarily.

All of this information has been given to emphasize the significance of the Lord's answer to Satan. Satan tried to get the Lord to give in to His human nature, in spite of the fact that the Heavenly Father had given Him the responsibility of being the perfect man. Satan wanted Jesus to be "human." God had commanded Jesus to be perfect. The Lord rebuked Satan's wily effort by reminding him that it was necessary to obey "every word." As Satan continued to "test" Christ, the Lord consistently resisted by quoting from the Scriptures, each time emphasizing that the Word of God was the source of His actions—not His situation or feelings.

The Lord later amplified this principle to His disciples:
". . .blessed are they that hear the Word of God and keep it" (Luke 11:28).
". . .if a man love me, he will keep my words" (John 14:23).
". . .the Scripture cannot be broken" (John 10:35).
". . .till heaven and earth pass, one jot or one

9

tittle shall in no wise pass from the law, till all be fulfilled'' (Matthew 5:18).

''. . .teaching them to observe all things whatsoever I commanded you'' (Matthew 28:20).

''Whosoever therefore shall break one of these least commandments, and shall teach men so, he shall be called the least in the kingdom of heaven'' (Matthew 5:19).

The Lord Jesus Christ put too much stock in each word of the Scriptures for Him to tolerate the breaking of even the ''least'' commandment. In fact, He used the Scriptures so precisely that it makes our pitiful efforts look very meager, indeed. On one occasion the Lord ''proved'' the spiritual nature of His kingdom by the use of two words found in Psalm 110:1. The Pharisees were always trying to ruin the ministry of the Lord, and frequently said that Jesus could not prove that he was truly a son of David. Rather than going through a lengthy court battle to prove His parental heritage, the Lord simply cut through to the heart of the matter and proved His diety.

He saith unto them, How then doth David in spirit call him Lord, saying 'The Lord said unto my Lord, Sit thou on my right hand, till I make thine enemies thy footstool?' If David then call him Lord, how is he his son?'' (Matthew 22:43-45).

The ''proof'' is through the modifiers ''the'' and ''my'' and by the fact that ''Lord'' is the object in both cases. Evidently every word is absolutely accurate and important.

Not only are the words important, but in an earlier instance the Lord verified the resurrection by the tense of one word. In this case the Sadducees were questioning that doctrine with a rather ridiculous hypothetical case of a woman who had been married to seven different husbands. These Sadducees gleefully asked who of the seven would be able to have the woman ''in the resurrection.''

Jesus answered and said unto them, Ye do err, not knowing the scriptures [please note where the Lord *gains His answers]* nor the power of God. For in the resurrection they neither marry, nor are given in marriage, but are as the angels of God in heaven. But as touching the resurrection of the dead, have ye not read that which was spoken unto you by God, saying *I am* the God of Abraham, and the God of Isaac, and the God of Jacob? God *is* not the God of the dead, but of the living (Matthew 22:29-32).

Note what the Lord is doing. The Sadducees asked Him a question to throw scorn on the doctrine of the resurrection which they did not believe. Jesus again cut through the sham and pointed out that they were wrong, "not knowing the Scriptures," and were overlooking the very obvious fact that God had told them that He "is" the God of the Patriarchs. That present tense verb, used twice, was the "proof" of the resurrection!

Perhaps a summary of thought is in order. Both the Old Testament and the Lord Jesus Himself insist on a very accurate examination of the words of the Scripture. However, since the Old Testament seems to be mostly given over to "laws" and "ordinances" which are difficult to understand in light of our twentieth-century environment, a lot of Bible study is done outside the Old Testament. The unfortunate result of that neglect is an indifferent attitude to the sober tone set in the Old Testament. Very few Christians approach the Scriptures with the reverence, awe, and care insisted upon by the Old Testament.

The writer to the Hebrews was forced to interrupt his discussion of that great Old Testament character, Melchisedek, because he knew that his readers were not able to understand the difficult applications of the teaching. "Ye ought to be teachers," he said, "but ye have need that one teach you again which be the first principles of the oracles of God; and are become such as have need of milk, and not of strong meat" (Hebrews 5:12). What an indictment! These Christians had evidently been saved long enough to have learned a good amount of the Scriptures, but were still mulling around in the "first principles." They had done little study, and had not used the Scripture to their own profit. "For every one that uses milk is unskillful in the word of righteousness: for he is a babe. But strong meat belongeth to them that are of full age, even those who by reason of use have their senses exercised to discern both good and evil" (Hebrews 5:12, 14). In other words, if all we learn about the Bible is what we manage to gain by listening to our pastor, Sunday school teacher, and various friends, we are "unskillful in the word of righteousness" and still "babes." The "strong meat" of the Scripture—the real nourishing food of the Holy Spirit—the spiritual energy that will enable us to grow up, comes through the "use" of the Word which will, in turn, "exercise" our senses so that we will be able to "discern both good and evil."

"But. . .but, I can't study that deeply! You have to know Greek and Hebrew, and theology, and...." That excuse has been used in one form or another almost every time solid Bible study is considered. Somehow, the impression has been made that only a "professional" minister is able to search out the "whole counsel of God," and that the "laymen" are only able to listen to what "they" preach, reading what "they" write, and rehashing what "they" have taught in various study groups, conferences, and schools.

It is easy to demonstrate that every student will remember something less than what he hears. If only "facts" are taught, then the ultimate result will be ignorance. If each generation only "hears" what someone else knows, then each generation will retain less than the generation that taught it. Obviously, that is not the case in the sciences. Each generation has become more knowledgeable than its predecessor. Well, why? The student is taught *method*. He is taught how to *research*. Each student is given the tools to *find,* to *originate,* to *develop* "facts." Therefore, each generation may begin by standing on the shoulders of their teachers—and may well surpass them in knowledge. In fact, that is exactly how the knowledge of our physical world has been expanded.

But there seems to be a deterioration of knowledge in the religious world. Fewer and fewer "scholars" have surfaced. The books that make the best seller lists are usually surface material, and often deal with the problems of carnal Christians or stimulate the imaginations on some "sensational" subject. When the average church member is asked to give a Scriptural defense of the doctrines of his church, many are unable to do so. Contrast today's situation with 100 years ago, 250 years ago, or 500 years ago, and a real difference is apparent. John Christian, in his marvelous book, *A History of the Baptists,* records this interesting fact about the Waldensian churches of the early fifteenth century:

In the time of the persecution of the Waldenses of Merindol and Provence, a certain monk was deputed by the Bishop of Cavaillon to hold a conference with them, that they might be convinced of their errors, and the effusion of blood prevented. But the monk returned in confusion, owning that in his whole life he had never known so much Scripture as he had learned in these few days that he had been conversing with the heretics. The Bishop, however, sent among them a number of doctors, young men, who had lately come from the Sorbonne, which, at that time, was the very center of theological subtlety at Paris. One of these publicly avowed that he had understood more of the doctrine of salvation from the answers of the little children in their catechisms than by all the disputations which he had ever heard (Veccembecius, Oratio de Waldensibus et Elbigensibus Christianis, 4).

Men are not born with knowledge. Before a little child can answer questions about deeper doctrines and concepts, that child has to be taught so that he remembers what he was taught. This was mostly done through the gifted men of the ministry in these early churches. However, the responsibility of teaching rested upon all of the believers since each person was responsible for the follow-up teaching of his or her convert. This made the church an efficient resource for moral impact when problems came up in and out of the assembly. G. H. Orchard, in *A Concise History of Baptists,* notes that even the worst of their enemies would admit that "They were very zealous, that they [men and women] never cease from teaching night and day." Orchard also quoted one man when asked to recount his experiences with the "heretics" who said,"They had the Old and New Testaments in the vulgar tongue; and they teach and learn so well, that I have seen and heard a country clown recount all Job, word for word; and divers, who could perfectly deliver all the New Testament; and that men and women, little and great, day and night, cease not to learn and teach."

Contrast that picture with what can easily be seen today. Serious Christian men and women in every part of the country are concerned about the condition of the churches. No doubt there has been such concern in each generation, but for at least the last fifty years there has been a worrisome condition which seems to express itself in preaching that is light and sentimental, with an effort made to be funny and "dramatize" the message. Quite frequently, sermons lack real doctrinal and expository content and are often developed around isolated texts used simply as a starting point from which to "preach" personal views. There seems to be an indifference—even a blissful ignorance among the members that feeds on a failure to teach individual responsibility to study and interpret the Scriptures. Many churches are using emotional or "dynamic" methods to motivate the service of their members, rather than encouraging them and teaching their hearts that the "love of Christ constraineth me." There is an emphasis on "fun" for many of our church activities, which may well be a reason for the failure to regard the Scripture as the authority for church practices and doctrine and for the unwillingness to put traditional views and practices to a Scriptural test. The sum total of these problems is a confusing and contradictory picture of the Lord's church.

It is no wonder that thousands of Christians are wandering from church to church, or from denomination to denomination for some stability. The rise of the Charismatic movement that sweeps across all "doctrinal" lines is due mainly to the peace and harmony that is experienced by the members of those groups. No wonder the "Bible study" groups are exploding all over this country. Christian people—God's people, hunger for the Word! When a teacher, or group, or book is found that provides some food, the Christian world "eats it up."

Well, what is the point? God's people need God's Word. They need it to grow, to live righteously, to find joy, to solve their problems, and to demonstrate unity to the world (John 17:21-23; I Corinthians 1:10; Ephesians 4:12-16). If all we do is listen to what is said by other people, read what is written by other people, and "think" with our friends about what the Bible "means," how are we ever going to know if we have heard, read, or thought wrongly? We must know enough about the Scriptures—or at least know enough about the technique to study the Scriptures, that we would be able to spot an incorrect doctrine or suspicious procedure where we hear it. Acts 17:11 records the praise that the Apostle Paul had for the Berean Christians because they did not simply "swallow" what he had to say, but "searched the Scriptures daily to see whether these things be so."

Are you aware that the Bible provides information on *how* to study? There is a wealth of specific information in the Scripture that tells us the procedures to use when we try to mine the wisdom it contains. Do you want to find out what it says? Read chapter two.

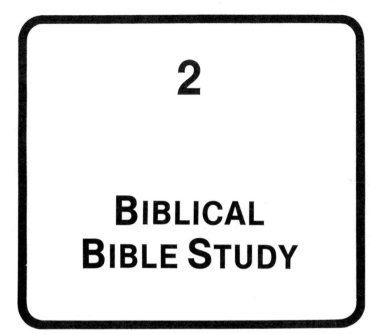

2

BIBLICAL
BIBLE STUDY

There seem to be only two ways to develop an understanding about something. One way is to begin with a general fact, and then try to find out why that fact is so by breaking the big fact down into smaller parts. That kind of reasoning is called *de*duction. The other way is to accumulate every fact possible about a general subject, and then let those facts dictate or shape the conclusions on that subject. That kind of reasoning is called, *in*duction.

Both methods are worthwhile. Sometimes, only one of the methods will work. But—and this is a big "but"—the *de*ductive method is terribly susceptible to human error and influence. It is very easy to say, "I know that such and such is true, now I'm going to find out why." When we assume "something" is so before we examine the data, it is very easy to ignore areas of data that may well conflict or disprove the "something." Or, more likely, we tend to "interpret" the data to fall in line with our "something" that we have already assumed is so.

The *in*ductive method is the basic method of all true science. That is the main reason why the sciences have developed so rapidly during the last two hundred years. The universities teach the *technique* of research to their students so that they will be able to discover more and more truth. The universe is not operating differently now since the great flood of Noah, so all a student has to do is collect the data available to him, correlate it, and arrive at the principles that help control and use the universe. That is *in*duction.

The same kind of thing is true for spiritual truth. The Bible contains all the truth that can be revealed to mankind (Deuteronomy 29:29). So, all we have to do is collect the data available, correlate it, and arrive at the principles that help us satisfy the requirements of God. That, also, is *in*duction. This is *especially* so in Bible study. If we start out with an assumed "truth," and then go to the Bible to "prove" it, it is entirely likely that we will miss a great deal of data that will affect the application of that "truth"—and may well contradict it.

As a matter of fact, induction is the only method of gaining knowledge openly supported by Scripture. Isaiah 28:9-10 expresses the method of study better than any single passage:

Whom shall he teach knowledge? and whom shall he make to understand doctrine? Them that are weaned from the milk and drawn from the breasts. For precept must be upon precept, precept upon precept; line upon line, line upon line; here a little, and there a little.

That passage contains a tremendous amount of information and requires careful examination. The Lord is looking for a certain kind of people, a type of people to whom He can "teach knowledge," and can "make to understand doctrine." Furthermore, these people must be mentally grown up. The Lord gives the specifications on who will receive teaching and doctrine by observing that those kinds of people must be "weaned from the

milk, and drawn from the breasts." That section in Hebrews, chapter five, which we looked at in the last chapter, clearly laments the same problem that Isaiah records.
"Why aren't people able to understand the knowledge
of the Scriptures?" The reason is that they are "become such as have need of milk, and not of strong
meat. For everyone that useth milk is unskillful in the
word of righteousness: for he is a babe." No wonder
the Lord is looking for the kind of people that do not
need milk anymore. Milk users are unskillful! They do
not know how to learn. Peter makes the comment in
his first epistle that we have to get rid of "all malice,
and all guile, and hypocrisies, and envies, and all evil
speakings, as newborn babes, desire the sincere milk of
the word, that ye may grow thereby" (I Peter 1:1-2). In
other words, we have to get our mind and mental attitude in shape—even before we can get enough *milk* of
the Word to grow up!

As a matter of fact, the Bible provides clear teaching
on just how we should approach the study of the Word
in that famous verse, II Timothy 2:15.

Study to shew thyself approved unto God, a workman that needeth not to be ashamed, rightly dividing the word of truth.

The word "study" in that verse is a very special word
that means "to use speed" or "to make an effort."
That word is frequently translated "labour" in the King
James Version because it has the idea of hard work. A
good example of how that idea is related to study is
found in Hebrews 4:11-12.

Let us *labour* therefore to enter into that rest, lest
any man fall after the same example of unbelief.
For the Word of God is quick and powerful, and
sharper than any two-edged sword, piercing even
to the dividing asunder of the soul and spirit, and
of the joints and marrow, and is a discerner of the
thoughts and intents of the heart.

We are to "study," to "work hard" to "shew" ourselves "approved" unto God. Again, those two words

are not incidental in the Scripture. "Shew is the word for "put, exhibit, recommend," or, in a more specific application, "be ready." The word translated "approved" is a word that means to be intellectually acceptable, or more precisely, "tested and found valuable." When we put all that together, we have a significant thought: "Work hard to put yourself on display to God, as having been tested and proven worthwhile, a workman that needeth not to be ashamed [disfigured or disgraced], rightly dividing the word of truth." "Rightly dividing" means to make a straight cut, or to dissect correctly. It comes from a combination of a word that means "honest" and a word that means "to cut by a clean, single stroke." In other twentieth-century words, we are to have the kind of mental attitude as we approach the Scriptures that is willing to work and display that work, having carefully examined each part of that work before we put it on display.

Before we go on, it is necessary to assume that we have graduated from the "babe" stage of our Christian life and have "nursed" enough on the "milk" of the Scriptures to understand basic principles. Remember, the Lord said in Isaiah 28:9-10 that He needed mature learners to whom He could teach knowledge and doctrine, *"For* precept must be upon precept. . .etc." The Lord is telling us that it is necessary to be above the "babe" stage simply because the "knowledge" and "doctrine" of the Scripture do not come easily. It requires enough spiritual and mental maturity to build a conclusion.

Look again at the words of Isaiah 28. "Whom shall he *teach knowledge?"* The word translated "teach" here is derived from another Hebrew word that means "to flow like water" and is very often translated "point out." It is even translated "shoot," as with a bow and arrow. The Lord has used a very special word here; a word that says, "I want to smoothly point out knowledge." The book of Ezekiel uses this same word in chapter 44, verse 23, to describe the purpose of the priests and the Levites in their ministry as teachers of the Israelites:

"And they shall *teach* my people the difference between the holy and profane, and cause them to discern between the unclean and the clean." The whole idea seems to be that this kind of teaching is very careful to explain and amplify the fine points so that the teaching arrives right "on target."

When we tie in this kind of "teaching" with the "knowledge" of Isaiah 28:9, we can begin to understand how much more specific the Lord is being. The word "knowledge" comes from the Hebrew word that literally means "to determine by observation." Therefore, that word is most often translated "opinion" in the Old Testament. If you substitute the literal descriptive meaning of these words "teach" and "knowledge" into that first phrase, the thought becomes somewhat more clear: "Whom shall he smoothly point out that which can be determined by observation?" God wants to teach us the "observable" things of His Word—not some mystical or allegorical meaning. Solomon provides an insight into the benefits of this kind of "knowledge" when he tells his son that the sweetness of honey is a good comparison to make, ". . .because it is good; and the honeycomb, which is sweet to the taste: So shall the *knowledge* of wisdom be unto the soul: when thou hast found it, then there shall be a reward, and thy expectation shall not be cut off" (Proverbs 24:13-14).

The passage in Isaiah continues with a further qualification of the kind of people for whom the Lord is looking, by asking the second question: "whom shall he make to understand doctrine?" Remember, we have already seen in the previous chapter that *every* word of the Word of God is important, so it becomes necessary to discover the reasons for the Lord's choice of words in this phrase. On the surface, the two questions seem quite similar. The one is looking for someone "to teach knowledge" and the other is looking for someone to "make to understand doctrine." However, by examining the literal definitions of the key words of the first question, we were able to expand the thought sufficiently for us to know that in the first instance, the Lord wants to "smoothly point out that which can be determined by observation."

In this second question, the English words, "make to understand," translate one Hebrew word that means "to finely distinguish" or "to separate." It is often translated "consider" or "discern." The English word "doctrine" is the translator's choice for a Hebrew word that literally means "an announcement." That Hebrew word developed from an earlier Hebrew word that meant "to stun" or "to stupify." The word that is translated "doctrine" in Isaiah 28:9 is more often translated "report." It is also translated "news, rumor, and tidings." When we examine these two key words in this second question and then insert those expanded literal meanings in the phrase, the question again becomes more significant: "Whom shall he [find] that will finely distinguish the report."

Keep that idea in mind and look at the use of the word "understand" in Nehemiah 8:3, 7, and 8.

And he read therein before the street that was before the water gate from the morning until midday, before the men and women, and those that could *understand*: and all the ears of the people were attentive unto the book of the law. *[Note that the "men and women," not "babes," were the ones that could "finely distinguish."]*

Also Jesua, and Bani. . .and the Levites, caused the people to *understand* the law. . . .So they read in the book of the law of God distinctly, and gave the sense, and caused them to *understand* the reading.

God wants to find men and women that are of the caliber to be able to distinguish the fine points of His Word, by being the kind of men and women that will be smoothly taught from that which can be observed in His Word.

Now that we can see what kind of people for whom the Lord is looking, we had better look closely at the "why" aspect. The Lord said in Isaiah 28:10 that He needed a certain type of student "for [because] precept must be upon precept. . .line upon line. . .here a little, and there a little." The word "precept" translates the Hebrew word that means "an injunction" or "basic commandment" and comes from a Hebrew word that means "to constitute" or "to appoint." The significance of this "precept upon precept" wording seems to be that it is difficult to be taught "knowledge" or understand "doctrine" because the "basic commandments" must be *built* into a readable thesis or principle. The process is lengthy, too: "Precept *must* be upon precept, precept upon precept."

Not only that, but we are instructed that the process also involves "line upon line. . . ." The word "line" describes a cord that was used for measuring. It comes from another word that meant to collect and bind together. The idea of the "line upon line" is that we are to develop those points in the "knowledge" and "doctrine" that will measure up to the truth. Note once again that the process is lengthy: "line upon line, line upon line." The Psalmist observes that the very glory of God is taught this way in the universe.

> The heavens declare the glory of God; and the firmament sheweth his handiwork. Day unto day uttereth speech, and night unto night sheweth knowledge. There is no speech nor language, where their voice is not heard. Their *line* is gone out through all the earth, and their words to the end of the world (Psalm 19:1-4).

And just to make sure that we do not think that this process of learning "knowledge" and understanding "doctrine" is too easy, Isaiah tells us that we have to find it "here a little and there a little." The word "little" means "that which is divided." The teaching is that the total truth is not found in one passage of Scripture. We must search "here" and "there" to build "precept upon precept" and then "line upon line."

Those verses, Isaiah 28:9-10, express the responsibility

23

of proper Bible study. Therefore, it would be worthwhile to write out those verses using expanded literal meanings of the words.

Whom shall He [the Lord] smoothly point out those things that can be determined by observation? And whom shall He [find] that will finely distinguish the announcement? Those that are weaned from milk and drawn from the breasts. For the basic commandment must be upon basic commandment; basic commandment upon basic commandment; measuring cord upon measuring cord, measuring cord upon measuring cord, here a divided part and there a divided part.

That is quite enlightening. If we are to study the Bible as the Bible demands, we are going to have to do it the Bible way!

But, that passage is more theoretical than practical. Isaiah tells us why it is necessary to approach the Scripture inductively, but it does not tell us how to develop the individual "precepts" and "lines" that we find "here" and "there." Fortunately, the Scriptures are adequate for "all things that pertain to life and godliness," and we are given excellent instruction for study techniques.

And moreover, because the preacher was wise, he still taught the people knowledge; yea he gave good heed, and sought out, and set in order many proverbs. The preacher sought to find out acceptable words: and *that which was* written *was* upright, *even* words of truth (Ecclesiastes 12:9-10).

This "wise preacher" did several things to insure that he was still able to teach the people knowledge: he "gave good heed," and he "sought out," and he "set in order many proverbs." If we boil down this verse to its simplest expressions, we will be able to gain a timeless technique for proper understanding of any verse or passage.

The "gave good heed" process of the preacher expresses the idea contained in one Hebrew word that means "to expand" or "to broaden out the ear." That word is most frequently translated "give ear" as is illustrated in Exodus 15:26.

> . . .if thou will diligently hearken to the voice of the Lord thy God, and wilt do that which is right in his sight, and wilt *give ear* to his commandments, and will keep all his statutes. . . .

The idea is that "the preacher" carefully thought through the wording of the verse and made sure that he understood what it was saying.

The "sought out" part of the preacher's technique is the examination, or more literally, the "penetration" of the passage. This special word is used by the writer of Deuteronomy in a way that demonstrates more clearly how much "penetration" is implied by the use of the word in Ecclesiastes 12:9.

> Then shalt thou enquire, and *make search,* and ask diligently; and behold, if it be truth, and the thing certain. . .(Deut. 13:14).

The connection of the synonyms "enquire" (to frequent, to follow) and "ask diligently" (to request, to demand) provide parallel amplification into the nature of the "sought out" action of the "preacher" in Ecclesiastes. He is to carefully exegete the text—each thought of the precious words, so that he can "set in order many proverbs."

The last of the three processes used by "the preacher" was the technique of "set in order many proverbs." That portion of the process can best be seen by a literal statement of the words used: "The preacher. . . equalized and/or composed many powerful sayings." The "set in order" phrase is most often translated "make straight" and obviously means that "the preacher" is to clearly organize the information that he gained during the process of "giving good heed" and "seeking out." These "proverbs" must be the kind of powerful sayings that have been constructed carefully and satisfy the criteria set out in the classic definition of a proverb in Proverbs 1:2-6.

These "proverbs" are further qualified in Ecclesiastes 12:10 as being "proverbs" that the preacher: "Sought to find out," proverbs that were "acceptable words," "And [that which was] written [was] upright," "[Even] words of truth." If we remove the italicized words from the King James text on that last phrase, we get, "and written, upright words of truth."

An overview of "the preacher's" technique provides the following principles:

1. The student must pay close attention to the wording of the text.
2. The student must examine the text by careful exegesis.
3. The student must correlate and systematize the information into carefully worded "proverbs" based solely upon the Word of God.

Please let me ask you a direct question. Did you enjoy digging down into those verses with me? If you did, then you are the kind of person that the Lord can use to "teach knowledge" and "make to understand doctrine." For those of you who may find such Bible research fascinating, let me offer this word of encouragement. Everything in this chapter was studied out and concluded by the *in*ductive method using only *one* other study tool in addition to the King James Version of the Bible: *The Strong's Exhaustive Concordance of the Bible.* Interested? Read on.

3

HOW TO BEGIN

The Scriptures are a marvelous collection of 66 different books written at different times through approximately 2,000 years by some 40 different authors. That in itself is a marvelous example of the interest that God had in men of all ages and backgrounds, but it does make the Bible a very complex Book. It is not the purpose of this little book to elaborate on the nature or structure of the Bible; that can be left to those men who have or will apply their minds to the literature and history of the Scriptures. However, since the Bible is a collection of different pieces, it might stand to reason that each piece would be an entity in itself. But that is not so. The Bible is unique in that it alone is inspired throughout by one God Who is revealing His truth to His creation.

Therefore, we may treat the Bible as a whole when studying inductively. Oh, yes, certain parts do apply to Israel, and certain parts to the church, and certain parts to this or that, but that is precisely the point! How do we know that? Did we read it somewhere? Did our professor tell us? How did he know? Who told him? When we approach the Word of God to try to determine what "knowledge" and "doctrine" the Holy Spirit has revealed to mankind, we have to approach it as the Bible has instructed us. That way is: precept on precept, line on line, here a piece and there a piece!

Remember, in the first chapter we looked at several Scriptures that emphasized the importance of *every* word? Think a minute about that. The written word is the most accurate of all methods of communication. Pictures are great, but without some "caption" they are subject to wide interpretation. Body or sign language is vague, and very difficult to get across. Some studies have been made about E.S.P. and "vibrations" and such like. What a margin for error! Even the spoken word is dependent on the attention of the hearer and his or her ability to sort out, evaluate, and retain what the speaker said. And if the speaker is bad, the problem is compounded.

The written word is the *best* way to transfer thought. The writer has the time to think through what he wants to say and to try several different words to find just the right one for the message he wants to get across. If it works for us, it does not seem to farfetched for God to to use the same method to deliver the messages He wanted to give to us. That is why *every* word is important. If a mere mortal author picks and chooses words to find *just* the right ones for his book, it does seem reasonable that God would choose precisely the words He wanted to get across the exact truth of His absolutely Holy nature.

Remember what we are dealing with. This is the Word of God. God caused His thoughts, which are absolutely Holy, to be recorded so that they were not subject to human error:

We have a more sure word of prophecy; whereunto
ye do well that ye take heed, as unto a light that

shineth in a dark place, until the day dawn, and the day star arise in your hearts: knowing this first, that no prophecy of the scripture is of any private interpretation. For the prophecy came not in old time by the will of man: but holy men of God spake as they were moved by the Holy Ghost (II Peter 1:19-21).

God, who at sundry times and in divers manners spake in time past unto the fathers by the prophets, Hath in these last days spoken unto us by his son. . .(Hebrews 1:1-2).

The secret things belong unto the Lord our God: but those things which are revealed belong unto us and to our children forever, that we may do all the words of this law (Deuteronomy 29:29).

We have already noted the emphasis that the Lord placed on the vitality of every word (Deuteronomy 8:3 and Matthew 4:4), the specific instruction by the Lord that His words are to be taken exactly as they were meant (Deuteronomy 4:1-2 and Revelation 22:18-19), that His Word is eternal and will never be changed (Psalm 119:89 and Matthew 5:17-18), and that all of His Word is to be obeyed (Deuteronomy 5:29 and Matthew 5:19).

However, we have a rather significant problem. The words that most of us are able to read are *at least* one step away from the words that the Lord used to speak His mind. The Old Testament was written in the Hebrew language for the most part, and hardly anybody speaks that language today. As a matter of fact, the Old Testament Hebrew in some parts of the Bible is 4,000 years old. The New Testament was written in an "ordinary" Greek language that has not been used for almost 1,800 years. All of the versions of the Bible that are available to us in our own language are at best translations of these original languages. Some of the versions are paraphrases of the translations or commentaries on the translations.

As a matter of fact, there is a surplus of "versions" on the market today, and we are constantly urged to get the "newest' and "most readable" or "best loved," etc., etc. Well, which Bible is best? For that matter, what is the difference between them? Those are valid questions for us to ask if we want to be as accurate in our Bible study as possible. If the Lord was so careful with each word, as seems to be taught in the Scripture, then it does seem likely that He would make sure those words were preserved for us to read and study. The problem for us is to find which one of the many Bibles on the market is the closest to the one that the Lord preserved!

There are really three different categories of Bibles into which all of the various "versions" fit: translations, interpretive translations, and paraphrases. Within each major group are several sub-categories based on different ent Greek texts, or different denominational councils, or different aims. However, for the purposes of our examination we can look at the differences on a general basis just so that we can narrow down the place to look.

A translation is an effort to express, in English, what the Greek and Hebrew words say, giving as nearly as possible a literal translation for each individual word. Additions are made only when it is necessary in order for the English reader to make sense out of the meaning. The basic assumption of the translator is that the Greek and Hebrew words are the precise words that the Holy Spirit inspired the original writers of the Bible to use, and therefore should be reproduced in English as accurately as possible. The King James Version of the Bible is the most popular translation in existence. There are other versions like the Revised Standard and the New American Standard, but they are based on different texts favored by other editors than the King James. The weight of evidence favors the King James Version as being the most nearly like the original Greek and Hebrew writings. An excellent book for further study on this subject is *Which Bible?* by David Otis Fuller, Grand Rapids International Publications, 1970.

An interpretive translation is not quite as reliable. The translator reads the Greek and Hebrew and then puts down in English those words that he feels will express the thoughts or general concept as he understands them. There is no effort to be literal or to avoid "adding" or "diminishing" words to the final product. The best known of this type of Bible is the *Good News for Modern Man* published by the American Bible Society. That work is essentially the preparation of Dr. Robert G. Bratcher, who then had it reviewed and edited by a panel of specialists. This version in its overall aim does "not conform to traditional vocabulary or style, but seeks to express the meaning of the Greek text in words and forms accepted as standard by people everywhere. . . " (Preface, *Good News for Modern Man)*. Well, there is nothing wrong with that. . .except that we are unable to *know* which words Dr. Bratcher chose to leave out or which words he added or changed according to his understanding.

The third category of Bible, the paraphrase, is probably the most popular "modern" version in our country. When Dr. Ken Taylor published *The Living Bible,* it seemed to take Christianity by storm. And, there is good reason for its wide acceptance. It is easy and pleasant to read. However, in Dr. Taylor's own words, "A paraphrase does not attempt to translate word for word, but rather, thought by thought. A good paraphrase is a careful restatement of the author's thoughts." The problem for us is, what thought belongs to Dr. Taylor and what thought to the Holy Spirit? There is no way, short of checking each verse with an accurate translation, for us to know.

One of the main arguments given by those who favor the more "modern" versions is that they are easier to read and understand. And that is true to a point. Those "modern" versions do use a more contemporary vocabulary and phrase their grammar in a more "readable" style. However, if we are not able to know which words or what thoughts are correct, how can we study effectively? The King James is somewhat lofty in its wording and does use some words that have lost their common meaning of three centuries ago, *but*—and this is a big "but"—the study tools, the concordances, the language dictionaries, and the overwhelming number of scholarly commentaries are geared to the King James text!

It may not be the easiest to read, or delightfully devotional, but the Lord told us that the "workman who needeth not to be ashamed" had to "study to shew" himself approved. Please do not misunderstand the emphasis here. Interpretive translations and paraphrases are not "worthless" or "blasphemous" as some have indicated. Many, many people have been blessed and nurtured in the Lord by using them. However, those types are *not* suited to serious Bible research. They were written primarily to be read devotionally.

So, what can we do? How can we be sure that we understand as much of the meaning of each word of the Bible as possible? We would really be in a fix if we had to learn to read Hebrew and Greek before we could understand the Bible. In the first place, most of us do not have the opportunity to go to a school that offers those languages, and in the second place, most of us have enough trouble learning the finer points of our mother tongue—let alone two more difficult languages! Fortunately, a lot of study has been done by hundreds of scholars over the centuries, trying to develop accurate tools of the languages of the Bible so that the average person will have the skill and expertise of the "scholar" available for their own personal use.

During the so-called "Dark Ages," the monasteries of the Roman Catholic church were training and developing dedicated men in the preservation and examination of the Scripture texts. These men diligently compared and analyzed the various copies and manuscripts from many parts of the world and were able to verify the wording of the original languages. With the rise of the "Rennaissance" and the explosion of scholarship among the "laypeople," a great effort was given by many more men and women in the development of lexicons or "dictionaries" of the Bible languages. These lexicons were refined and amplified as "modern" scholars continued to examine the languages and texts of Scriptures, so that we now have a wide pool of knowledge available for our use.

But, as valuable as these "dictionaries" are to the average person, they cannot measure up to the information contained in a special kind of study tool called the concordance. There are two different kinds of English concordances: the analytical and the exhaustive. Both of these types list all of the words of the English Bible in such a manner to enable the student to find every reference in the Scripture, the words of the original language used in those references, and the basic meanings of all the Hebrew and Greek words used in the original writings. The two most accurate and complete concordances are the *Young's Analytical Concordance* and the *Strong's Exhaustive Concordance of the Bible.* Both of these tools are excellent! They provide essentially the same information in different formats and are designed so that layman and scholar alike may be able to use them for inductive study of the Scriptures. Of the two, Strong's concordance is preferable for finding various words and references. It lists everything alphabetically under the English words as they appear in the King James Version of the Bible, and the dictionaries of the Hebrew and Greek words are much more thorough and amplified than the index-lexicons of the Young's concordance.

The major difference between the *Strong's Exhaustive Concordance* and the *Young's Analytical Concordance* is the manner in which the English words of the King James text are arranged. Both works list them in alphabetical order, but Young's then arranges the verse references under the respective original words, all in their own proper alphabetical order. This arrangement permits a rapid comparison of the various locations of any given English translation for any given Greek or Hebrew word.

The language dictionaries of Young's concordance are also arranged differently than those of Strong's concordance. There is no numerical code affixed to the verse listings, but the word headings in the main concordance cite the English equivalent of the Greek or Hebrew word as the key for dictionary location. Each dictionary is then arranged under the *English* alphabetical order for the various transliterated words of the two languages. The language dictionaries do *not* provide any definitive studies for the Hebrew or Greek, but do list each leading English word used to translate the given Hebrew or Greek word. These listings also cite the number of times a given English word is used.

There are two advantages to the Young's concordance over the Strong's concordance. First, there are times when the rapid comparison of a given Greek or Hebrew word usage is quite valuable. Although this is possible in the Strong's, it is not as rapid. Secondly, the glossaries of Young's concordance provide the totals of word usage frequency for the various Hebrew and Greek words. It is sometimes valuable to know how frequently a word is used and also to know what English word is chosen by the translators most frequently. That information is available in Strong's only by counting the various occurrences individually.

There are also two disadvantages to the Young's concordance. First, it is more difficult to locate a given reference in the listings, since they are arranged under the respective Hebrew and Greek words as well as under the English headings. Furthermore, the English headings are only given for the leading word, not for the various forms of it. This can make location of a given word or reference more time consuming. Second, the word definitions and word meanings are not nearly as complete as they are in Strong's dictionaries. Nor is there any word history or word derivative information in Young's.

It is the opinion of this writer that the Young's concordance is slightly inferior to the Strong's concordance for the above disadvantages. If a Bible student can only afford to purchase one concordance, he should get the Strong's. However, it would be well worthwhile to own both works. Each has its own value, and both books can be used more effectively together than can either alone.

The Scriptures tell us to "search the Scriptures daily, to see whether those things be so" (Acts 17:11). It would take a lifetime just to read the Bible through each time we had a question about a doctrine in order to make sure that we had read every "precept" and every "line" in the Bible about the doctrine we were questioning! Yet, that is what the Word of God tells us to do (Isaiah 28:9-10). How can we possibly "search the Scriptures daily" in such a complete fashion? There must be some way for all of us, for the educated and the uneducated, the urban and the rural, the old and the young. . .whatever classification we might like to suggest; there must be some way for every person with a sincere desire to find out what God has revealed in His Word to do so with what he or she may have available. Otherwise, God's people are left at the mercy of the select few who have opportunity or inclination to be trained in the "theology" of religious thought.

We cannot simply sit back and let the public figures in our religious environment pour their thoughts into our waiting brain. In the first place, that is the *worst* way to learn anything, and in the second place, there is every probability that we will get some wrong data. If we are unable to know or at least find out that the data is wrong, we will probably let that wrong data affect our lives in some way. This is true especially if we are not checking out the data we are hearing, since "wrong" data often coincides with the natural philosophy and logic of man. ("There is a way that seemeth right to man, but the end thereof are the ways of death" Proverbs 16:25.) Our job, the responsibility of *every* born again man or woman is to "study to shew thyself approved unto God, a workman that needeth not to be ashamed, rightly dividing the Word of truth'' (II Timothy 2:15). The Lord is going to call everyone of us before Him one day and ask each of us what we have done with His Words (John 12:48-50 and 14:21-24). He has put His Word above His very Name (Psalm 138:2) and will relegate those believers who have mistaught His Word to a position of "least in the kingdom of Heaven" (Matthew 5:19). *That* should cause us to be very careful! Fortunately, the exhaustive concordance provides the tool that will enable us to check everything for ourselves. Do you want to know how it works? Read the next chapter.

4

STRONG'S EXHAUSTIVE CONCORDANCE

It would be good to have a Strong's concordance while reading the rest of this book. While these pages are arranged to provide illustrations and examples of the concordance, more will be gained by comparing the various sections along with the concordance and by being able to use the concordance itself as this book demonstrates.

The Strong's concordance is designed to provide an exhaustive listing of *every* single word in the King James Bible. That's right, every single word . . . even down to the "a's," "the's," "and's," "but's," etc. It is a monumental work: it contains about 1,600 pages, weighs about five pounds, and took about forty years to write. It has proven to be the most valuable single tool for Bible study in this century. This concordance will allow a layman to get an accurate definition and explanation of each word of the original languages. It will permit objective comparison of Scriptural data on any subject in the Bible, thereby providing the only adequate resource for inductive study. It can be used by the trained professional for thorough analysis of Bible content. This chapter will explore the sections of that tool and provide initial exposure to its design and use.

THE MAIN CONCORDANCE

This is the "guts" of the concordance. It lists all of the words in the Bible except for some 47 unimportant particles (the "a's," "the's," "but's," etc.). Each word is listed alphabetically, exactly as it appears in the text of the King James.

Word Heading

Numerical Codes

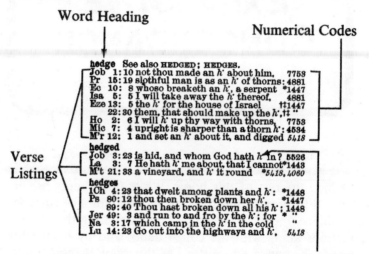

Verse Listings

Word Listing

[NOTE: The word headings are in bold type. The word listing is noted only by the italicized first letter of the word.]

The listing of each word in its immediate context is very valuable for a quick scan of the verses and for locating a verse that may be "right on the tip of your tongue." However, the words have much more significance when we know what they mean in the original languages. Check back at that last example. The listing under "hedge" shows nine verses in the Bible where the English word "hedge" is used. But, that heading also shows that there are five *different* Hebrew and Greek words used by the Holy Spirit! Look at the numerical code on the right side of the listings. These are given numbers 7753, 4881, 1447, 4584, and *5418*. The bold, upright numbers represent Old Testament Hebrew words and are located in the Dictionary of the Hebrew Bible in the back of the concordance. The light, italicized numbers represent New Testament Greek words and are located in the Dictionary of the Greek Bible behind the Hebrew dictionary.

When we check the numbers listed in the main concordance with the numbers in the corresponding dictionary, we are assured of knowing the reason for the translator's choice of the words. But what about those English words that the translators felt were necessary to add to help express the concept of the Greek or Hebrew word? How can we know which English word is the specific word and which word is a "helper" word? Once again, Dr. Strong anticipated that problem and designed the listings so that we could check the very word order of the translators.

Remember the verse we examined in Ecclesiastes 12:9 where "the preacher gave good heed; and sought out, and set in order many proverbs"? If we try to check the words in the "gave good heed" phrase, we will quickly find out which of the English words is the "main" word.

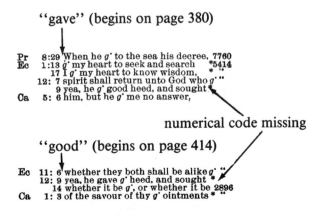

"gave" (begins on page 380)

Pr	8:29 When he g' to the sea his decree,	7760
Ec	1:13 g' my heart to seek and search	*5414
	17 I g' my heart to know wisdom,	* "
	12: 7 spirit shall return unto God who g' "	
	9 yea, he g' good heed, and sought	
Ca	5: 6 him, but he g' me no answer,	

numerical code missing

"good" (begins on page 414)

Ec	11: 6 whether they both shall be alike g' "	
	12: 9 yea, he gave g' heed, and sought *	
	14 whether it be g', or whether it be	2896
Ca	1: 3 of the savour of thy g' ointments * "	

39

"heed" (located on page 477)

```
Pr   17:  4 wicked doer giveth h' to false lips ;7181
Ec    7: 21 Also take no h 'unto all words 5414,3820
     12:  9 he gave good h', and sought out,  * 238
Isa   7:  4 Take h', and be quiet; fear him,   8104
```

numerical code given

The *absence* of a numerical code indicates that the word is supplied as a grammatical or syntactical help to *another* English word which will represent the root meaning of the word in the original language. The words "gave" and "good" are helpers to the word "heed" which is the root translation of the Hebrew word AZAN (#238 in the Hebrew dictionary). "Gave" and "good" *do not* have the #238 following their listing. "Heed" does. Using this procedure, the student is able to determine precisely which words represent original words and which words are supplied by the translators.

THE ADDENDA, APPENDIX, AND COMPARATIVE CONCORDANCE

These three sections are not used as much as the main concordance and the language dictionaries. However, they are quite valuable in their own right.

The Addenda   The Addenda contains the listing of those words and particles that were not included in the original work. It also contains the listing of those passages considered to be copy additions, i.e., titles, subscripts, etc. It is arranged exactly like the main concordance and should be consulted when a search of the main concordance fails to locate a specific word in a specific passage.

The Appendix   The Appendix lists 47 unimportant words that occur too frequently to list in the main concordance ("a's," "and's," "but's," etc.). It is arranged alphabetically as is the main concordance, but does *not* cite the passage context. It only lists the reference of the word. It also contains, in the upper right-hand corner of the column directly opposite the English word heading, the numerical code of the Hebrew and/or Greek word(s) that are used for those instances where there is a specific Greek or Hebrew word. However, most of the references in the Appendix will not have a corresponding Greek or Hebrew word. They are mainly English "helper" or grammatical filler words supplied by the translators.

The Comparative Concordance

The Comparative Concordance appears only in the Abingdon edition. It has been dropped from newer works. It contains only those passages in which the text of the Revised Version has a different word from the King James and is arranged alphabetically under the leading word as it appears in the King James text. The student will not find this section used too frequently, since the Revised Version has fallen into disuse.

These three portions of the concordance can be used to good advantage for certain types of study. However, it will be seldom used by the normal Bible student. Some scholars will find their data indispensible, but we will not refer to these sections again in this book.

THE LANGUAGE DICTIONARIES

If the main concordance is the "guts" of Strong's, then the dictionaries are the "brains." Other concordances have glossaries, or definitions of the languages, but Strong's is the only work that is meant to be used as a lexicon, with word explanations, development, and comparison studies. These dictionaries are designed to provide ease of use for the layman and depth of content for the scholar. They are unequaled in any other concordance.

The Dictionary Of The Hebrew Bible

All the original words are listed in the Hebrew language's alphabetical order. Each word is numbered consecutively, making location possible without knowing the language characters. The numbering corresponds to the numerical code in the main concordance. The exact English equivalent of the original word immediately follows the word listing.

Next follows the exact pronunciation.

Then comes a tracing of the etymology (word history), radical meaning, and applied meaning(s) of the word. These definitions are stated in the most precise manner that can be given in a few words. Sometimes synonyms will be given for additional clarification, and an explanation of the sense of the word is often given.

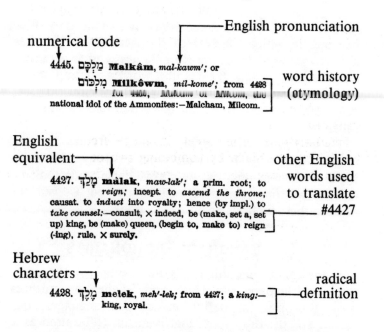

The radical definition and the implied meanings of that definition are always most complete in those words designated "a prim. root." A trace should always be made back to the source, or primitive word.

Finally, after the punctuation mark (:-), each leading English word is listed that is used in the KJV text to translate that specific Hebrew word. By locating the leading word(s) in the main concordance and noting the passages where the same number that corresponds to the Hebrew word under consideration appears in the marginal column, the student will be able to use the concordance just like a complete Hebrew concordance.

There are several abbreviations and symbols used in these word definitions. A complete list of various meanings is contained in the front of each dictionary. Do *not* assume that the meaning is clear.

The Dictionary To The Greek Testament

This dictionary is arranged just like the Hebrew dictionary. All the original words are listed in the Greek language's alphabetical order. Each word is numbered consecutively so that the student does not have to know the language characters. Then the exact English equivalent of the original word appears immediately after the word listing, followed by the exact pronunciation. The tracing of the word history comes next, followed by the radical and applied meanings of the word.

Combinations: The Greek language frequently has words that are made by combining two or more other words. These combinations are noted by citing the corresponding numbers of the words from which the word in question is composed. The Greek word, EPISUNAGŌ (#1996) is "from #1909 and #4863;" a check of those numbers will reveal the separate words (EPI and SUNAGŌ) that combine to form EPISUNAGŌ. Such a check will also amplify the additional shades of meaning assumed by the composite word.

1996. ἐπισυνάγω **ĕpisunagō**, *ep-ee-soon-ag'-o;* from *1909* and *4863;* to *collect upon* the same place:— gather (together).

comes from

1909. ἐπί **ĕpi**, *ep-ee';* a prim. prep. prop. mean. *superimposition* (of time, place, order, etc.), as a relation of *distribution* [with the gen.], i.e. *over, upon,* etc.; of *rest* (with the dat.) *at, on,* etc.; of *direction* (with the acc.) *towards, upon,* etc.:—about (the times), above, after, against, among, as long as (touching), at, beside, × have charge of, (be-, [where-]) fore, in (a place, as much as, the time of, -to), (because) of, (up-) on (behalf of), over, (by, for) the space of, through (-out), (un-) to (-ward), with. In compounds it retains essentially the same import, *at, upon,* etc. (lit. or fig.).

and

4863. συνάγω **sunagō**, soon-ag'-o; from 4862 and 71; to lead *together*, i.e. *collect* or *convene*; spec. to *entertain* (hospitably):— + accompany, assemble (selves, together), bestow, come together, gather (selves together, up, together), lead into, resort, take in.

NOTE: the last word SUNAGŌ (4863) is itself composed of 4862 and 71.

Comparisons: Often a synonym will be cited for a comparative study.

AGAPAŌ (#25) is the Greek word "to love." The

25. ἀγαπάω **agapaō**, ag-ap-ah'-o; perh. from ἄγαν **agan** (*much*) [or comp. 5689]; to *love* (in a social or moral sense):—(be-) love (-ed). Comp. 5368.

5368. φιλέω **phileō**, fil-eh'-o; from 5384; to be a *friend to* (*fond of* [an individual or an object]), i.e. *have affection* for (denoting *personal* attachment, as a matter of sentiment or feeling; while 25 is wider, embracing espec. the judgment and the *deliberate* assent of the will as a matter of principle, duty and propriety: the two thus stand related very much as 2309 and 1014, or as 2372 and 3563 respectively; the former being chiefly of the *heart* and the latter of the *head*); spec. to *kiss* (as a mark of tenderness):— kiss, love.

student is referred to #5368, PHILEŌ which is, in turn, derived from #5384, PHILOS, "a friend." Under the radical meaning of #5368, an amplification of

the relationship *between* #25 and #5368 appears. The student is thus given the ability to develop comparative word studies. Again, the radical meaning (in italics) is the most precise expression that can be put into a few words. Sometimes, to provide additional clarification, a synonym will be given along with an explanation of the sense of the word (usually in parentheses).

Finally, after the punctuation (:-), appears each leading English word that is used in the KJV text to translate that specific Greek word. An explanation of all abbreviations is located in front of the language dictionary. Do *not* assume their meaning.

Both the Hebrew and Greek dictionaries are arranged

44

in the same basic order so that there is as little confusion as possible. However, there is a lot of information in the Strong's concordance! As a matter of fact, the massive amount of data in that book is somewhat intimidating. Take heart, the fright begins to vanish when we get closer to the front line and begin to see why the battle is necessary. The next chapter will help explain the mechanics of the most basic and most necessary of all studies—the study of the words. If you feel a little overwhelmed by the complexity of this chapter, please read on. It really begins to make sense later!

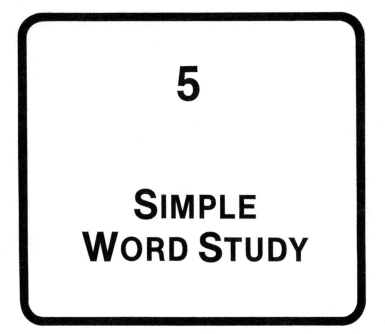

5

SIMPLE WORD STUDY

Perhaps the first negative reaction a student faces when he begins to think about *all* those words that have to be looked up is that there could never be enough time to do it. Well, it really is not that bad. In the first place, it is not necessary to look up the "a's," "the's," "but's," etc. And, most of the time it is not necessary to look up the "upon's" and "therefore's" and other connecting or introductory words. So, 20% of the work has been eliminated already! This kind of study simply provides us with the technique necessary to discover the meanings of those words about which there may be some question. Or, to clarify those words that describe a condition or doctrine with which we are not familiar and those words that seem to be unusual to the structure of the passage.

A good example of that last problem can be found in the Gospel of John, chapter 21, verses 15-17.

So when they had dined, Jesus saith to Simon Peter, Simon, son of Jonas, lovest thou me more than these? He saith unto him, Yea, lord; thou knowest that I love thee. He saith unto him, feed my lambs. He saith to him again the second time, Simon, son of Jonas, lovest thou me? He saith unto him, Yea, Lord; thou knowest that I love thee. He saith unto him, Feed my sheep. He saith unto him the third time, Simon son of Jonas, Lovest thou me? Peter was grieved because he said unto him the third time, lovest thou me? And he said unto him, Lord, thou knowest all things; thou knowest that I love thee. Jesus saith unto him, feed my sheep.

A surface reading of that passage produces a quizzical response to the way that the Lord kept repeating the same question to Peter. Surely, the Lord was not repeating for emphasis alone. Nor, was Peter *that* thick-headed. But what is the reason? Why did Jesus ask the same question three times, and give the same response each time to Peter's answer? A check of the key words will help.

Find The Word In The Main Concordance

The first step in this process is to locate the word we want to check in the main concordance. The words are listed in alphabetical order, exactly as they appear in the King James text. In this case, the key words are "lovest," "love," and "feed." These words are the heart of the Lord's question to Peter ("lovest thou me"?), the response of Peter ("you know I love you"), and the instruction of the Lord to Peter ("feed my sheep"). We now have to find the word headings in the concordance.

Locate Specific Verse Listing

After we have found the page that contains the word heading, we have to locate the specific verse listing.

word heading ——▸lovest
Ge 22: 2 thine only son Isaac, whom thou *l*.157
J'g 14:16 dost but hate me, and *l*' me not: "
2Sa 19: 6 In that thou *l*' thine enemies, and   "
Ps 45: 7 Thou *l*' righteousness, and hatest * "
     52: 3 Thou *l*' evil more than good; and   "
          4 Thou *l*' all devouring words, O thou "

48

verse listing

```
Ec   9:  9 joyfully with the wife whom thou l' "
Joh 11:  3 behold, he whom thou l' is sick.   5368
     21:15 Jonas, l' thou me more than these? 25
        16 Simon, son of Jonas, l' thou me?    "
        17 Simon, son of Jonas, l' thou me?  5368
        17 him the third time. L' thou me?    "
```

numerical code

Determine The Numerical Code

Once we have located the verse listing, we can then check for the numerical code. That code corresponds to a specific word in one of the language dictionaries. In this case, since we are dealing with a New Testament passage, we will be checking for words in the Greek dictionary. However, the style of number will tell us which dictionary to check. The bold, upright numbers (#157 in the example) correspond to the Hebrew dictionary, and the light italicized numbers #5368 and 25 in the example) correspond to the Greek dictionary.

Right away it should be apparent that there is an unusual factor to the Lord's question. In verses 15 and 16, He used word number 25 when He said, "lovest thou me." But in verse 17, the Lord used word number 5368. Why? What is the difference?

Find The Number In Appropriate Language Dictionary

The way that we can shed some light on the choice of the Lord's words, is by knowing what the difference is between them. Find the numbers of the words in the Greek dictionary, and then try to develop an understanding of the definitions.

24. ἀγανάκτησις **aganaktēsis**, *ag-an-ak'-tay-sis;* from *23; indignation:—*indignation

25. ἀγαπάω **agapaō**, *ag-ap-ah'-o;* perh. from ἄγαν **agan** (*much*) [or comp. 5689]; to *love* (in a social or moral sense):—(be-) love (-ed). Comp. *5368.*

26. ἀγάπη **agapē**, *ag-ah'-pay;* from *25; love,* i.e. *affection* or *benevolence;* spec. (plur.) a *love-feast:—*(feast of) charity ([-ably]), dear, love.

This definition (#25) tells us that the word *agapaō* means "to love (in a social or moral sense)." And it tells us to compare #5368. That is the other word the Lord used.

49

5368. φιλέω **phileō**, *fil-eh'-o;* from *5384;* *to be a friend to* (*fond of* [an individual or an object]), i e. *have affection* for (denoting *personal* attachment, as a matter of sentiment or feeling; while *25* is wider, embracing espec. the judgment and the *deliberate* assent of the will as a matter of principle, duty and propriety: the two thus stand related very much as *2309* and *1014,* or as *2372* and *3503* respectively; the former being chiefly of the *heart* and the latter of the *head*); spec. to *kiss* (as a mark of tenderness):— kiss, love.

This word (#5368) has a basic meaning of "to be a friend to." But this listing gives a lot of information about both #25 and #5368. We now have to sort out and understand what this dictionary has stored up for us.

Trace Out All Information About The Word

If all that we do is just read the major definition, we will not be much better off than if we had left well enough alone. When we use words, we are expressing a mental thought or picture with those words. We are usually familiar enough with our own language to be able to grasp more than just the words when we listen or read. However, we cannot know the mental thought or picture of the Greek or Hebrew words—unless we are given more than a mere definition. We need to understand the history of the word *use,* the comparison of that word with other synonyms, and some of the ways that the word is used in normal conversation. Strong's dictionaries provide all of that information for us. We just have to dig it out.

Check The Source Word

5368. φιλέω **phileō**, *fil-eh'-o;* from *5384;* *to be a friend to* (*fond of* [an individual or an object]), i e. *have affection* for (denoting *personal* attachment, as a matter of sentiment or feeling; while *25* is wider, embracing espec. the judgment and the *deliberate* assent of the will as a matter of principle, duty and propriety: the two thus stand related very much as *2309* and *1014,* or as *2372* and *3503* respectively; the former being chiefly of the *heart* and the latter of the *head*); spec. to *kiss* (as a mark of tenderness):— kiss, love.

5384. φίλος **philos**, *fee'-los;* prop. *dear,* i.e. a *friend;* act. *fond,* i.e. *friendly* (still as a noun, an *associate, neighbor,* etc.):—friend.

#5368 comes from #5384

comparison words

Check The Comparisons

2309. θέλω **thělō**, *thel'-o;* or ἐθέλω **ěthělō**, *eth-el'-o;* in certain tenses θελέω **thělěō**, *thel-eh'-o;* and ἐθελέω **ěthělěō**, *eth-el-eh'-o*, which are otherwise obsol.; appar. strengthened from the alt. form of *138;* to *determine* (as an act. *option* from subj. impulse; whereas *1014* prop. denotes rather a pass. *acquiescence* in obj. considerations), i.e., *choose* or *prefer* (lit. or fig.); by impl. to *wish,* i.e. *be inclined* to (sometimes adv. *gladly*); impers. for the fut. tense, to *be about to;* by Heb. to *delight in:*—desire, be disposed (forward), intend, list, love, mean, please, have rather, (be) will (have, -ling, -ling [ly]).

and

1014. βούλομαι *boo'-lom-ahee;* mid. of a prim. verb; to "*will,*" i.e. (reflex.) *be willing:*—be disposed, minded, intend, list, (be, of own) will (-ing). Comp. *2309.*

2372. θυμός **thumŏs**, *thoo-mos';* from *2380;* *passion* (as if *breathing* hard):—fierceness, indignation, wrath. Comp. *5590.*

compare 5590

5590. ψυχή **psuchē**, *psoo-khay';* from *5594;* *breath,* i.e. (by impl.) *spirit,* abstr. or concr. (the *animal* sentient principle only; thus distinguished on the one hand from *4151,* which is the rational and immortal *soul;* and on the other from *2222,* which is mere *vitality,* even of plants: these terms thus exactly correspond respectively to the Heb. 5315, 7307 and 2416):—heart (+ -ily), life, mind, soul, + us, + you.

and

3563. νοῦς **nŏus**, *nooce;* prob. from the base of *1097;* the *intellect,* i.e. *mind* (divine or human; in thought, feeling, or will); by impl. *meaning:*—mind, understanding. Comp. *5590.*

Analyze And Summarize The Definition

Very few words require this much work, but if we understand the complex words, we can understand the simple ones. In our passage of John 21:15-17, the Lord used two words to question the love of Peter. We should be able to learn what He was thinking when He used them.

1. *Agapaō* (#25) seems to mean a "head" love, as opposed to "heart" love. Or more probably, a "spiritual" love as opposed to an "emotional" love. Because:
   a. "Wish" (#2309) and "will" (#1014) compare to "friendly" and "love"
   b. "Passion" (#2372) and "intellect" (#3563) compare to "emotion" and "spirit"
   c. The expanded definition of #25 (*agapaō*) given under #5368, explains that "25 is wider, embracing espec. the judgment and the *deliberate* assent of the will as a matter of principle, duty, and propriety:"
2. *Phileō* (#5368) is an affectionate type of love, a fondness rooted in the emotion rather than the intellect.
3. Therefore, we can say that the Lord was asking Peter the first two times if he had come to the point in his spiritual life where he had come to "love" the Lord with his "judgment and the deliberate assent of the will." But, something changed the Lord's mind by the time He asked the third question, because He used the word *phileō* which asked Peter if he was even emotionally fond of Him.

We must now find out what Peter said that made such a difference in what the Lord said. So, we have to go back to the passage and find the key words in the answers of Peter, then look them up in the main concordance and trace the definition in the language dictionary.

```
Joh 10:17 Therefore doth my Father l˙ me,       "
    13:34 give unto you, That ye l˙ one another;"
       34 loved you, that ye also l˙ one another."
       35 disciples, if ye have l˙ one to another.26
    14:15 If ye l˙ me, keep my commandments.25
       21 and I will l˙ him, and will manifest   "
       23 a man l˙ me, he will keep my words:    "
       23 my Father will l˙ him, and we will     "
       31 may know that I l˙ the Father; and     "
    15:  9 I loved you: continue ye in my l˙.    26
       10 ye shall abide in my l˙; even as I     "
       10 commandments, and abide in his l˙.     "
       12 That ye l˙ one another, as I have      25
       13 Greater l˙ hath no man than this,      26
       17 command you, that ye l˙ one another.25
       19 world, the world would l˙ his own: 5368
    17:26 l˙ wherewith thou hast loved me       26
    21:15, 16, 17 thou knowest that I l˙ thee. 5368
```

verse listing

The word heading is "love." It actually begins on page 637, but our verse is located on page 638. The word numerical code is 5368. All three times.

Peter used *phileō* in his response to the Lord. That is the word for "fond" or "affectionate." If we reconstruct these questions and answers in these verses, we can begin to get a clearer picture of what was happening.

First: Jesus asked Peter, "Do you love me with your intellect and will?"

Second: Peter replies, "Lord, I am fond of you."

Third: Jesus asks again, "Peter, are you intellectually and judgmentally loving me?"

Fourth: Peter replies again, "Lord, you know I am fond of you."

Fifth: The Lord now asks, "Peter, are you *fond* of me."

No wonder the Bible then says "Peter was grieved because he said unto him the third time. . . ."

The words *do* play an important part in the meaning of this passage. We would *not* have understood that difference in this interchange by just reading the verses in the Bible.

But, wait! There is more. The Lord gave some instructions to Peter after each of the three times He questioned him. He told him twice to "feed my sheep," and once to "feed my lambs." Is the difference merely the difference in the age of the sheep?

Find The Word In The Main Concordance

Feed is on page 343

Locate The Specific Verse Listing

verses 15-16 of John

Determine Numerical Code

numbers 1006 and 4165

Da	11:26 that *f* of the portion of his meat*	398
Ho	4:16 the Lord will *f* them as a lamb	7462
	9: 2 and the winepress shall not *f* them,"	"
Jon	3: 7 let them not *f*, nor drink water:	"
Mic	5: 4 and *f* in the strength of the Lord,	"
	7:14 *F* thy people with thy rod, the	"
	14 let them *f* in Bashan and Gilead,	"
Zep	2: 7 they shall *f* thereupon: in the	* "
	3:13 for they shall *f* and lie down,	"
Zec	11: 4 *F* the flock of the slaughter;	"
	7 And I will *f* the flock of slaughter,	"
	9 Then said I, I will not *f* you:	"
	16 nor *f* that that standeth still:	3557
Lu	15:15 him into his fields to *f* swine.	1006
Joh	21:15 He saith unto him, *F* my lambs.	"
	16 He saith unto him, *F* my sheep.	*4165
	17 Jesus saith unto him, *F* my sheep.	1006
Ac	20:28 overseers, to *f* the church of God,	4165
Ro	12:20 if thine enemy hunger, *f* him; if	5595
1Co	13: 3 bestow all my goods to *f* the poor,	"
1Pe	5: 2 *F* the flock of God which is	*4165
Re	7:17 midst of the throne shall *f* them, *	"
	12: 6 that they should *f* her there a	*5142

Find The Number In The Appropriate Language Dictionary

1006. βόσκω **bŏskō**, *bos'-ko;* a prol. form of a prim. verb [comp. *977, 1016*]; to *pasture;* by extens. to *fodder;* reflex. to *graze:*—feed, keep.

and

4165. ποιμαίνω **pŏimainō**, *poy-mah'ee-no;* from *4166;* to *tend* as a shepherd (or fig. *superviser*):—feed (cattle), rule.

Trace Out All Information About The Word

#1006 comes from:

977. βιβρώσκω **bibrōskō**, *bib-ro'-sko;* a reduplicated and prolonged form of an obsol. prim. verb [perh. causative of *1006*]; to *eat:*—eat.

and

1016. βοῦς **bŏus**, *booce;* prob. from the base of *1006;* an *ox* (as *grazing*), i.e. an animal of that species ("beef"):—ox.

Check The Source Word

#4165 comes from:

4166. ποιμήν **pŏimēn**, *poy-mane';* of uncert. affin.; a *shepherd* (lit. or fig.):—shepherd, pastor.

Check The Comparison

#1006 comes from 977 ("to eat") and 1016 ("ox" as grazing).

#4165 comes from 4166 ("a shepherd").

Analyze And Summarize The Definition

1. #1006 means to "pasture," to "fodder," to "graze." It is a passive word: "let them graze—like an ox grazes, foraging for its own food."
2. #4165 means "to tend as a shepherd or supervisor." It is an active word: to lead to food, to direct correct eating habits.

It now becomes necessary to tie all of the information together. The Lord asked Peter if he loved Him with a deep, spiritual kind of love, and Peter replied that he "liked" Him. Jesus then said, "Let my lambs graze." Then, the second time the Lord asked Peter if he had an intellectual and spiritual commitment to Him, but Peter still said, "I like you." So, the Lord strengthened His advice to Peter by saying, "Pastor, or shepherd, or supervise the feeding of my sheep." Evidently, Peter did not take the hint, because the Lord changed His question to, "Peter, do you like me?" Peter got mad and said, "You know I like you!" Peter saw that the Lord was now using his own "like" in place of the Lord's "love" and Peter "was grieved." Well, the Lord then gave His final advice to Peter, "Let my sheep graze."

What a difference the words make! The passage comes to life with an understanding of what the conversation was really like. This insight is not just for the "learned"; it is available to every one of us if we are willing to learn a very basic research skill and spend a little time and energy to "study to show thyself approved."

Unfortunately, most of the passages of the Bible are more complex than that section from John's gospel. It, therefore, becomes necessary to use the skill of "the preacher" that we discovered in Ecclesiastes 12:9-10. In those verses we were told that the process of Bible study was threefold:

1. "give good heed" or pay close attention to the wording.
2. "seek out" or penetrate and exegete the text.
3. "set in order many proverbs" or equalize and compose powerful sayings.

These three processes are very broad and may be applied specifically to any kind of Bible study. Even though we did not carefully think of those three things in the study of John 21, we did use them. However, in more complex passages, it is best to follow the Biblical procedure consciously. If a careful attention to God's instruction is given, the Holy Spirit will be less hindered in His effort to teach us the truth. Are you willing to give Him a chance? Read on.

6

COMPLEX PASSAGE WORD STUDY

Since most of the Bible passages are more complex than the simple narrative in John 21, we must be more careful to apply some specific skill to the examination of the words. If we take the time, and have enough respect for the instructions from God's Word to use the technique suggested by the Holy Spirit, we will be delighted with the result!

One section that can be examined profitably is in Romans 7 where Paul discusses the stress he feels between the old, sinful nature and the "new man" that has been given him by the Lord.

For that which I do I allow not: for what I would, that do I not; but what I hate, that do I. If then I do that which I would not, I consent unto the law that *it is* good. Now then it is no more I that do it, but sin that dwelleth in me. For I know that in me (that is, in my flesh,) dwelleth no good thing: for to will is present with me; but *how* to perform that

which is good I find not. For the good that I would
I do not: but the evil which I would not, that I do.
Now if I do that I would not, it is no more I that
do it, but sin that dwelleth in me. I find then a law,
that, when I would do good, evil is present with
me (Romans 7:15-21).

That is confusing! Not only is the Old English hard to
read, but the "would's" and "do's" and "I's" really
make a jumble. However, God has promised us that His
Word is available for our understanding, so all we have
to do is try. We can understand *any* passage of the Bible,
if we will simply take the time to let the Bible comment
on itself and let the words that the Holy Spirit has chosen
speak in their full strength to our hearts and minds.

STEP ONE
GIVE GOOD HEED

**Make A List Of
The Words To
Be Studied**

The first thing we have to do with
a passage this long and this difficult, is to develop a list of the
words that must be checked out.

The best way is to start with the first verse in the passage
and jot down, in a column, those words that "jump" out
while reading.

verse 15 - For that
        which I *do* I
           allow not: for what I
           would, that
           do I not; but what
      I hate, that *do* I.

verse 16 - If then I *do* that which I
           would not, I
           consent unto the law that *it is* good.

verse 17 - Now then it is no more I that
           do it, but sin that
           dwelleth in me. For I know that

verse 18 - in me (that is, in my flesh)
dwelleth no good thing: for to
will is present with me; but
how to *perform* that which is good I
find not.
verse 19 - For the
good that I *would* I
do not: but the evil which I
would not, that I
do.
verse 20 - Now if I *do* that I
would not, it is no more I that
do it, but sin that
dwelleth in me.
verse 21 - I find then a law, that,
when I *would*
do good, evil is
present with me.

There is no hard and fast rule for picking out the key words in any passage of Scripture, but there are a few basic principles that will help you make a judgment.

1. Look for the action words—the verbs. Many times they will clarify the message more than the other kinds.
2. Look for the object words—the "who" and "what" words. Often they will help pin down the intent of the message.
3. Look for unknown words. Every time you run across a word in English that you do not know, find out the proper definition from the language dictionaries.

One note that should be made here is the necessity of some sort of worksheet. The more orderly and systematic we are with our work, the more easily we can sort out and analyze the information. Since we already know that it is necessary to find the original word, its number, and its definition, it stands to reason that our worksheet should have at least three columns:

WORD	WORD #	DEFINITION

The column of words outlined in the preceding example should be listed on the worksheet in order of their verse appearance in the Bible text.

Find The Word
In The Main
Concordance
⋮
Locate The
Specific
Verse Listing
⋮
Determine The
Numerical
Code

We now have several words to check. The best way to work is from "A" to "Z," writing down the numerical codes of the various words as they relate to the word order on the list that was prepared.

	WORD	WORD#
15	do	2716
	allow	1097
	would	2309
	do	4238
16	do	4160
	would	2309
	consent	4852

"allow" - page 49

allow See also ALLOWED; ALLOWETH; ALLOWING; DISALLOW.
Lu 11:48 ye *a'* the deeds of your fathers: *4909*
Ac 24:15 which they themselves also *a'*, *4327*
Ro 7:15 that which I do I *a'* not: *1097*

"consent" - page 216

Lu 14:18 with one *c'* began to make excuse.
Ro 7:16 I *c'* unto the law that it is good. *4852*
1Co 7: 5 except it be with *c'* for a time, *4859*
1Ti 6: 3 and *c'* not to wholesome words, *4334*

"do" - page 273

Ro 3: 8 Let us *d'* evil, that good may come? ··
31 *D'* we then make void the law
7:15 For that which I *d'* I allow not: *2716*
15 for what I would, that *d'* I not; *4233*
15 but what I hate, that *d'* I. *4160*
16 If then I *d'* that which I would not ··
17 it is no more I that *d'* it, but sin *2716*
19 the good that I would I *d'* not: but *4160*
19 evil which I would not, that I *d'*. *4233*
20 Now if I *d'* that I would not, *4160*
20 no more I that *d'* it, but sin that *2716*
21 I would *d'* good, evil is present *4160*
8: 3 law could not *d'*, in that it was weak

	WORD	WORD#
17	do	2716
	dwelleth	3611
18	dwelleth	3611
	perform	2717
	find	2147
	will	2309
19	would	2309
	do	4160
	would	2309
	do	4238
20	do	4160
	would	4160
	do	2716
	dwelleth	3611
21	would	2309
	do	4160
	present	3873

"dwelleth" - page 287

Ro 7:17 that do it, but sin that *d* in me. *3611*
     18 is, in my flesh,) *d* no good thing: "
     20 I that do it, but sin that *d* in me. "
    8:11 bodies by his Spirit that *d* in you. *1774*

"find" - page 350

Ro 7:18 that which is good I *f* not. *2147*
     21 If then a law, that, when I would "
    9:19 Why doth he yet *f* fault? For who

"perform" - page 785

Lu 1:72 *p* the mercy promised to our **4160*
Ro 4:21 promised, he was able also to *p*. "
    7:18 how to *p* that which is good I find*2716*

"present" - page 807

Ro 7:18 for to will is *p* with me; but how *3873*
     21 would do good, evil is *p* with me. "
    8:18 sufferings of this *p* time are not *3568*
     38 nor things *p*, nor things to come, *1764*
   11: 5 then at this *p* time also there is a *3568*
   12: 1 ye *p* your bodies a living sacrifice,*3936*

"will" - page 1172

Ro 4: 8 to whom the Lord *w* not impute sin.
    5: 7 for a righteous man *w* one die:
    7:18 for to *w* is present with me; but *2309*
    8:27 the saints according to the *w* of God.

"would" - page 1192

Ro 1:13 Now I *w* not have you ignorant, *2309*
    5: 7 good man some *w* even dare to die.
    7:15 for what I *w*, that I do not; but *2309*
     16 If then I do that which I *w* not, "
     19 For the good that I *w* I do not: "
     19 the evil which I *w* not, that I do. "
     20 Now if I do that I *w* not, it is no "
     21 when I *w* do good, evil is present "
   11:25 For I *w* not, brethren, that ye "
   16:19 yet I *w* have you wise unto that "

STEP TWO
SEEK OUT

After that work, we have boiled down the problem to nine key words that will require reference to the language dictionary. Each of these words will have to be located, traced, compared, and defined. Once again, the easiest way to work is from "A" to "Z," or in this case, from smallest number to largest number. Each word will require the use of the skills learned in the study of the passage in John. We must:

Explore The Word

1. Locate the number in the appropriate dictionary.
2. Trace out all information about the word.
3. Check the source word.
4. Check the comparisons.
5. Analyze and summarize the definition.

#1097 - "allow"

1097. γινώσκω **ginōskō**, *ghin-oce'-ko;* a prol. form of a prim. verb; to "*know*" (absol.), in a great variety of applications and with many impl. (as follow, with others not thus clearly expressed):—allow, be aware (of), feel, (have) know (-ledge), perceive, be resolved, can speak, be sure, understand.

- idea is to understand

#2147 - "find"

2147. εὑρίσκω **heuriskō**, *hyoo-ris'-ko;* a prol. form of a prim.

εὕρω **heurō**, *hyoo'-ro;* which (together with another cognate form

εὑρέω **heureō**, *hyoo-reh'-o*) is used for it in all the tenses except the pres. and imperf.; to *find* (lit. or fig.):—find, get, obtain, perceive, see.

- no change from English

#2309 - "will" and "would"

2309. θέλω **thelō**, *thel'-o;* or ἐθέλω **ethelō**, *eth-el'-o;* in certain tenses θελέω **theleō**, *thel-eh'-o;* and ἐθελέω **etheleō**, *eth-el-eh'-o*, which are otherwise obsol.; appar. strengthened from the alt. form of *138;* to *determine* (as an act. *option* from subj. impulse; whereas *1014* prop. denotes rather a pass. *acquiescence* in obj. considerations), i.e., *choose* or *prefer* (lit. or fig.); by impl. to *wish*, i.e. *be inclined* to (sometimes adv. *gladly*); impers. for the fut. tense, to *be about to;* by Heb. to *delight in:*—desire, be disposed (forward), intend, list, love, mean, please, have rather, (be) will (have, -ling, -ling [ly]).

- an active exercise of the mind:
  to determine, to choose, to prefer

#2716 - "do" and "perform"

2716. κατεργάζομαι **katergazomai**, *kat-er-gad'-zom-ahee;* from *2596* and *2038;* to *work fully*, i.e. *accomplish;* by impl. to *finish, fashion:*—cause, do (deed), perform, work (out).

- the combination of *kata,* which has the idea of intensity, and *ergazomai,* which carries the idea of a job, or an assignment, results in an "intensive job" or "hard work" idea for *kataergazomai.*

from

2596. κατά **kata,** *kat-ah'*; a prim. particle; (prep.) *down* (in place or time), in varied relations (according to the case [gen., dat. or acc.] with which it is joined):—about, according as (to), after, against, (when they were) × alone, among, and, × apart, (even, like) as (concerning, pertaining to, touching), × aside, at, before, beyond, by, to the charge of, [charita-] bly, concerning, + covered, [dai-] ly, down, every, (+ far more) exceeding, × more excellent, for, from . . . to, godly, in (-asmuch, divers, every, -to, respect of), . . . by, after the manner of, + by any means, beyond (out of) measure, × mightily, more, × natural, of (up-) on (× part), out (of every), over against, (+ your) × own, + particularly, so, through (-oughout, -oughout every), thus, (un-) to (-gether, -ward), × uttermost, where (-by), with. In composition it retains many of these applications, and frequently denotes *opposition, distribution* or *intensity.*

and

2038. ἐργάζομαι **ĕrgazŏmai,** *er-gad'-zom-ahee;* mid. from *2041;* to *toil* (as a task, occupation, etc.), (by impl.) *effect, be engaged in* or *with,* etc.:—commit, do, labor for, minister about, trade (by), work.

#3611 - "dwelleth"

- the idea is "to live at home with"

3611. οἰκέω **ŏikĕō,** *oy-keh'-o;* from *3624;* to *occupy a house,* i.e. *reside* (fig. *inhabit, remain, inhere*); by impl. to *cohabit:*—dwell. See also *3625.*

from

3624. οἶκος **ŏikŏs,** *oy'-kos;* of uncert. affin.; a *dwelling* (more or less extensive, lit. or fig.); by impl. a *family* (more or less related, lit. or fig.):—home, house (-hold), temple.

see

3625. οἰκουμένη **ŏikŏumĕnē,** *oy-kou-men'-ay;* fem. part. pres. pass. of *3611* (as noun, by impl. of *1093*); *land,* i.e. the (terrene part of the) *globe;* spec. the Roman *empire:*—earth, world.

#3873 - "present"

-the idea is "to be right alongside - ready to be available"

3873. παράκειμαι **parakĕimai,** *par-ak'-i-mahee;* from *3844* and *2749;* to *lie near,* i.e. *be at hand* (fig. be prompt or easy):—be present.

from

3844. παρά **para,** *par-ah';* a prim. prep.; prop. *near,* i.e. (with gen.) *from beside* (lit. or fig.), (with dat.) *at* (or *in*) the *vicinity* of (obj. or subj.), (with acc.) to the *proximity* with (local [espec. *beyond* or *opposed* to] or causal [*on account* of]):—above, against, among, at, before, by, contrary to, × friend, from, + give [such things as they], + that [she] had, × his, in, more than, nigh unto, (out) of, past, save, side . . . by, in the sight of, than, [there-] fore, with. In compounds it retains the same variety of application.

and

2749. κεῖμαι **kĕimai**, *ki'-mahee;* mid. of a prim. verb; to *lie* outstretched (lit. or fig.):—be (appointed, laid up, made, set), lay, lie. Comp. *5087.*

compare

5087. τίθημι **tithēmi**, *tith'-ay-mee;* a prol. form of a prim.

θέω **thĕō**, *theh'-o* (which is used only as alt. in cert. tenses); to *place* (in the widest application, lit. and fig.; prop. in a passive or horizontal posture, and thus different from *2476,* which prop. denotes an upright and active position, while *2749* is prop. reflexive and utterly prostrate):— + advise, appoint, bow, commit, conceive, give, × kneel down, lay (aside, down, up), make, ordain, purpose, put, set (forth), settle, sink down.

#4160 - "do"

4160. ποιέω **pŏiĕō**, *poy-eh'-o;* appar. a prol. form of an obsol. prim.; to *make* or *do* (in a very wide application, more or less direct):—abide, + agree, appoint, × avenge, + band together, be, bear, + bewray, bring (forth), cast out, cause, commit, + content, continue, deal, + without any delay, (would) do (-ing), execute, exercise, fulfil, gain, give, have, hold, × journeying, keep, + lay wait, + lighten the ship, make, × mean, + none of these things move me, observe, ordain, perform, provide, + have purged, purpose, put, + raising up, × secure, shew, × shoot out, spend, take, tarry, + transgress the law, work, yield. Comp. *4238.*

- refers to a single act (check the comparison in word - number 4238)

compare

#4238 - "do"

4238. πράσσω **prassō**, *pras-so;* a prim. verb; to "*practise*", i.e. *perform repeatedly* or *habitually* (thus differing from *4160,* which prop. refers to a. *single* act); by impl. to *execute, accomplish,* etc.; spec. to *collect* (dues), *fare* (personally):—commit, deeds, do, exact, keep, require, use arts.

- means to perform repeatedly as a habit

#4852 - "consent"

4852. σύμφημι **sumphēmi**, *soom'-fay-mee;* from *4862* and *5346;* to *say jointly,* i.e. *assent to:*—consent unto.

from

-to speak together so that the thoughts are known

4862. σύν **sun**, *soon;* a prim. prep. denoting *union; with* or *together* (but much closer than *3326* or *3844*), i.e. by association, companionship, process, resemblance, possession, instrumentality, addition etc.:—beside, with. In comp. it has similar applications, includ. *completeness.*

and

5346. φημί **phēmi**, *fay-mee';* prop. the same as the base of *5457* and *5316;* to *show* or *make known* one's thoughts, i.e. *speak* or *say:*—affirm, say. Comp. *3004.*

Now, after having done that bit of gold digging, it is necessary to put all the nuggets into their proper place. The worksheet is the best place to coordinate the data. Write down the summary definition that was obtained from the dictionary work alongside the word to which it corresponds.

	WORD	**WORD#**	**DEFINITION**
verse 15	do	2716	to work fully: to work hard to do
	allow	1097	to understand
	would	2309	to determine: to choose
	do	4238	to perform repeatedly: as a habit
	do	4160	to do a single time
verse 16	do	4160	to do a single time
	would	2309	to determine: to choose
	consent	4852	to speak together to express thought
verse 17	do	2716	to work fully: to work hard to do
	dwelleth	3611	to live at home with
verse 18	dwelleth	3611	to live at home with
	will	2309	to determine: to choose
	perform	2716	to work fully: to work hard to do
	find	2147	to find
verse 19	would	2309	to determine: to choose
	do	4160	to do a single time
	would	2309	to exercise the mind: to choose
	do	4238	to perform repeatedly: as a habit
verse 20	do	4160	to do a single time
	would	2309	to exercise the mind: to choose
	do	2716	to work fully: to work hard to do
	dwelleth	3611	to live at home with
verse 21	would	2309	to determine: to choose
	do	4160	to do a single time
	present	3873	to be alongside: to be available

STEP THREE
SET IN ORDER MANY PROVERBS

That exercise is most profitable. A pattern is beginning to develop that should trigger a small light. In order for us to direct that light with its maximum intensity toward the Scripture passage we are studying, it is necessary to rewrite this passage, using the expanded definitions that have been gained by the previous work.

Expand The Passage

"For that which I (try hard to work), I do not (understand): For what I (choose), that I am not (repeating); but what I hate, that I (do a single time). If then I (do a single time) that which I do not (choose), I (speak together in a clear thought) unto the law that is good. Now then it is no more I that (works hard to do) it, but sin that (lives at home with) me. For I know that in me, that is, in my flesh, no good thing (lives at home): For to (determine) is present with me, but how to (work hard to accomplish) that which is good, I find not. For the good that I (choose), I (do not do a single time), but the evil which I do not (choose), that I (perform repeatedly). Now if I (do a single time) that which I do not (choose), it is no more I that (am working hard to do) it, but sin that (lives at home with) me. I find then a law, that when I (choose) to (do good a single time) evil is (right alongside and available) with me."

What a difference the words make! The precise word choices by the Holy Spirit make a magnificent doctrinal explanation about the two natures in the born-again person, and provide us with excellent insight into the way those two natures operate. Just reading that account in *any* version would not have given us the depth that this short study has provided. However, we must "set in order" the information that is now available to us from this passage. Although the expanded wording is much more clear, we will remember the data better and be able to teach others more clearly, if we organize the data into "proverbs."

Reread The Expanded Passage

Initially, it is vital that we reread the expanded passage several times to help our minds grasp the thrust of the message. In effect, we are repeating the "give good heed" step in order to understand the *real* words.

Look For The Key Words Or Thesis

Every passage is trying to tell us something. Since the Word of God is not "secret," we should be able to detect the key thought(s) of the passage, or be able to discover the key words. Frequently, the "action" words are the important cornerstones. Sometimes the "description" words help unlock the thought process. The "who" and "what" words are always necessary to make the "action" and the "description" make sense.

Use The Worksheet

On page 60 there is an example of the kind of worksheet that could be used for this study. Initially, there were three columns: "Word," "Word #," and "Definition." We should now add a "Thesis" and a "Key Word" column, unless it seems easier to make a new worksheet. The objective is to locate and define the main points of the passage. We already have a worksheet that provides a quick overview of the major words and their definitions, so it would seem reasonable to start with work already done rather than re-do it. By simply making a check mark (✓) in the "Key Word" column next to those words that seem to be most important, we can quickly review the situation. Then we can write down in the "Thesis" column the key thoughts as they appear in the text.

It may not be necessary to make a formal notation of the key words or key thoughts for some passages. In fact, as you become familiar with the procedure, you will find that the work is almost automatic. However, in passages where the thoughts are somewhat complex, it is always worthwhile to take whatever extra time is necessary to analyze as completely as possible. In this passage, the theses (key thoughts) are not much more than the main clauses of each verse. The key words all seem to be the action words. If you will reread the expanded passage, then read the text as it appears in the King James, and then follow down the ''thesis'' and ''key word'' columns on the worksheet example, you should begin to get a feel for the procedure.

WORD	WORD#	DEFINITION	THESIS	KEY WORD
do	2716	to work fully	don't know how	✔
allow	1097	to understand		
would	2309	to determine		
do	4238	to repeat	can't do it	✔
do	4160	to do singularly	hate it	✔
do	4160	to do singularly		
would	2309	to determine		
consent	4852	to speak together		
do	2716	to work fully	sin does it	✔
dwelleth	3611	to live at home	sin lives in me	✔
dwelleth	3611	to live at home		
will	2309	to determine		
perform	2716	to work fully		
find	2147	to find	don't know how	✔
would	2309	to determine		
do	4160	to do singularly		
would	2309	to determine		
do	4238	to repeat		
do	4160	to do singularly	do evil a lot	✔
would	2309	to determine		
do	2716	to work fully	it is not me	✔
dwelleth	3611	to live at home		
would	2309	to determine		
do	4160	to do singularly	evil is alongside	✔
present	3873	to be alongside		

Organize The Information

Once we have set down the key words and the key thought(s), we must put them into a usable form for memory and teaching. Inductive study is a close study. It is like going into a deep forest to find a certain kind of tree for microscopic examination and jotting down the various discoveries. The discoveries are exciting in themselves, and it is very easy to forget that we are in the forest! We must, therefore, take the microscopic data and relate it to the tree, and then relate the tree to the forest. Once that is done, we then have the "many proverbs" that were the goal of the wise "preacher in Ecclesiastes.

Make Another Worksheet For The "Proverbs"

In this particular passage, the key words are seen to be the different usages of "do." The "thesis" of each "do" word is the key to the progression of the thought throughout the entire passage. When we reread the expanded passage, it is fairly easy to see that Paul is trying to explain the difference between the way he "does" sin and the way he "does" righteousness. He is also trying to explain why there is such a problem. Our job is to "set in order many proverbs." We are told by the passage in Ecclesiastes that those "proverbs" are to be prayerfully sought and based upon the desirable written words of truth. Therefore, the "proverbs" we make must be based only on the information we have gained from the words of Scripture—not some personal experience or clever illustration we heard somewhere.

List The Thoughts In Bible Order

The first step in this organization process is to follow the Biblical order. That is, we must not try to force the ideas of the Scripture to fit some preconceived notion or system of theology. Let God's Word present the doctrine in its own manner. If we follow that basic principle—all the time—we will be less likely to "interpret" the Scripture incorrectly. In this case the Biblical order is as follows:

1. Paul does not understand what he tries to fully accomplish.

2. Paul is unable to repeat what he determines to do.
3. Paul does do a single time that which he hates.
4. Paul reasons that the single act which he does, even though it is hated, verifies his agreement to the holiness of the law.
5. Paul recognizes that he is not fully accomplishing the deed, but sin that is at home with him.
6. Paul knows that it is because nothing good is in the flesh .
7. Paul understands that he has the ability to choose.
8. Paul also recognizes that he repeatedly does the evil which he does not choose.
9. Paul therefore concludes that every time he determines to do a single act of good, evil is right alongside and available with him.

Isolate And Correlate The Data

Every passage of the Bible is trying to communicate truth. Sometimes it is simple and sometimes quite complex. If we keep to the previous pattern of listing the truth in our own words following the Biblical order, the major truths should become more clear. Usually, there will be one central truth with supporting arguments. Or, as in this case, contrasting or complementary truths with supporting arguments. Our job is to isolate the major truth(s) and correlate the supporting data into an understandable "proverb that can be remembered and taught.

There are nine "points" made by Paul in his discussion in Romans 7:15-21. Some of these "points" are supportive rather than specific. The main thrust of the whole discussion seems to be contained in points five and nine. Since this is a narrative argument, as though the speaker would be trying to persuade the hearer, the conclusion would follow the argument. In the outline format, the student or teacher usually places the conclusion as the Roman numeral heading for the outline. The arguments then follow under the appropriate Roman numeral as capital letters. Thus, our "proverbs" would be as follows:

I. Sin lives in our home and fully accomplishes its work.
   A. We cannot understand what we fully accomplish.
   B. We are unable to repeat those things we choose to do.
   C. We instantly do the things we hate.
   D. We verify the righteousness of the law because of our recognition of sin.
II. Sin is constantly available and alongside us.
   A. Our flesh is all evil.
   B. Our will can choose good.
   C. Our flesh repeatedly overcomes our will with evil.

That last outline can now be used to help you remember the message of the passage—and to teach someone else. It would probably be a good idea to expand the outline with the information you gained through the word definitions themselves. And you would certainly want to apply the message to your own life. That is, check your own circumstances against the teaching that you have uncovered to discover how you can improve your own Christian testimony and effectiveness. The Scriptures are not merely for academic knowledge. They are "living and abiding" and must be obeyed as well as learned.

OTHER BIBLE TOOLS

The Bible Dictionary These valuable tools are almost a necessity for the serious Bible student. They are designed to provide geographical, historical, and technical data that the average person is unable to find. Although one can study the Bible accurately without knowledge of geography or history, it is certainly enlightening to have that portion of truth available. Frequently, a knowledge of the customs of the Bible period will open up a curious verse meaning. Sometimes, it is helpful to have a visual perspective of the cities and countries involved in a Biblical narrative. A Bible dictionary will provide that information in summary form.

The Bible Atlas   This is an expansion of the geographical and archaeological information contained in a good Bible dictionary. These books usually contain excellent maps with far more detail than the normal maps in the back of most Bibles. They will give more archaeological information than the Bible dictionary and usually provide more technical information on the social, political, and economic climate of the Bible times. These books are especially valuable for pastors and Sunday school teachers.

The Word Study Books   These books are part dictionary and part commentary. They are designed to compare the differences between key words of the Bible languages and are usually structured so the non-linguist can use them. There are many levels of these books; some are designed for the scholars, others for the curious. Two of the best and easiest to use are: *An Expository Dictionary of New Testament Words,* by W. E. Vine, and *Old Testament Synonyms,* by Girdlestone. Both of these books are arranged alphabetically under the main English term, with good cross-reference indexes. They will assist the Bible student in making a finer comparison between similar words than is easily possible through the concordance dictionaries.

SUMMARY OF THE WORD STUDY PROCESS

The work for this kind of study is not complex, and is absolutely basic to every kind of study that can ever be done with the words of Scripture. It is vital that any serious student of the Word of God know this procedure well. Therefore, these next few pages will review the process in outline form, adding those notes that will make retention more probable.

THE SIMPLE WORD STUDY

Purpose

This procedure should be used whenever there is a key word in a Scriptural passage. Unless the student is *sure* that he or she knows what the word means in the original language, the word should be checked in the concordance.

Procedure

This format should be followed for *every* word study. Attempts to shortcut will only produce error. Never assume to know any point. When there is doubt, consult the instructions in the concordance or this book.

    A. Locate the study word in the main concordance.

    B. Locate the specific verse listing where the word appears.

    C. Locate the numerical code of the word.

        1. Old Testament verses have bold upright numerals and represent Hebrew words.

        2. New Testament verses have italicized numerals and represent Greek words.

    D. Locate the appropriate language dictionary in the back section of the concordance.

    E. Locate the study word number in the appropriate dictionary.

    F. Trace out all the information about the word.

        1. Check back until the source word is found.

        2. Check all of the root or source words.

        3. Check for the comparison words.

    G. Analyze and summarize the definition.

        1. Check the radical meaning.

        2. Compare the root or source word radical meaning.

        3. Examine the radical meaning of any comparison words.

        4. Examine any synonyms or explanitive information given in each applicable word.

        5. Write a definition in sentence form, if necessary.

        6. Summarize the definition in a few words.

        7. Record other English translations, if necessary.

THE COMPLEX PASSAGE WORD STUDY

Purpose   This procedure should be followed for every section of Scripture that requires more than a few word studies. The student will soon learn the limitation of memory alone and will find that organized, written study is far more reliable.

Procedure   This format should be followed, allowing only those modifications which assist the *accuracy* of the study procedure. Time is valuable only if it can be used to produce that which is valuable. Any short cuts that may develop with practice should be used with caution and should be used when testing has proven them a valuable time and energy saver.

A. Make a list of the words to be studied.
  1. Prepare a worksheet with adequate space for the information to be recorded.
  2. Record the words vertically, proceeding from the top to bottom of the worksheet, in the order of the word's appearance in the study passage.
B. Perform a simple word study on each word.
  1. See previous section for instructions.
  2. Record all information on the worksheet.
C. Rewrite the passage using the expanded word definitions.
D. Reread the expanded passage.
  1. Look for key words or key themes.
  2. Check those points on the worksheet.
  3. Look for organized patterns in the passage.
E. Organize the information into outline form.
  1. List the thoughts in Bible order.
  2. Develop the information as an outline, placing main points in proper relationship to the sub-points.
      a. Place the conclusion, or central truth, as the heading or main point.
      b. Place the supportive or argumentative logic as the sub-points under the heading.

These two outlines should be sufficient for your review until you become proficient in this work through your own practice. The next section will cover a more complex type of study that assumes a working knowledge of this information. Make sure you feel comfortable with this procedure before going on. The word study process will clarify Scripture in a delightful way, but it definitely does not provide the capacity to dig out the marvelous truths hidden in other pages of God's Word. Do you want to know how to do that? Read on.

Penetrating Bible Study

7

PENETRATING BIBLE STUDY:
AN OVERVIEW

The remainder of this book makes the assumption that you have mastered the basic procedures involved in the word study process. If you do not feel comfortable with that level of study, please go back and reread the summary section in chapter six. Then work through several passages of your favorite section of Scripture. After you have actually done four or five sections of the Bible, you should have committed the procedure to heart. You will have a good "feel" for the development of definitions from the word histories, and you will be comfortable with the structure of the concordance. With those tools, you will be able to develop your skills so that you can mine the whole of the Bible for additional information which will amplify and clarify any passage.

However, before we go any farther, it is necessary to draw a perspective from which we can see the direction of our work. And, the best way to do that is to review the two Scripture passages that we have discussed earlier.

The passage in Isaiah 28:9-10 gave us the general information on how to uncover "knowledge" and "doctrine." We were to build our information by finding the "precepts" and the "lines" in several different parts of the Bible. The "precepts" are the basic commandments or principles of whatever "knowledge" or "doctrine" we are trying to study. The "lines" are the supportive points that will fill out and complete the idea of the "precepts." The whole study process is *in*ductive; that is, a process of building a conclusion from the many pieces of information. The conclusion is withheld until the research has been done.

Ecclesiastes 12:9-10 provides a more mechanical framework by which we can organize our efforts to find the "precepts" and "lines" required by Isaiah.

1. The student must first pay close attention to the wording of the text ("Give good heed").
2. The student must next penetrate and examine the message of the text ("Seek out").
3. The student must then compose an ordered structure of the penetrated message that will be valuable for teaching and retention ("Set in order many proverbs").

Those three steps are our Biblical guidelines for effectively researching out the bits of information which will ultimately make the message of any passage the clearest. We will have to go into some detail in order to learn those procedures adequately, but we should take time initially to view each of them conceptually.

GIVE GOOD HEED

This is the first stage of research. It is much the same as the "Attentive Bible Study" procedures covered in the previous section of this book but does require a little more analysis.

Isolate The Total Thought To begin with, it is necessary to make a more careful approach to the passage under study. Frequently, we are impressed by a partial thought in our devotional reading, or from a stimulating message from the pulpit. When such an impression takes place, it is easy to repeat the impression verbally often enough for it to become "Scripture" in our lives. What must be done for proper study of such impressions is to first insure that we have isolated the *total* thought in its proper context *before* we begin to examine the message. That work is not difficult, but it is vital. The Word of God must never be knowingly misused or treated lightly. We must be as sure as we can be that we are not using a phrase out of context, a partial thought, or an incomplete teaching.

Analyze The Purpose And Thesis Of The Thought
Once the context has been determined and the complete thought isolated for study, it then becomes necessary to examine the structure of the thought so that we can properly work through the various elements. Every thought is composed of words, and it does not require too much analytical ability to pick out the key words. However, when it becomes necessary to outline the components of a thought, the job becomes a little more demanding. In this step, we must determine the main thesis or major point of the thought. This is critical to our evaluation of the many pieces of data which we will be locating later on. If we do not know what the thrust of the message is, it is *likely* that we will be led far afield when actual research begins.

Perform A Word Study On Each Key Word
With a good visual representation of the study passage in front of you on a worksheet, you can begin to use the basic word study procedure acquired in the previous section of this book. Each of the key words have to be researched for the accurate meanings in the original language and must be kept in a proper relationship to the flow of the message in the study passage. Hence the necessity of clear worksheet organization. Furthermore, since we are going to look for other passages of Scrip-

ture that bear on the thesis of our study passage, we will have to note any other English term which may have been used by the translators in other passages. It is not necessary to rewrite the study passage after the word study step, since we will be doing that later.

SEEK OUT

This stage of our work is the most tedious. There is the frequent temptation to short-cut or ignore certain elements in an effort to save time. But, time is only valuable when it is used effectively to produce a quality product. Since we are dealing with the Word of God, we cannot take any haphazard chances with the efforts made to discover its truth. We must be careful! Therefore, when we "seek out" the information, we must be sure that we search for "precept upon precept . . . line upon line . . . here a little and there a little."

Locate The Parallel Scriptures When we develop the word definitions, we are able to get a clearer picture of the immediate significance of the message, but there is always the feeling that "something" is missing. There is! That "something" is the rest of the teaching in other portions of the Bible. But how can we find it? That is the whole point of this "seek out" stage. We can use the concordance to locate every other reference in the Bible that uses any of the key words of our study passage, thereby making sure that we examine the bulk of the Bible's teaching on that particular message. If we are careful to penetrate each component of the thought under study, we will be rewarded with a rich cache of parallel information.

The work for this procedure is not complex, but it is involved. We will be sorting through many references and will have to select those that are more likely to apply to the main thesis and context of our study passage. Then we will have to read each potential reference in its contextual setting to determine if it does apply. Once that is done, we have to check out other words and concepts that have been revealed by the research to make sure we understand how they apply to our original study passage. Again, the work is not complex, but it does demand the patience of a research scientist and the dedication of a spirit submitted to the authority of the Word of God.

The main danger of this kind of research is that it is easy to go after that "neat" verse or "wonderful" idea that is bound to be uncovered. There will never be an end to the new discoveries in this process. In fact, that is one of the most delightful reasons for doing it. You will never run out of things to study or reach an end to your learning. However, and this is a big "however," it is absolutely necessary to confine the study process to the study passage. Every parallel reference must either amplify or clarify the message of the passage. If it is merely "interesting" or if it is neutral to the message, it must not be used. The objective is to "seek out" the information of the Scripture on a specific thought—not to wander around in search of "neat" ideas.

SET IN ORDER MANY PROVERBS

Here is the stage that turns the raw ore into precious metal. Every mining operation involves the "dirty" work of extracting the ore from the rock that hides it. But that ore is unusable. It has to be refined. Sometimes the refining process is nothing more than hand sorting of big pieces from little ones. Sometimes a mere color selection process is adequate. Most of the time, however, the ore has to be crushed to a powder and melted in a crucible. As the rock and ore melt, the true precious metal separates from the "slag." The slag is then discarded and the melted metal poured into waiting molds for use in special projects. That is what is done when the Bible student "sets in order many proverbs."

**Categorize
The Verses**
Initially we have to go through a sorting of the "big" pieces from the "little" ones. We have to separate the "precepts" from the "lines," as Isaiah has

told us. Also, we can make recognition of the various *kinds* of precepts and lines within a given area. All of this is done under the organizational framework of our study passage. That is, we are looking for categories of verses which fit *within* the various points of the message of the study passage.

Pinpoint The Relationships

Once we have a rough sorting of the verses, it is then necessary to go through each of those categories to develop the relationships. There will be a relationship *between* the categories and a relationship *within* the categories. For all practical purposes, we will be using a finer and finer sieve with which to organize the information gained during the research stage. Some verses will be eliminated. As we begin to exact a better "order" to the information, it will become clear that some data will not "fit" the message of the study passage.

Prepare The Final Outline

That message, if it is going to be effective, must be "set in order" into "many proverbs." That is, we are going to have to compose an organized presentation of the "powerful sayings" contained in the message. We have to make an outline—a sentence outline of all the information which has been uncovered as relating to that message. You will soon learn, if you have not already, that your memory is undependable. The only way to insure that the truth uncovered through this study is preserved accurately is to carefully record that information in such a fashion that it can be reused time and again. If this is not done, all the work will have to be done over again the next time you want to know what the Bible says in that area. Not only that, but you will be unable to teach the information to others as clearly or to retain the information in your memory as effectively. The more "ordered" the information becomes, the more easily it is retained and taught.

GET READY TO WORK

Well, if you are still anxious to develop your skills in this vital area, then find a good work area; get your Bible, concordance, scratch pad, pencils, and patience; now turn the page to the next chapter.

8

PAY ATTENTION

The best way to approach this study is to define terms. A "thought" is the orderly progression of words, connected in a recognizable pattern, designed consciously to express a mental concept. Usually the sentence is the least complex form of a thought. Sometimes a sentence is not sufficient to adequately express a thought, so the author connects a series of sentences together to form a paragraph. Less frequently, but none the less necessary, some thoughts are too complex to express even in a paragraph and therefore require additional paragraphs to properly explain and convey the thought. It was necessary to say all of that rather basic information, because the normal Bible text is not easily read that way. Most Bibles are printed in chapter and verse sub-headings that were designed as aids in *location,* not as aids in *understanding.* Unfortunately, the verse indentations give the impressions of new material, or new thoughts. They are *not* intended to do so! More often than not, the verse listings do *not* indicate a new thought. Even the punctuation within the text of the English Bibles is not always correct. Remember, the words were inspired—not the verses or the punctuation as it has been given to us from the translators. That is not to say that the student should disregard the work of the translators. In most cases they were godly men with great respect for the accuracy of the original languages. But they were men. Therefore, we cannot *assume* that they were infallible. We must follow the Biblical process given to us in Ecclesiastes: Give good heed, seek out, set in order many proverbs.

This first step, while fairly basic, is key to the whole operation. If not done properly, it is entirely possible to throw the whole study into error. Some of the things we must discuss may well be "old hat" to some students, but it will be profitable to review the information anyway . . . especially since it is necessary to connect these skills with the whole procedure.

Isolate The Total Thought

The objective in this important step is to locate and clarify the complete thought. There is a tendency to over or undershoot the point of the Bible writer. This happens because our study desire is normally triggered through surface devotions or friendly discussion with other Christians. Usually, we are directed to a verse or passage that is only a part of the thought being expressed by the writer. This requires us to carefully read the passage *surrounding* the verse in question to determine the complete thought. It is entirely likely that the total thought will be isolated in one single sentence. Most often, however, the student is really dealing with a subpoint in a larger, more complex thought. The type of study discussed in this chapter *will not* be adequate for a large, complex, interrelated doctrine. Therefore, it is best to confine the search to the *smallest* complete thought. By examining the immediate paragraph, or chapter, if necessary, the student will be able to isolate all of the words that are required to express that complete thought.

The major problem there is to determine what "context" is necessary for proper isolation of the verse or verses to study. That term, "context," is very broad and can mean anything from the preceding verse to the entire Bible. In the type of study that we are now considering, the context should be limited to the immediate chapter or two, certainly no more than the setting of the book itself. Essentially, "context" is a composite word (con and text) that means "with writing." Many, many books have been written that contain information on how to find and use context, and not many of them agree. Therefore, it is somewhat presumptuous to think that we will be able to settle all the problems now. However, there are a few simple steps that will help any student find adequate context.

Normally, the thought will begin with a new paragraph. If the Bible being used has paragraph indentations or paragraph symbols (¶), drop backward in the passage to the point where the paragraph that contains the study verse begins. If there are no paragraph indentations or symbols, begin reading at the chapter division prior to the study verse and read forward through and beyond that verse until the thought seems complete. In this manner, the paragraph break should become apparent. There will be some occasions where the chapter division is either too close or too distant to use as a starting point. If so, a good "rule of thumb" is to drop back 10-15 verses from the study verse. Usually, that will be sufficient to locate the immediate context.

The paragraph is merely a convenient writing form that signals the start of a different thought. There is no "mechanical" way to form a paragraph, and the writers of the Scriptures did *not* use the same style of paragraphing that we do. However, we are better able to isolate thoughts by containing them in a paragraph. What the Bible student *must* look for is the sentence or sentences that express the total thought as contained in the immediate wording surrounding the verse or verses under study. Many parts of the Bible are quite complex, and all of the Bible is interrelated. Therefore, it is vital that the student remember to isolate the *least* complex thought for initial study. It may well become necessary to expand the study in order to accurately express the teaching, but that must only be done when the Scriptures themselves demonstrate the necessity. First, deal with the simplest, most self-contained, most complete thought that can be isolated in the immediate context. Sometimes, it will be necessary to read the argument and teaching flow of more than one previous chapter. Since each of the books of the Bible tend to have one overriding purpose in their message, the supporting points within that message may be difficult to understand unless the student "feels" the reason for the message. If after reading the immediate context the complete thought still remains elusive, the student should take the time to read the teaching through the preceding two chapters. During that process it will be helpful to jot down the major thoughts that seem to "pop out" of the reading. After that step, the "flow" of the teaching will be fairly easy to recognize. Once that is done, the student can then narrow down the thought to be studied.

Break Down The Thought To Its Major Sub-Points

Every thought is composed of several incomplete thoughts that together make up the total idea. If the thought is very simple, the incomplete parts may be nothing more than the words themselves. However, most Bible thoughts are complex enough to require more careful analysis. The objective in this step is to locate and define those groups of words that have a bearing on the composite picture. Usually, they will be set apart by some form of punctuation and are easily identified. However, the punctuation was *supplied* by the translators and could confuse the student. A helpful, initial practice is to rewrite the thought *without* punctuation, and then read it over several times until a pattern of sub-points becomes clear. Each of these sub-points will be incomplete by itself, but will change the total thought if left out. It is difficult to describe the various factors involved in this step. Practice is the best way for a student to become proficient in breaking down the thought structure.

One helpful skill and technique is to pinpoint the major parts of speech in the thought. Any language is only valuable when it is structured so that the various words can be used in different ways to express varying functions of these words. Those different functions are called parts of speech. Those "parts" are grouped into four major kinds: the subject, verb, object, and modifier. While there are many variations and fine points within these four kinds, it is not necessary to explain their function for our purpose here.

THE SUBJECT is usually the most obvious of all parts of speech. It can be a person, a place, or a thing of some sort, and is briefly, the person, place, or thing that is being spoken about. For Bible study purposes, the subject is important because it will identify the main emphasis of the thought. Quite frequently, the subject is "you" understood. That is, the writer is speaking to us and will address us by a command or rhetorical question. The object of that kind of writing is to gain our direct, personal attention. We must know who or what is the subject of the thought in the Scripture passage, or we will not know how to treat the information we have been given.

THE VERB is the word or words that describe the action of the subject. Normally the verb expresses something that the subject is doing, but sometimes the subject gets acted upon. When the subject does the activity, the verb is called an *active verb*. When the subject is receiving the action, the verb is called a *passive verb*. That difference is important since many of the commands that the Scriptures give to us are given in a *passive* form: that is, we are to let something happen to us. Baptism is a good example. We do not baptize ourselves, we are baptized by someone else. Usually, *passive* verbs have "helper" words like "have been" or "should have." Active verbs normally stand alone.

THE OBJECT receives the action that the subject does.

Not every thought has an object, but most do. This is obviously important because we must find out the result or purpose of the action that the subject is doing. Sometimes the subject does something *for* or *to* an object. Either way, it is important for us to know what happens to the action of the thought. The object provides the place to look.

THE MODIFIER is a word that changes or limits the description of another word. A modifier may be applied to any of the other three parts of speech and is very important. Since the Holy Spirit inspired every word, the modifier makes a big difference in the total thought. We must know what words are affected and why they are there.

Analyze The Purpose And Thesis Of The Thought

After locating and relating the various parts of the thought, the student needs to determine the main thrust of the writer. This is somewhat akin to the "context" of the passage and is vital for setting the limit on what other sections of Scriptures will apply to the thought under study. Every thought has a "thesis" or main point. Usually the thesis is found in the subject/verb/object words of the sentence and normally will be obvious to the reader. However, some of the Bible writers were complex men. Their thought structures are more difficult to pin down and must be carefully sought. It is very important that we limit our study to those verses of Scripture that are dealing with the same thought thesis. A random comparison of other sections of Scripture will only serve to confuse the thought, not clarify and amplify.

Part of the process involves the analyzation of the purpose of the thought. Why was the thought thought? Is it a command? If so, to whom or to what is it directed? Is the thought a question? If so, what kind of question? Does that question demand an answer, or is the question merely teaching a point? Is the thought a teaching point in a larger doctrine? If so, what doctrine?

92

Is the thought self-contained; does it express a complete idea? If so, what is the reason for that idea? All of this is necessary to enable the student to evaluate the information that will be obtained in a search through the Scriptures for additional data.

Obviously, it would be very difficult to try to remember every question or every possibility during a preliminary approach to Bible study. Each passage will have its own peculiarities, and, thankfully, its own similarities to other Biblical structure. Remember, the Scriptures are the *revelation* of God. That is, they were written to *reveal* the truth of God to men. It is true that much of the Bible is written in such a way to keep the truth from those who will not hear (Matt. 13:10-17). But, it is possible—indeed, exciting—for the children of God to discover the "pearls" of God's Word.

Do you remember the discussion of Isaiah 28:9-10 in chapter two? That section described the logical approach to "understand doctrine" from the Scripture. We were told that "knowledge" and "doctrine" were difficult to get, even for the spiritually mature, because "precept must be upon precept...line upon line...here a little and there a little." That building process is applicable to every portion of Scripture and is the key to unlocking even the most complex "knowledge" or "doctrine." In the type of study that we are now considering, the Isaiah process is equally important for unlocking the "thesis" of the passage.

Perhaps a short review is in order. The word "precept" in that Isaiah passage means "basic injunction" or "command." The word "line" was the word that described the measuring device used by those ancient cultures to subdivide the major measures in much the same manner as our ruler. The "here a little and there a little" could best be paraphrased by noting that the sub-points ("little" = that which is divided) are not going to be found in one spot, or one phrase for that matter. In other, more twentieth-century-like words, Bible doctrine must be built by first finding the basic thought, then by locating the sub-points of that thought, finding both by examining more than one single spot in the Scripture. When we relate that approach to the immediate problem of finding the thesis and/or purpose of our study thought, we discover some relatively simple procedures.

Find The Independent Clause

Since the first procedure recommended by Isaiah was to find the "precept," the first step for this basic process is to locate that part of our study passage that stands by itself as a complete unit. That is, an independent clause (perhaps, a sentence) that has no need for any other words to make the concept understandable. One caution: this process is done *after* we have isolated the complete thought (verse, passage) which we wish to study and is not intended to repeat that step. This effort is to break down and analyze the thought under study to its component parts. And, the first thing to be done is to find the "precept"— the basic commandment. Some passages may have multiple "precepts" in the major thought because the "knowledge" or "doctrine" is complex enough to require a building of "precept upon precept." However, it is wise to be cautious here. If the thought under study seems to have five or six "precepts", it is entirely possible that the area for consideration is too large. Try to limit the study (at least until practice has produced proficiency) to a thought that has no more than three "precepts."

Find The Dependent Clause

Almost every complete thought will be supported by explanatory or definitive argumentation. The Isaiah instruction requires us to build upon the "precepts" by finding the "lines" of the thought. Usually, those will be structured in the same sentence as the independent clause (the "precept") and will be set off by commas (,). Sometimes the supportive points will be contained within another, separate sentence. When that is the case, there will normally be some word signal, such as "for," or "and," or "because," or "upon," etc. Those words should signal the reader that the information to follow is related to the information that has preceded it. More often than not, however, the supporting points will be in the same sentence as the main point and will frequently be nothing more than descriptive or modifying words. There is a simple test that the student can apply to check out the relationship of these clauses. The "precept" should make sense all by itself. That is, it will be readable and sound comfortable without the rest of the information. The "lines" will not make sense by themselves. They are not complete without the "precept." The "precept" will be made clearer by the "lines," but the "lines" need the "precept" to be understood.

AN EXAMPLE seems to be in order now. We have discussed a good bit of information, and much of it is fairly complex. However, it all ties together rather easily when we actually apply it to a "real life" situation.

One of the most sobering instructions in the Scriptures is given by the Apostle Paul to young Timothy near the end of Paul's life.

I charge thee therefore before God, and the Lord Jesus Christ, who shall judge the quick and the dead at his appearing and his kingdom; Preach the word; be instant in season, out of season; reprove, rebuke, exhort with all longsuffering and doctrine. For the time will come when they will not endure sound doctrine; but, after their own lusts shall they heap to themselves teachers, having itching ears; And they shall turn away their ears from the truth, and be turned unto fables. But watch thou in all things, endure afflictions, do the work of an evangelist, make full proof of the ministry (II Timothy 4:1-5).

This passage is very important—especially to anyone who is involved with a ministry of teaching the Word of God. And, since everyone is told to check out the things that they have been taught (Acts 17:11), it is equally important that we know the kind of things that the teachers are supposed to teach. But, we must *study* the passage to find out its real truth.

Isolate The Total Thought

This first step involves an examination of the contextual setting so that we can get a "feel" for the flow of the teaching. In this case, the passage begins at the start of a chapter division which will require that we go back into the previous chapter. Since there do not appear to be any paragraph symbols (¶), we should drop all the way back to the beginning of the preceding chapter to begin the contextual isolation. It is a good practice to write down the impressions gained during this process. A simple scratch pad is more than adequate for the work here, but it is wise to keep all work in as organized a fashion as possible.

THE PRECEDING VERSES seem to divide up into different topics fairly easily. Verse one of chapter three begins "This know also, that in the last days perilous times shall come." Then verses two through nine proceed to describe the various conditions and types of people that will characterize those "last days." On the scratch pad a simple notation should be made as follows: "3:1-9—last days, description." Reading on, we can notice that verses ten through thirteen contain a different thought. Verse ten starts out, "But thou hast fully known my doctrine. . . ." The "but" is a signal that the thought is either changing or being contrasted with the previous section. The following verses outline the ministry of Paul and conclude with a promise of persecution for godly believers (vs. 12) and a warning about increasing wickedness (vs. 13). So, the notation on the scratch pad could be: "3:10-13—Paul's example and warning." Verse fourteen begins with another "but." This would tend to signal another topic, especially since there is a change of subjects. Paul says, "But continue thou in the things thou hast learned. . . ," and then proceeds to tell Timothy of the importance of the Scriptures. This section seems to tie in with the "charge" given to Timothy in the section in chapter four—especially since verse one begins "I charge thee *therefore*. . . ." The scratch pad should now look like this:

3:1-9—last days, description
3:10-13—Paul's example and warning
3:14-17—importance of the Scriptures
4:1-5—charge to Timothy about the Scriptures

THE STUDY PASSAGE, however, is not related directly to the sections in 3:1-9 or 3:10-13. Therefore, we are justified in excluding consideration of those sections from the thought we want to isolate in chapter four. The section dealing with the Scriptures themselves in 3:14-17 does have some bearing on the passage in 4:1-5, but it seems to be self-contained. That is, the teaching in 3:14-17 does not need the teaching in 4:1-5 to make it clear. And the "charge" of 4:1-5 is not dependent upon the instruction in 3:14-17—except as an explanation as to why the charge is given. Paul's command to "preach the word" would be just as valid if it stood by itself. Therefore, we would be justified in excluding exegetical consideration of the 3:14-17 section from the thought in chapter four. We must note the relationship created by the context; however, Paul is giving the "charge" *because* the Scripture is inspired.

ISOLATING THE SIMPLEST THOUGHT is now possible. With the context established and the general flow of argument understood, we can now try to pin down the most critical, or most concise thought in our passage for careful study. The "charge," introduced in verse one, is not really given until verse two. Although Paul supports the necessity of the charge by calling on "God, and the Lord Jesus Christ. . . ," etc. he does not actually give the command until verse two. Verses three and four are provided as reasons for the command in verse two, and verse five seems to amplify the command of verse two with additional instructions. Once again, the scratch pad is necessary to jot down the passage sequence so that it can be visualized prior to study.

4:1-5 - Charge to Timothy about the Scripture
vs. 1 - Charge based on 3:14-17

Charge made solemn by:
God
Christ
His Judgment
His Coming
His Kingdom
vs. 2 - preach the word
be instant in season, out of season
reprove, rebuke, exhort
with all longsuffering and doctrine
vs. 3 - Because:
not endure sound doctrine
heap teachers to themselves after own lusts
vs. 4 - turn away ears from truth to fables
vs. 5 - Watch in everything
endure afflictions
do the work of an evangelist
make full proof of the ministry

This process is vital. Later on, when we begin to examine the various words, it will be easy to forget what related to what. This first isolation process will be the "picture" which will restore the "vision" of the passage. It is absolutely necessary to write down this information on a sheet of paper. If this is not done, not only will the isolation of the study thought be made more difficult, but the likelihood of improper study (either too much or too little) is increased significantly. In this passage, the main thought is contained in verse two. That verse is the "isolated thought" because of its relationship to the other verses. As was pointed out earlier, verses one, three, and four are all supporting information to the actual command contained in verse two. Verse five, although related to the activity of the general subject, is not directly tied to the simple command "preach the word." All of the instructions of verse five *could* be connected to the command to preach—especially since the subject ("you") is the same. However, both verse two and verse five are able to stand alone. Therefore, we should limit our initial search to the main thought. If, after completing the initial study, we find that a further examination of verse five is helpful, we can develop that verse in the same way we are going to do verse two.

Break Down The Thought Into The Major Sub-points

Having isolated the simplest, most complete thought in the passage, we can now begin to break it down into its component parts. This procedure is much the same as the process we just went through to isolate the thought, but is more critical and microscopic in its approach. Perhaps the first thing to do is to locate and relate the various parts of speech in the thought. This need not be done in writing if the student is fairly competent in grammatical skills. However, it is wise to pinpoint the key elements as an assistance to later study. In this instance, the subject of the entire thought is "you" as understood by the command language. Paul is writing to Timothy and is writing in the form of a personal letter. Since this is also the Word of God, the "you" means both you and me.

This subject is given a series of actions to follow. "You" is told to "preach," to "be instant" and to "reprove, rebuke, exhort." Obviously, there is a great deal of instruction here. Our job is to sort it out. There is also an object for each of the actions. The subject is told to preach "the word," be instant "in season," reprove, etc. "with all longsuffering and doctrine."

Analyze The Purpose And Thesis Of The Thought

After locating and identifying the key parts of speech in the thought, we can begin to separate the parts into the major and minor points of the thought. Normally, the natural word order will outline the relationships. That is, the most important point will be first, and the supporting points will follow in descending importance. Obviously, that is not always the case, but it is true often enough that the student should certainly examine that possibility first. If the natural order does not seem to allow for logical relationship, then recourse has to be made to simple common sense. Remember, the Holy Spirit revealed the Scriptures and designed them so that the truths could be understood by born-again children of God. If for some reason the relationship does not fall satisfactorily into place, establish the best possible sequence and proceed with study. During the study of the Scriptures themselves, the proper order *will* be revealed. The Holy Spirit promised to help us (John 16:13).

Find The Independent Clause
The beginning point has to be the location of that phrase, sentence, —whatever—that stands on its own as the thesis or main point of the passage. In this passage, "preach the word" seems to fill the bill. Look back at the note pad (the example is on page 98). All of the action phrases or words are either incomplete (reprove, rebuke, exhort), or they seem to be vague and dependent upon some other thought for ample clarity (be instant in season). Therefore, the first independent clause, "[you] preach the word," stands by itself as the main thesis of this thought. All of the other ideas will be either explanations of or supporting arguments to the command to "preach to the word."

Find The Dependent Clause
Knowing the main thought now enables us to relate the various sub-points. In this case there are several! As always, the scratch pad is imperative. Please do not think that you are that "special" person who does not need to go through these "silly" steps. As the Lord helps you to become proficient in Bible study, you may find some other form or procedure that helps you become more rapid, but please do not be tempted to skip these elemental steps of passage outline and analysis. If you do, the result will only be harmful to you and your hearers (read Matthew 5:19). Back to the point. Paul has told Timothy (and us) to preach the word *and* to preach that word under some strict guidelines. The best way to see those guidelines is

to describe the thoughts fairly carefully on the scratch pad.

> preach the word (thesis)
>> instant in season, out of season (when to preach)
>
> reprove, rebuke, exhort (how to preach)
>> with all longsuffering and doctrine (how to reprove, etc.)

The result of all this effort has been to produce a visual representation of the thought relationships. If we wanted to make a formal outline (which we will do later), we would only have to put in the Roman numerals and capital letters that would add the "dress." This visual relationship is the basis for all further study within the passage. If we have done it correctly, we will be rewarded with real insight into the information. If we have done it poorly, we will have real trouble "reading" the information and may well come to improper conclusions. Usually, if the preceding steps have been followed, the Holy Spirit will assist our efforts through His "enlightenment" (Eph. 1:17-18) to direct our minds to the truth.

But, this is only the edge of the water. If you really want to go swimming, you have to get all the way in. The next chapter does just that. Hold your breath and dive in!

9

LOOK AT THE WORDS

All of that previous work is just the start—just a portion of the "give good heed" part of our study. But take courage! It takes far less time to actually do the work than it does to read about how to do it! The main focus during the previous chapter was on the grammar and structure of the message. We must now attempt to dig into the treasures of the words themselves and try to locate the concrete truth of the message.

Perform A Word Study On The Key Words

Obviously, the first thing to be done is to make sure of the definitions of the key words used in the thought. If proper preparation has been made during the previous step, the student will have located the key words in the thought by determining the parts of speech. Usually this process is quite simple and will, with practice, become quite rapid. In this case, we can transfer the key words to a worksheet similar to the one we used in chapter five.

WORD	WORD #	DEFINITION
preach	2784	to herald, cry out
word	3056	the logos
instant	2186	to be present
season	2121	well-timed, convenient
season	171	inopportunely
reprove	1651	admonish, convict
rebuke	2008	to tax, to censure
exhort	3870	to call near, invite
longsuffering	3115	forbearance
doctrine	1322	instruction

The word study process is summarized in chapter six. If you do not recall how it was done, or cannot see from the worksheet example what is being done, then please go back and skim over those outlines. That should bring you up to our position here.

Determine The Other English Words Used

Almost every one of the Hebrew and Greek words of the Bible are translated by more than one English word. It is virtually impossible to find an exact comparison between one language and another, so the translators must try to choose a word that will fit the message as well as the definition. That is why there are so many different words used in the English for the same Greek or Hebrew word. In our study process, we must "penetrate" the Scriptures to try to find additional Biblical data that will shed light on the subject we are studying. Since the Holy Spirit used the Biblical languages, we must resort to those languages for such study. And, since the translators have rendered the same Greek or Hebrew word by different English words, we must know what those different words are. Thankfully, the Strong's concordance provides such information for us.

Back in chapter four we examined the structure of Strong's concordance and spent some time going through the construction of the two language dictionaries. In each word listing within the dictionaries, there is cited every other English word chosen by the translators to replace that specific Greek or Hebrew word. Those words were given at the end of the word history and definition information, and followed the punctuation mark, (:-).

word history—
and
definition

982. בָּטַח **bâṭach**, *baw-takh'*; a prim. root; prop. to *hie* for refuge [but not so *precipitately* as 2620]; fig. to *trust*, be *confident* or *sure:*—be bold (confident, secure, sure), careless (one, woman), put confidence. (make to) hope, (put, make to) trust.

translated words

The words that appear inside parentheses are words that are sometimes used by the translators to give special emphasis to the principal word. In the above example, BATACH, number 982, is translated by "be bold (confident, secure, sure), careless . . . ." The same Hebrew word, number 982, appears in Proverbs 28:1 as "bold," in Psalms 27:3 as "confident," in Judges 18:7 as "secure," and in Proverbs 11:15 as "sure." However, the next word, "careless," is followed by the parenthetical notation (one, woman). This shows that some of the usages of BATACH (number 982) are followed by a *supplied* English word to carry out the sense of the linguistic context. In Isaiah 32:10, BATACH appears in a context where "daughters" are spoken to, so the translators rendered the word "careless *women*." And, in verse 11, rather than being redundant in their language, they translated the same word "careless *ones*." Dr. Strong makes that information available to us by noting, in parentheses, that "careless" sometimes appears with "one" and sometimes with "women."

The last two parenthetical notations in the example of BATACH, *precede* the translated word, and are there to note *helping* words for translated accuracy. The dictionary notes the following: "(make to) hope, (put, make to) trust." In Proverbs 22:9, the Scriptures note that God "didst *make* me *hope* . . . ." Psalms 4:5 simply says, "*put* your *trust* in the Lord." Both of these examples are repeated many times throughout the languages of the Bible. The translators were trying to make the transition from one language to another as smooth as possible while still preserving the accuracy of the original language. They did a remarkable job! Dr. Strong has made our job considerably easier by providing the linguistic information which will help us see what was supplied by the translators and which single word was actually the core meaning. Once we have found the word listing in the dictionary, we must record the other English words under that listing on our worksheet.

Determine Other Forms Of The Key Words

While we were breaking down the key thought, it was necessary to locate the various parts of speech. This was valuable then in gaining a more accurate understanding of the thought, but it is also very helpful in "penetrating" the thought throughout the rest of Scripture. Every language is composed of "root" words. That is, words that are the source for several closely related words. Normally, the "root" word is the action word, and is expressed in slightly different form to show a different part of speech. A good example is the word "thought." That word is a noun. That is, it expresses a specific concept—a "thing." If we want to show that concept taking place, we use the word "think." That word is a verb. It expresses the activity of thought. If it becomes necessary to describe a person who uses thought activity a lot, that person is said to be a "thinking" person. In this form, the word is an adjective or modifier. All of these "different" words are really the same word expressing another view of the same concept. The scholars who cataloged the various Hebrew and Greek words used in the original books of the Scripture, listed each form of the word as a separate word.

It is necessary to locate the other forms of the key words in our study since the Scripture may use those other forms in other passages which will provide critical information for our understanding of the study concept.

The dictionaries of the Strong's concordance do not directly identify the parts of speech, but are arranged in such a manner to make discovery of them relatively easy.

LOCATE THE SOURCE WORD. As was pointed out back in chapter two, a proper trace of each word should begin with the source, or primary word. In most cases this "source" word will be designated "a prim. root" by the dictionary.

EXAMINE THE RADICAL MEANING. This concise definition will pinpoint the part of speech fairly well. If the word is a verb, the definition will always have the English word "to" in front of the main word. That infinitive construction is our key that the Hebrew or Greek word is an action word. The other forms are designated by the explanative wording in the definition.

TRACE OUT THE PARALLEL WORDS. Usually, those words that are parallel in meaning but different in form will have very close spelling to the source word. That means that they will follow in fairly close alphabetical order and can be located by the numerical sequence of the language dictionary.

radical meaning ⎤

8104. שָׁמַר **shâmar,** *shaw-mar';* a prim. root; prop. to *hedge* about (as with thorns), i.e. *guard;* gen. to *protect, attend to,* etc.:—beware, be circumspect, take heed (to self), keep (-er, self), mark, look narrowly, observe, preserve, regard, reserve, save (self), sure, (that lay) wait (for), watch (-man).

⎤ source word verb

uses the infinitive "to hedge"

8105. שֶׁמֶר **shemer,** *sheh'-mer;* from 8104; something *preserved,* i.e. the *settlings* (plur. only) of wine:—dregs, (wines on the) lees.

⎤ noun form

8106. שֶׁמֶר **Shemer,** *sheh'-mer;* the same as 8105; *Shemer,* the name of three Isr.:—Shamer, Shemer.

⎤ proper name

8107. שִׁמֻּר **shimmûr,** *shim-moor';* from 8104; an *observance:*— × be (much) observed.
שֹׁמֵר **Shômêr.** See 7763.

⎤ noun form

8108. שָׁמְרָה **shomrâh,** *shom-raw';* fem. of an unused noun from 8104 mean. a *guard; watchfulness:*—watch.

107

8109. שְׁמֻרָה **shᵉmûrâh,** *shem-oo-raw';* fem. of
pass. part. of 8104; something *guard.*
ed, i.e. an *eye-lid:*—waking. ⎤ participle

8110. שִׁמְרוֹן **Shimrôwn,** *shim-rone';* from 8105 ⎤ noun or
in its orig. sense; *guardianship;* adjective
Shimron, the name of an Isr. and of a place in Pal.:—
Shimron.

Obviously, not every source word will have this many
forms, nor will every source word generate parallel
forms that are as closely related alphabetically as the
above example. But, each major word does have some
varying forms. The objective here is *not* to determine
the precise part of speech, but to locate those words
that *may* have some bearing on the subject under study.
We do not need to perform an exhaustive word analysis,
but only gain the *list* of those words (numbers, for our
purposes) that are parallel to the word used in our study
passage.

Make A New Worksheet

The best way to clear up the confusion that you are no doubt now
feeling, is to provide a demon-
stration of this process. But before we can do that, it
is advisable to make a new worksheet. So far, we have
a worksheet that lists the key words and their definitions. However, that sheet may not leave enough room
for the information that we need to obtain now. It is
possible to use one worksheet here, but it would be
best to become familiar with the new procedure before
attempting to combine steps. Once you are comfortable
with this work, it will be easy to plan ahead on the
worksheet for adequate material. For now, however, we
should separate the steps.

WORD	WORD #	OTHER #	OTHER ENGLISH WORDS
preach	2784	2782-84	proclaim, publish

word	3056	3048-56	oracle, doctrine, matter, tidings, treatise, utterance
instant	2186	----	assault, come, be at hand, present, stand
season	2121	2120-22	opportunity, convenient, in time of need
season	171	170	lack opportunity
reprove	1651	1649-51	rebuke, evidence, convict, convince, fault
rebuke	2008	----	charge
exhort	3870	3874-75	advocate, beseech, comfort, desire, intreat, pray, consolation
longsuf-fering	3115	3114-16	suffer, patience, bear long
doctrine	1322	1321	teach

Remember where we are. We have begun an analysis of II Timothy 4:2 in an effort to find out a little more about the command given to "preach the word." We have done a word study on each of the key words, and have now begun to find the other English and Greek words that are parallel to each of the key words in the II Timothy passage. The purpose in this exercise is to prepare ourselves to search the Scriptures for the additional information they may contain which will enhance our understanding of the II Timothy passage. Before we can search the Scriptures, we must know where to look. And, since the concordance is arranged according to our English Bibles, we have to know the English words before we can look up other Scriptures. OK? OK!

109

Locate The Source Word

⋮

Examine The Radical Meaning

⋮

Trace Out The Parallel Words

This procedure should be done as one step. It is really not complex and will be accomplished quite rapidly. However, it is important that each point be observed carefully, since it is easy to overlook a thought or a word that might very well be a crucial point. Frequently, the word that we are trying to find in the dictionary will not be the source word. That requires us to trace back the word history information provided by the dictionary in order to obtain the most complete data. Normally, this will be done during the process of gaining the word definition and may not have to be repeated here. However, it is necessary to examine the source word from the perspective of locating those additional English words that might be used to relate to the study we are considering.

The radical meaning of the source word and the radical meaning of the parallel words, will be valuable in helping us to determine how the English words are used. As was discussed a few paragraphs back, the part of speech can be identified by the way the dictionary describes the definition of the word. That part of speech will help us decide which of the various English words are most likely to afford parallel information to our study. Since our objective is to gain only that perspective which is directly parallel to a specific passage (in this case II Timothy 4:2), it is not necessary to examine every passage in the Bible where a certain word appears. But, it is necessary to examine those passages that speak to the same subject. The difference is not always easy to see, however, and we must rely on the "unction from the Holy One" (I John 2:20) to assist our thinking process.

3048. λογία **lŏgia**, *log-ee'-ah;* from *3056* (in the commercial sense); a *contribution:*—collection, gathering.

3049. λογίζομαι **lŏgĭzŏmai**, *log-id'-zom-ahee;* mid. from *3056; to take an inventory,* i.e. *estimate* (lit. or fig.):—conclude, (ac-) count (of), + despise, esteem, impute, lay, number, reason, reckon, suppose, think (on).

3050. λογικός **lŏgĭkŏs**, *log-ik-os';* from *3056; rational* ("*logical*"):—reasonable, of the word.

3051. λόγιον **lŏgĭŏn**, *log'-ee-on;* neut. of *3052;* an *utterance* (of God):—oracle.

3052. λόγιος **lŏgĭŏs**, *log'-ee-os;* from *3056; fluent,* i.e. an *orator:*—eloquent.

3053. λογισμός **lŏgĭsmŏs**, *log-is-mos';* from *3049; computation,* i.e. (fig.) *reasoning* (*conscience, conceit*):—imagination, thought.

3054. λογομαχέω **lŏgŏmachĕō**, *log-om-akh-eh'-o;* from a comp. of *3056* and *3164; to be disputatious* (on trifles):—strive about words.

3055. λογομαχία **lŏgŏmachĭa**, *log-om-akh-ee'-ah;* from the same as *3054; disputation* about trifles ("*logomachy*"):—strife of words.

3056. λόγος **lŏgŏs**, *log'-os;* from *3004; something said* (including the *thought*); by impl. a *topic* (subject of discourse), also *reasoning* (the mental faculty) or *motive;* by extens. a *computation;* spec. (with the art. in John) the Divine *Expression* (i.e. *Christ*):—account, cause, communication, × concerning, doctrine, fame, × have to do, intent, matter, mouth, preaching, question, reason, + reckon, remove, say (-ing), shew, × speaker, speech, talk, thing, + none of these things move me, tidings, treatise, utterance, word, work.

•••

3004. λέγω **lĕgō**, *leg'-o;* a prim. verb; prop. to '*lay*" forth, i.e. (fig.) *relate* (in words [usually of systematic or set *discourse;* whereas *2036* and *5346* generally refer to an *individual* expression or speech respectively; while *4483* is prop. to *break silence* merely, and *2980* means an *extended* or random harangue]); by impl. to *mean:*—ask, bid, boast, call, describe, give out, name, put forth, say (-ing, on), shew, speak, tell, utter.

The main thesis in our study passage is "preach the word." In *examining* "preach," the dictionary does not present much complex information. However, "word," number 3056 in the dictionary, is a different story! To begin with, the definition is confusing. And, if that were not bad enough, it comes from number 3004 whose definition is equally complex. Besides that, the English words given for the various translations seem to run the entire spectrum of conversation. How in the world can we make sense out of that?

Surprisingly enough, it really is not as bad as it seems. There is one overriding factor in this kind of study—the thesis of the passage. We are not interested at this point in anything that does not relate to preaching the Word. Therefore, we can eliminate all the data that does not pertain. The source word, number 3004, seems to be the common word for speaking. But our thesis uses "preach," number 2784, an entirely different word. The thing "preached" (the word) is only related to number 3004 through the concept of speaking. Remember, the thesis is "preach the word." "Preach is the action, and "word" is the thing upon which the action is taking place. Therefore, we do not have to be concerned with the action of number 3004 or the various words that are used to translate it. But, we do have to discover what parallel words are important.

In this case, as seems to be the case most frequently in the Greek language, the noun is the source or basic word rather than the verb, as is the case in the Hebrew language. So, to find those parallel forms of word number 3056, we must check backward (and sometimes forward) to see if there are any other words that have number 3056 as *their* source. And, sure enough, there are several. Number 3054 is "a comp. of 3056 and 3164." Numbers 3052, 3050, 3049, and 3048 all say that they are "from 3056." And, number 3055 says that it is "from the same as 3054," which means that it also comes from 3056, as does number 3051 which says that it is the "neut. of 3052." Therefore, every word from 3048 and through 3055 is another form of our study word, number 3056. That is the information that needs to be recorded in the "other #" column on our worksheet.

Now that we know what words (what numbers) are legitimate forms of this study word, we have to determine what additional English words have a legitimate relationship to our study thesis. Remember, the thesis is "preach the word." We only need to look up those words that have a bearing on that concept. The best way to check that out is to repeat the thesis, substituting the various English words in the place of the study word. Word number 3048 is translated by "collection" and "gathering." If we substitute those two words in the thesis, they do not make sense: "preach the collection; preach the gathering." Therefore, word number 3048 is not a valid parallel of our study. The same is true of words numbered 3049 and 3050. None of the English words used for those two Greek words would make any sense in our thesis. But, the one English word which translates number 3051 does seem to make sense: "preach the oracle." So, we would jot that word down in the "other words" column on our worksheet.

The words numbered 3052 and 3055 both seem to be a specialized form of "word" and do not "fit" our thesis easily. And, since it is never good practice to force a thought or word into the Scriptures, we are most often safe to ignore those words or concepts that do not seem to "fit." Later on, we will discuss how to examine every passage of Scripture that uses a particular word and compile an accurate study of it. However, for this type of study, it is necessary to stick with those words and passages that are obviously related.

That brings us back to our main word, number 3056. The radical meaning (the definition) of the word shows that it is a rather broad word that can mean anything from "something said" to "a computation." That is not all that unusual for any language, and just means that the way in which the word is used will determine the various shades of meaning. In this case, we have the thesis to help us determine which usages will be valid. We should substitute the message of the thesis into the various translated terms. Preach the:

> "account, cause, communication, X concerning, *doctrine,* fame X have to do, intent, *matter,* mouth, preaching, question, reason, + reckon, remove, say (-ing), shew, X speaker, speech, talk, thing, + none of these things move me, *tidings, treatise, utterance,* word, work."

[These are the words listed in the dictionary under 3056.]

Of all these words, only five seem to make sense when we substitute them into the thesis phrase. Those are the words that we would put in our "other words" column on the worksheet.

All of that process can be done in about one or two minutes when it becomes familiar and will help establish a good perspective on the study passage. It is necessary to follow the same procedure for each of the key words in the study passage—each time relating the process to the thesis of the passage. When we study these initial pieces of information, it is very easy to forget what we are looking for. Always repeat the thesis in your mind while dissecting the various words!

Now look back at the word study worksheet. Take the time to perform these word expansion steps on your own for each of the other key words in the study passage. As you finish each word, check your work against mine in the worksheet I have shown. They may not be exactly the same, but they will not be very different either. If you do not understand what is going on, please reread this chapter and examine each of the examples provided. You should have a reasonable grasp of this process before you go on.

The various mechanics involved in this initial step of "listening" to the message are not too complex, but they are necessary to provide an adequate base from which to "seek out" the additional information within the Scriptures that will make the message clearer. Make sure that you have followed the basic procedure up to this point. You may not yet see why all of this is necessary. That will come in the next chapter. Interested? Read chapter ten.

10

PENETRATE
THE MESSAGE

Now comes the exciting part! All the work up to this point has been just plain work. Now we can begin to look "here and there" in the Word for the "knowledge" and "doctrine" that the Lord said would be there if we were willing to do it His way. So, it is necessary for us to examine the general guidelines of this phase before we examine the specifics.

LOOK UP THE BASIC ENGLISH WORD that appears in the King James text as it has been listed on the worksheet. The "other words" column on the worksheet will be used to fill out the study, but we must first consult those passages where the basic word appears. After all, the translators did choose the same word for other places because that English word seemed the best choice for the message. Probably, we will find the bulk of parallel information in these passages.

EXAMINE EACH WORD LISTING, but look *only* for those passages that use the same numbers as the word in the study passage. We are studying II Timothy 4:2, in which the thesis is "preach the word." When we look for parallel passages under "preach," we will only look for the words that have the numbers 2782 through 2784 as was determined by the previous process.

JOT DOWN THE REFERENCES that seem to relate to the main thesis. Once again, it is a good idea to substitute the word or phrase into the thesis to make sure that the relationship is valid. It will probably be necessary to make another worksheet now since there should be several references. A good way of keeping the information in order is to relate this worksheet to the basic outline worksheet that was made initially. That is, keep the references in the section of the worksheet that is visually separated from different points

---

preach the word
    preach
    word
be instant in season out of season
    instant
    season   season
reprove
rebuke
exhort
with all longsuffering and doctrine
    longsuffering
    doctrine

The whole objective here is to dig down into the Word of God and find the additional truth which will make the study passage meaningful. However, if we do not take careful pains to "give good heed" while we "penetrate" the passage, it is entirely likely that we will run off after some piece of interesting information that has absolutely nothing to do with our thesis. Hence, the necessity of some "visual" reminder of our study's relationship. And since it is so easy to lose the perspective of the passage in detailed study, it is best to proceed with the research in the order of the Biblical thoughts. That is, look for additional information for "preach" first, then for "word," then for "instant," etc. That will force a continuity to the research which will encourage objectivity.

The word heading in the main concordance usually will provide the other English words that are immediately associated with the leading word. In this case, we are told to: "see also preached; preachest; preacheth; preaching." This is valuable information since we have only recognized the leading word, "preach," in our study pro-

```
preach  See also PREACHED; PREACHEST; PREACH-
        ETH; PREACHING.
Ne   6:  7 prophets to p' of thee at Jerusalem,7121
Isa 61:  1 anointed me to p' good tidings      1319
Jon  3:  2 p' unto it the preaching that I bid 7121
M't  4: 17 From that time Jesus began to p', 2784
    10:  7 as ye go, p', saying, The kingdom of "
         27 ear, that p' ye upon the housetops. *"
    11:  1 to teach and to p' in their cities.    "
M'r  1:  4 p' the baptism of repentance for the*"
         38 next towns, that I may p' there also:"
     3: 14 that he might send them forth to p',"
    16: 15 and p' the gospel to every creature. "
Lu   4: 18 me to p' the gospel to the poor;    2097
         18 to p' deliverance to the captives,  *2784
         19 p' the acceptable year of the Lord.* "
         43 I must p' the kingdom of God to    2097
     9:  2 he sent them to p' the kingdom of  2784
         60 thou and p' the kingdom of God. *1229
Ac   5: 42 not to teach and p' Jesus Christ.   2097
    10: 42 he commanded us to p' unto the     2784
    14: 15 and p' unto you that ye should turn*2097
    15: 21 hath in every city them that p' him,2784
    16:  6 Holy Ghost to p' the word in Asia, *2980
         10 us for to p' the gospel unto them.  2097
    17:  3 this Jesus, whom I p' unto you, is*2605
Ro   1: 15 I am ready to p' the gospel to you  2097
    10:  8 is, the word of faith, which we p';   2784
         15 shall they p', except they be sent?  "
         15 of them that p' the gospel of peace,*2097
    15: 20 so have I strived to p' the gospel,   "
1Co  1: 17 not to baptize, but to p' the gospel: "
         23 But we p' Christ crucified, unto the2784
     9: 14 they which p' the gospel should    *2605
         16 For though I p' the gospel, I have   2097
         16 woe is unto me, if I p' not the gospel!"
         18 when I p' the gospel, I may make    "
    15: 11 they, so we p', and so ye believed.  2784
2Co  2: 12 I came to Troas to p' Christ's gospel,*
     4:  5 For we p' not ourselves, but Christ2784
    10: 16 p' the gospel in the regions beyond2097
Ga   1:  8 p' any other gospel unto you than  "
          9 man p' any other gospel unto you * "
         16 I might p' him among the heathen;"
     2:  2 which I p' among the Gentiles,     2784
     5: 11 if I yet p' circumcision, why do I     "
Eph  3:  8 I should p' among the Gentiles the2097
Ph'p 1: 15 Some indeed p' Christ even of envy2784
         16 The one p' Christ of contention,    *2605
Col  1: 28 we p', warning every man, Whom * "
2Ti  4:  2 P' the word; be instant in season,2784
Re  14:  6 to p' unto them that dwell on the  *2097
```

cess. The same point would follow in the use of remaining study words as well as the various synonyms discovered earlier. One point that should be made, even though it may seem obvious, is that we should not be concerned at this stage with information in the other Testament. That is, since we are now studying the New Testament passage II Timothy 4:2, we should not try to uncover information in the Old Testament. This is primarily because of our limitation from the specific words used in our study passage. Since the Holy Spirit used a certain word to express a certain thought, we must have adequate and accurate linguistic parallel between Greek and Hebrew before we can interchange the words. During this level of study, we will not deal with that information. Later, we will discover the technique for such transfer, and you can then use it for other studies.

Now, however, it is necessary to examine the data in the concordance and glean from it those Scripture references that *may* provide some parallel truth for our edification. As can easily be seen from the one small section under "preach," there are a lot of verses cited. And, when one tries to imagine repeating this step for *all* those different words . . . well, it does seem a bit involved! Please do not give up yet. The job is not as immense as it may seem on the surface, and the fruits of the labor are well worthwhile. Remember, the objective is to discover *parallel* truth. We are to search for those "precepts" and "lines" from all the short, incomplete phrases in the concordance listing.

That "trick" is nothing more than the "give good heed" process that we have already done. During that work, we outlined the passage in its relationship to the thesis and uncovered the "flow" of the argument. Our job now is to use that information as a sieve to sort out only those verses that apply to the study passage. The thesis "preach the word," will be the main funnel through which we will pour all the verse phrases listed in the concordance, and the argument flow or passage outline will act as the sifter to help us place the various verses into the proper category. If we have done the "give good heed" preparation work correctly, we should have little difficulty with the "seek out" process.

PREACH THE WORD
After locating the leading word heading in the concordance, we must begin to examine each phrase that con-

tains one of the word numbers that we have previously determined to be applicable to our thesis. We need to use the word study worksheet as a constant reference during this stage of our research. In this case, the word numbers for "preach" could be anything from 2782 to 2784. Under the main heading in the example, we can see that there are several references that use 2784.

However, it would be unwise to try to tie in every verse that uses 2784, so we shall only look for those that have something to do with "preaching the word." A good initial practice is to see if there are any other passages that have the same thesis. Acts 16:6 uses the same English phrase, but uses a different Greek word for "preach." Therefore, it would be unwise to use that reference unless we were positive that the other Greek word, number 2980, was a definite parallel to number 2784. Romans 10:8 seems to deal with the same thesis when it says "the word of faith, which we preach. . . ." The word number in that passage is the same, so we can jot that reference down on our worksheet.

It is usually wise to continue the same search (looking for the same phrase or thesis) through the immediate parallel English words (preached, preacher, etc.). In this case, Mark 2:2; Acts 8:25; Acts 13:5; Acts 14:25; Acts 15:36; Acts 17:13; Hebrews 4:2; Acts 8:4; Acts 11:19; and Acts 15:35 all deal directly with preaching the Word, but they used word numbers 2980, 2605, 2097, or 189. Since there seem to be a good many verses here that may deal with the thesis even though they do not use the same Greek word, it is worthwhile to note those references for possible application later. The best way to do that is to make an isolated area on the worksheet in the same general vicinity as the place where "preach" is located and list the extra verses under their respective words. That is, the references Mark 2:2; Acts 8:25; 11:19; 14:25; 16:6 would all be listed under word number 2980. References Acts 13:5; 15:36; 17:13 would all be listed under word number 2605. References Acts 8:4; 15:35 would be under word number 2097, and Hebrews 4:2

listed under word number 189. These verses *may* apply to our study, but before we would be justified in using them as support for the teaching in II Timothy 4:2, we would have to know that the different words (2980, 2605, 2097, and 189) were proper synonyms to the source word, number 2784. That will be done later. All that needs to be done now is to record the *possibility* of their application on the worksheet.

To complete this initial run through the verses, we must note that I Corinthians 2:4 and Titus 1:3, listed under "preaching," are both phrases that contain the thesis idea and use the thesis word. They should be recorded on the worksheet as probable sources of parallel truth.

To this should be added those verses that in some way identify with the *purpose* of the thesis. In this case, the thesis is a command to preach the word. We must try to locate any verses that give another such command, or that seem to provide information concerning such a command. So, when we look back through the verses under the heading "preach," we find that Acts 10:42 is listed with the phrase "he commanded us to preach to the. . . ." And Romans 10:15 cites the phrase, "shall they preach except they be sent." Both of these references may be added to the worksheet.

preach the word	#2980 - Mk. 2:2; Acts 8:25; 11:19; 14:25; Acts 16:6
	#2097 - Acts 8:4; 15:35
preach - Rom. 10:8	#2605 - Acts 13:5; 15:36;
I Cor. 2:4; Tit. 1:3	17:13
Acts 10:42; Rom. 10:15	# 189 - Heb. 4:2
word -	

The other English words, "proclaim" and "publish," which we had determined earlier to be appropriate synonyms to check, should now be checked under their listing in the concordance. However, when this is done we find that the eight references do not have any bearing on our study thesis (by the way, those words are located on page 813 and 819 in the concordance). We may now move on to the next word.

But when we do, we discover that the next word, "word," has almost four full pages of references! How in the world can we make sense out of that? Well, we do not have to examine the Old Testament references, so that eliminates all but about one page. And, we only have to check those references that use those Greek words (numbers 3048-3056) which were relevant to our study passage. Besides that, there still remains the limiting factor of the thesis. That is, of all the passages that use word numbers 3048 through 3056, we are only interested in the ones that have some direct bearing on the command to "preach the word." Furthermore, since this is an object word, that is, it is used as the "what" or "why" of the action word, we do not have to be concerned with searching for the action portion of the command since we already did that under "preach." Therefore, the only verses that we have to locate are those that might tell us some of the reasons *why* we are to preach the word—or some information on what "word" is.

Obviously, we could spend a great deal of time developing such an approach—even as limited as it is. Our objective is to develop II Timothy 4:2, not to develop the doctrine of preaching. Therefore, we must limit ourselves in this form of study to that which is most helpful to the study passage. Often, the initial approach made when searching out the action of the thesis ("preach," in this case) will be enough to satisfy the scope of a particular study. If not, it is usually sufficient to locate a few supporting verses within the secondary concept.

This study is immediately concerned with the phrase "preach the word." We have already examined the "preach" aspect, have located three key verses which have the same basic thesis, and have found several other verses that seem to deal with the same thought but use different words. Now we are confronted with a very large number of references which use the same word as the object of the "preach" action, the word "word."

Since there are so many, and since we already have a fairly good number of supporting verses, it should not be necessary to search through every reference using "word" for some new insight. However, it is always valuable to scan the columns in the concordance to see if there are books of the Bible that use the study word very frequently. Usually, that is an indicator that the book of the Bible deals with the concept in some depth. In this case, John's gospel seems to be one book that majors in that theme.

```
Joh 1: 1 In the beginning was the W',    3056
        1 and the W' was with God,         "
        1 and the W' was God.              "
       14 the W' was made flesh, and dwelt "
    2:22 and the w' which Jesus had said.  "
    4:41 believed because of his own w';   "
       50 man believed the w' that Jesus had"
    5:24 He that heareth my w', and        "
       50 ye have not his w' abiding in you"
    8:31 If ye continue in my w', then are "
       37 because my w' hath no place in you,"
       43 even because ye cannot hear my w'."
   10:35 unto whom the w' of God came,     "
   12:48 the w' that I have spoken, the same"
   14:24 the w' which ye hear is not mine. "
   15: 3 w' which I have spoken unto you.  "
       20 Remember the w' that I said unto "
       25 that the w' might be fulfilled that"
   17: 6 me; and they have kept thy w'.    "
       14 I have given them thy w'; and the "
       17 through thy truth: thy w' is truth."
       20 believe on me through their w';  "
```

A closer examination of those listings provides us with three or four familiar passages that give us some "why" to the command of our study thesis. John 5:24 is a famous salvation verse, John 8:31 notes that the continuance in the Word is necessary for discipleship, and John 17:17 verifies that holiness comes through truth, which is the Word of God. These selections are somewhat arbitrary. However, we should be able to select references that are in line with the thrust of the message of our study passage, as long as we constantly filter the selections through the thesis of the passage. By asking the normal questions about the thesis (who, what, when, where, why), we will be able to stay within the scope of the message. Once such selections have been made, the verse references must be added to the worksheet.

preach the word	#2980 - Mk. 2:2; Acts 8:25; 11:19; 14:25; Acts 16:6
	#2097 - Acts 8:4; 15:35

preach - Rom. 10:8   #2605 - Acts 13:5; 15:36;
  I Cor. 2:4; Tit. 1:3   17:13
  Acts 10:42; Rom. 10:15 # 189 - Heb. 4:2

word - John 5:24; 8:31;
    17:17

BE INSTANT IN SEASON OUT OF SEASON

Now we can go on with the study. This initial thesis examination is usually the most difficult, in that it requires a fairly careful analysis of the thrust of the message. Once we have done that work, however, it is much easier to search the Scriptures for the related points.

instant
Isa 29: 5 yea, it shall be at an *i* suddenly. 6621
    30:13 breaking cometh suddenly at an *i*. "
Jer 18: 7 At what *i* I shall speak concerning 7281
      9 at what *i* I shall speak concerning "
Lu 2:38 she coming in that *i* gave thanks *5610
  23:23 And they were *i* with loud voices, ‡1945
Ro 12:12 continuing *i* in prayer;   *4342
2Ti 4: 2 be *i* in season, out of season; 2186

season
Ac 19:22 he himself stayed in Asia for a *s*. *5550
  24:25 when I have a convenient *s*, I will 2540
2Co 7: 8 sorry, though it were but for a *s*. 5610
Ga 6: 9 for in due *s* we shall reap, if we 2540
2Ti 4: 2 Preach the word; be instant in *s*, 2121
      2 be instant...out of *s*; reprove, 171
Ph'm 15 he therefore departed for a *s*, that5610
Heb11:25 enjoy the pleasures of sin for a *s*; 4340
1Pe 1: 6 rejoice, though now for a *s*, if   3641
Re 6:11 they should rest yet for a little *s*. *5550
  20: 3 that he must be loosed a little *s*. * "

seasoned
Lu 14:34 his savour, wherewith shall it be *s*? 741
Col 4: 6 be alway with grace, *s* with salt, "

seasons
Ge 1:14 let them be for signs, and for *s*, 4150
Ex 18:22 them judge the people at all *s*: 6256
    26 they judged the people at all *s*: "
Le 23: 4 which ye shall proclaim in their *s*.*4150
Ps 16: 7 reins also instruct me in the night *s*.
 104:19 He appointed the moon for *s*: 4150
Da 2:21 He changeth the times and the *s*: 2166
M't 21:41 render him the fruits in their *s*. 2540
Ac 1: 7 for you to know the times or the *s*, "
  14:17 us rain from heaven, and fruitful *s*. "
  20:18 I have been with you at all *s*, *5550
1Th 5: 1 of the times and the *s*, brethren, 2540

convenient
Pr 30: 8 feed me with food *c* for me: *2706
Jer 40: 4 whither it seemeth good and *c* 3477
     5 go wheresoever it seemeth *c* unto "
M'r 6:21 And when a *c* day was come, 2121
Ac 24:25 when I have a *c* season, I will call 2540
Ro 1:28 do those things which are not *c*; *2520
1Co 16:12 come when he shall have *c* time. *2119
Eph 5: 4 nor jesting, which are not *c*: * 433
Ph'm 8 to enjoin thee that which is *c*. * "

conveniently
M'r 14:11 he sought how he might *c* betray 2122

This next phrase, ''be instant in season, out of season,'' seems to have no other direct Scriptural counterpart . . . that is as it applies to preaching the word. A quick check of the references listed under the various words and synonyms reveals that the words themselves are not at all frequent in the New Testament, and are not used in any other

123

lack See also LACKED; LACKEST; LACKETH; LACKING.
Ge 18:28 there shall *l* five of the fifty   2637
      28 destroy all the city for *l* of five?
Ex 16:18 he that gathered little had no *l*;   2637
De 8: 9 thou shalt not *l* any thing in it;
Job 4:11 old lion perisheth for *l* of prey,   1097
     38:41 God, they wander for *l* of meat.   "
Ps 34:10 The young lions do *l*, and suffer   7326
Pr 28:27 giveth unto the poor shall not *l*:   4270
Ec 9: 8 and let thy head *l* no ointment.   2637
Ho 4: 6 are destroyed for *l* of knowledge: 1097
M't 19:20 from my youth up: what *l* I yet?   5302
2Co 8:15 that had gathered little had no *l*.   1641
Ph'p 2:30 to supply your *l* of service toward*5303
1Th 4:12 that ye may have *l* of nothing.   *5302
Jas 1: 5 If any of you *l* wisdom, let him   *3007

lacked
De 2: 7 with thee; thou hast *l* nothing.   2637
2Sa 2:30 *l* of David's servants nineteen   6485
      17:22 the morning light there *l* not one   5737
1Ki 4:27 man in his month: they *l* nothing.*   "
     11:22 But what hast thou *l* with me,   2638
Ne 9:21 wilderness, so that they *l* nothing;   2637
Lu 8: 6 away, because it *l* moisture. *3361,2192
     22:35 scrip, and shoes, *l* ye any thing?   5302
Ac 4:34 was there any among them that *l*:1729
1Co 12:24 honour to that part which *l*:   5302
Ph'p 4:10 also careful, but ye *l* opportunity. 170

opportunity
M't 26:16 time he sought *o* to betray him.   2120
Lu 22: 6 sought *o* to betray him unto them   "
Ga 6:10 As we have therefore *o*, let us do 2540
Ph'p 4:10 were also careful, but ye lacked *o*. 170
Heb11:15 have had *o* to have returned.   2540

passage where they are connected to preaching. Therefore, the only thing that will be of value to us in this study will be to verify the definition of the study words through their use in unrelated passages, "Instant" is used several other times, but no reference is particularly valuable as a further definition.

"In season" is used in Mark 6:21, translated as "convenient," and in Luke 22:6, translated as "opportunity." Both of these verses are merely good usage examples and need not be recorded on the worksheet. The fact that we have visually verified the language use is sufficient. "Out of season" is cited in Philippians 4:10 where it is translated "lacked opportunity" in such a manner that it *may* have value for our study, so we should jot that reference down on the worksheet.

REPROVE, REBUKE, EXHORT

The next three action words are all used in an effort to show *how* the preaching is to be done. We have been told *what* to preach—"the word," we have been told *when* to preach—"instant in season out of season," and now the Apostle Paul is telling us *how*. We are to preach the word by reproving, rebuking, and exhorting. Obviously, we must search the concordance for parallel Scripture references and must be careful to stay within the textual framework. Once again, a good practice is to insert the wording of the main thesis into the phrase of the potential parallel reference in an effort to insure actual application. This is the best check that we can make short of examining the Scriptural passage itself (which, by the way, we will and must do eventually). However, in this step, we are merely trying to locate those *potential* passages that *may* bear directly to our study passage.

reprove See also REPROVED; REPROVETH; UNRE-PROVABLE.

Joh 16: 8 is come, he will r' the world of sin,*1651
Eph 5:11 of darkness, but rather r' them. "
2Ti 4: 2 r', rebuke, exhort with all "

reproved
Ge 20:16 with all other: thus she was r'. *3198
    21:25 Abraham r' Abimelech because "
1Ch 16:21 yea, he r' kings for their sakes. "
Ps 105:14 yea, he r' kings for their sakes; "
Pr 29: 1 being often r' hardeneth his neck,8433
Jer 29:27 why hast thou not r' Jeremiah 1605
Hab 2: 1 what I shall answer when I am r'.*8433
Lu 3:19 being r' by him for Herodias his 1651
Joh 3:20 light, lest his deeds should be r'. "
Eph 5:13 that are r' are made manifest by "

reprover
Pr 25:12 is a wise r' upon an obedient ear. 3198
Eze 3:26 dumb, and shalt not be to them a r':"

reproveth
Job 40: 2 he that r' God, let him answer it. *3198
Pr 9: 7 He that r' a scorner getteth to 3256
    15:12 scorner loveth not one that r' him:*3198
Isa 29:21 a snare for him that r' in the gate, "

This first verb, "reprove," is also translated "rebuke." That means that the meanings are similar enough that they may be used interchangeably on occasions. However, the Holy Spirit used *both* words in our study passage which means that He does see a difference—at least as far as preaching the Word is concerned. It is our job to find out the differences and to pin down some *scriptural* examples of "reproving" with the Word and "rebuking" with the Word.

In the sections of the concordance that list "reprove" and "rebuke," there are eleven references that use the

rebuke See also REBUKED; REBUKES; REBUK-ETH; REBUKING; UNREBUKABLE.

M'r 8:32 took him, and began to r' him. "
Lu 17: 3 trespass against thee, r' him; and "
    19:39 unto him, Master, r' thy disciples. "
Ph'p 2:15 the sons of God, without r', in the* 298
1Ti 5: 1 R' not an elder, but intreat him as 1969
    20 Them that sin r' before all, that *1651
2Ti 4: 2 r', exhort with all longsuffering 2008
Tit 1:13 Wherefore r' them sharply, that *1651
    2:15 exhort, and r' with all authority. * "
Jude 9 but said, The Lord r' thee. 2008
Re 3:19 many as I love, I r' and chasten: *1651

Greek word number 1651. Of those, only Luke 3:19 and Hebrews 12:5 do not seem to apply to our thesis. All of the others,

rebuked

M't 8:26	and r' the winds and the sea; and 2008
17:18	And Jesus r' the devil; and he "
19:13	pray: and the disciples r' them. "
20:31	the multitude r' them, because they' "
M'r 1:25	And Jesus r' him, saying, Hold thy "
4:39	he arose, and r' the wind, and said "
8:33	he r' Peter, saying, Get thee behind "
9:25	he r' the foul spirit, saying unto "
10:13	his disciples r' those that brought "
Lu 4:35	And Jesus r' him, saying, Hold thy "
·39	and r' the fever; and it left her: "
8:24	he arose, and r' the wind and the "
9:42	Jesus r' the unclean spirit, and "
55	he turned, and r' them, and said, "
18:15	his disciples saw it, they r' them. "
39	they which went before r' him, "
23:40	But the other answering r' him, * "
Heb12: 5	nor faint when thou art r' of him:*1651
2Pe 2:16	But was r' for his iniquity: the 2192,1649

rebuker

Ho 5: 2	I have been a r' of them all. 4148

rebukes

Ps 39:11	When thou with r' dost correct 8433
Eze 5:15	and in fury and in furious r'. "
25:17	upon them with furious r'; and "

rebuketh

Pr 9: 7	he that r' a wicked man getteth *3198
28: 23	he that r' a man afterwards shall "
Am 5:10	They hate him that r' in the gate,* "
Na 1: 4	He r' the sea, and maketh it dry, 1605

rebuking

2Sa 22:16	discovered, at the r' of the Lord, *1606
Lu 4:41	he r' them suffered them not to 2008

convicted

Joh 8: 9	being c' by their own conscience. *1651

convince See also CONVINCED; CONVINCETH.

Tit 1: 9	exhort and to c' the gainsayers. *1651
Jude 15	to c' all that are ungodly among *1827

convinced

Job 32:12	there was none of you that c' Job, 3198
Ac 18:28	For he mightily c' the Jews, *1246
1Co 14:24	unlearned, he is c' of all, he is *1651
Jas 2: 9	c' of the law as transgressors. "

convinceth

Joh 8:46	Which of you c' me of sin ? *1651

fault See also FAULTS; FAULTLESS.

M't 18:15	and tell him his f' between thee 1651
M'r 7: 2	unwashen, hands, they found f' *3201
Lu 23: 4	I find no f' in this man. 158
14	have found no f' in this man "
Joh 18:38	I find in him no f' at all. * 156
19: 4	know that I find no f' in him. * "
6	for I find no f' in him. * "
Ro 9:19	Why doth he yet find f' ? For who 3201
1Co 6: 7	there is utterly a f' among you, *2275
Ga 6: 1	if a man be overtaken in a f', *3900
Heb 8: 8	For finding f' with them, he saith, 3201
Re 14: 5	are without f' before the throne * 299

could have some bearing on the study passage in II Timothy. The only way to be sure is to look up each reference in the Bible and read the verse in its context. That we will do later. For now, we must simply record the *potential* references on the worksheet along with those potential references that we find listed under the other English words which have been used to translate word number 1651.

Our worksheet should now look like this:

preach the word	#2980 - Mk. 2:2; Acts 8:25; 11:19; 14:25; Acts 16:6 #2097 - Acts 8:4; 15:35

preach - Rom. 10:8   #2605 - Acts 13:5; 15:36;
   I Cor. 2:4; Tit. 1:3   17:13
   Acts 10:42; Rom. 10:15   # 189 - Heb. 4:2

word - John 5:24; 8:31;
         17:17

be instant in season out of season
   instant -
   season - Mk. 6:21; Lk. 22:6   **season** - Phil. 4:10

reprove - John 16:8; Eph. 5:11; Jn. 3:20;
            Eph. 5:13; I Tim. 5:1; Titus 1:13; 2:15; 1:9;
            I Cor. 14:24; Jas. 2:9

This process must be continued for the next two action words. We have some information on "rebuking with the Word," but the Holy Spirit gave us *three* different methods of preaching in this marvelous passage. We cannot overlook any point. In the concordance listings of "rebuke" (the example is back on page 125-26), we can quickly notice that our word, number 2008, is used fairly frequently. But remember, we are limited to those usages that relate to the thesis, "preach the word." Therefore, we should be able to eliminate those references in the gospels that show Jesus "rebuking" the demons, or the crowd "rebuking" Jesus, etc.

charged See also CHARGEDST; OVERCHARGED.
Ge 26:11 And Abimelech *c'* all his people,   6680
    28: 1 and *c'* him, and said unto him,   "
M't 9:30 Jesus straitly *c'* them, saying,   1690
    12:16 And *c'* them that they should not   2008
    16:20 Then *c'* he his disciples that they   1291
    17: 9 Jesus *c'* them, saying, Tell the   *1781
M'r 1:43 he straitly *c'* him, and forthwith   1690
     3:12 straitly *c'* them that they should   2008
     5:43 he *c'* them straitly that no man   1291
     7:36 *c'* them that they should tell no   "
       36 but the more he *c'* them,   "
     8:15 he *c'* them, saying, Take heed,   "
       30 he *c'* them that they should tell   2008
     9: 9 *c'* them they should tell no man   1291
    10:48 And many *c'* him that he should   *2008
Lu   5:14 And he *c'* him to tell no man: 3853
     8:56 but he *c'* them that they should   "
     9:21 straitly *c'* them, and commanded   2008
Ac 23:22 *c'* him, See thou tell no man   *3853
1Th 2:11 *c'* every one of you, as a father   *3143
1Ti 5:16 and let not the church be *c'*;   * 916

And, when we look back at our "other words" worksheet we find that word number 2008 is also translated "charge." A check of that listing in the concordance reveals four more references that use our study word, but they are also in the gospels in settings that do not seem to relate to the thesis "preach the word." The only reference out of all those that use "rebuke" which might apply to our thesis is Jude 9. That is an unusually small ratio—unless the verses are predominantly *method* verses. That is, the normal use of the word "rebuke" is to show or describe how someone responded in certain circumstances.

Remember, these three action words were given to show us *how* to preach the Word. Since "reprove" and "rebuke" are fairly close words, close enough for one of them to be used interchangeably with the other, we must take whatever Scriptural evidence is available to draw an accurate distinction between them. In this case, "reprove," number 1651, was translated "rebuke." But "rebuke," number 2008, was not translated "reprove." Evidently, "rebuke," number 2008, is the *stronger* of the two words. This seems to be borne out by the various references in the gospels wherein the Lord "rebukes" the demons. The Scriptures must only be used for that which they plainly say. We are not at liberty to "force" an application and must therefore be very careful how we connect passages. Our thesis is "preach the word." We are told to "rebuke" with that word, but are not given any other Scripture passage that directly amplifies that kind of preaching. However, the Scripture does provide *examples* of rebuking. Therefore, we may use those Scriptures as illustration of the mechanic, all the while making sure the mechanic is tied to "the word."

The last of these three action words is "exhort." In our previous worksheet digging out the "other words," we found that this word seems to be fairly broad. It is translated by several different English words, and seems to be used in different ways. That means that we must be all the more careful in keeping our research in the context of the thesis of the passage under study.

On pages 133-35 are each of the pertinent excerpts

from the Strong's concordance that contain listings using the Greek word 3870 and its parallel forms. Our job now is to check through these various listings to find those references that might have a bearing on our study passage in II Timothy. As was noted in our digging through the listings on "rebuke," many of the references may only have a bearing by way of example. This is fairly common when the study words themselves are used as "how to" descriptions of the main thesis. However, this does not release us from checking the examples in the Scripture—especially when the word under study seems to have two meanings.

In this case, "exhort," number 3870, is translated by two different *kinds* of English words. On the one hand, "beseech," "desire," and "intreat" all have the common idea of begging. On the other hand, "comfort" and "consolation" seem to carry the idea of help and assistance to promote peace and assurance. Remember, this is the same Greek word, yet there are two diverse applications. It is possible to see a relationship between the two meanings since it is often necessary to "beg" someone to do a certain thing in order to "help" them. But the two meanings must be related to some other key than the mere whim of the translators. And, indeed that is true. As was mentioned earlier, it is often necessary to judge a word's meaning by the way that it is used in a sentence. A good English example that is somewhat parallel to our word in II Timothy is the word "fuss." If we say, "she fussed at him," the meaning is that she was angry at him and was probably shouting. If we say, "she made a fuss over him," the meaning is that she was concerned about his welfare. If, however, we say "she fussed with the flowers," the meaning is that she was worrying with the visual appearance and was probably concerned with the effect that the flowers would have on her acceptance by the people who would look at the flowers.

The same English word is used in three different ways . . . each one depending on the "context" of the word.

Obviously, the same thing is true in any language. Our job, as Bible students, is to be aware of that simple fact in our research and be wise enough to discern *which* use is applicable to the section of Scripture under current study. In this case, we are trying to find how to "preach the word" and how to "exhort" with the word. The translators have chosen that word over the other possibilities because they felt that it expressed the idea of the context better than the others. And since we can be fairly confident that the translators had more than mere whim as the basis of their choice, it stands to reason that we would find more parallel information in those parts of Scripture where the same English word, "exhort," was chosen. Therefore, that is where to start.

exhort See also EXHORTED; EXHORTETH; EXHORTING.

Ac	2:40	did he testify and *e'*, saying, Save	3870
	27:22	now I *e'* you to be of good cheer:	3867
2Co	9: 5	it necessary to *e'* the brethren.	*3870
1Th	4: 1	and *e'* you by the Lord Jesus.	"
	5:14	we *e'* you, brethren, warn them	"
2Th	3:12	and *e'* by our Lord Jesus Christ.	"
1Ti	2: 1	I *e'* therefore, that, first of all.	"
	6: 2	These things teach and *e'*.	"
2Ti	4: 2	rebuke, *e'* with all long suffering	"
Tit	1: 9	to *e'* and to convince the gainsayers.	"
	2: 6	likewise *e'* to be sober minded.	"
	9	*E'* servants to be obedient unto their	"
	15	speak, and *e'*, and rebuke with all	3870
Heb	3:13	But *e'* one another daily, while it	"
1Pe	5: 1	I *e'*, who am also an elder.	"
Jude	3	me to write unto you, and *e'* you*	"

exhortation

Lu	3:18	*e'* preached he unto the people.	*3870
Ac	13:15	any word of *e'* for the people,	3874
	20: 2	and had given them much *e'*.	3870
Ro	12: 8	Or he that exhorteth, on *e'*:	*3874
1Co	14: 3	edification, and *e'*, and comfort.	† "
2Co	8:17	For indeed he accepted the *e'*;	"
1Th	2: 3	For our *e'* was not of deceit,	"
1Ti	4:13	to reading, to *e'*, to doctrine.	"
Heb	12: 5	forgotten the *e'* which speaketh	"
	13:22	brethren, suffer the word of *e'*:	"

exhorted

Ac	11:23	and *e'* them all, that with purpose	3870
	15:32	*e'* the brethren with many words.	"
1Th	2:11	As ye know how we *e'* and	*

exhorteth
Ro 12: 8 Or he that *e*', on exhortation: 3870

exhorting
Ac 14:22 *e*' them to continue in the faith,   3870
    18:27 *e*' the disciples to receive him: *4389
Heb 10:25 but *e*' one another: and so much   3870
1Pe 5:12 written briefly, *e*', and testifying   "

These listings contain quite a few references that seem to have some direct bearing on the study passage in II Timothy. When this is so, the student is faced with the problem of sorting out the references into some semblance of order. Remember, the objective is to *understand* the doctrine better. That means that we must be careful in each procedure to keep the information as organized as possible. The best way to allow the Holy Spirit to help us is to try very hard not to hold some preconceived notion about the information under study. That is much easier to say than it is to do, since all of us have built-in biases to some degree or other. However, the more Bible study we do, the easier it is for us to develop an objective, wait-and-see attitude—because, we will have found ourselves to have been wrong as often as not. It does not take too many "I-told-you-so" experiences to help develop the proper humility for serious Bible study.

At any rate, the first approach to multiple references in a concordance listing is to read them all—without trying to make any notations. During that initial reading some patterns or categories will suggest themselves to our mind. That way, we are allowing the objective data to speak, rather than establishing some assumed categories in which to place the data. In the above example, as in most cases, the words in the phrases themselves tend to suggest ways of sorting out the references. There seem to be several verses that tell *who* was exhorted. There are several verses that provide information on *what* to exhort about. Other verses show *how* exhortation was to be done, and a few others tell us *by whom* it was done, or that something was *said* in exhortation. Therefore, on a separate piece of scrap paper, we need to jot down the verses under the various categories in an effort to catalog the *kinds* of information. This is what it would look like:

WHO	HOW	BY WHOM	WHAT
II Cor. 9:5	I Th. 2:3	I Th. 4:1	Acts 27:22
I Th. 5:14	I Tim. 4:13	II Th. 3:12	Tit. 2:6, 9
Tit. 1:9	Tit. 2:15		Acts 14:22
I Pet. 5:1	Ro. 12:8		
Jude 3	I Cor. 14:3		**SAYING**
Lk. 3:18	Acts 11:23;		Acts 2:40
Acts 13:15;	15:32		I Tim. 2:1;
20:2	I Th. 2:11		6:2
I Cor. 8:17	I Pet. 5:12		Heb. 12:5;
Heb. 10:25			13:22

With this much information, we could easily build a doctrinal study on exhortation. However, that is *not* the objective in our study of II Timothy 4:2. We are *only* trying to find the information that is relevant to preaching the word through exhortation. Therefore, we have to use judgment and some selection process to "weed out," or, more correctly put, to "filter in" those verses that are most applicable.

It is worthy of note that of these three action words, "reprove," "rebuke," and "exhort," this last one has, by far, more references that seem applicable. We had only found some ten possible references for "reprove" and virtually none for "rebuke." However, "exhort" has some 30 potential references already, and we have not yet checked through the other word listings! Obviously, this kind of preaching was done fairly frequently. And, since that is so, it is necessary that we establish some *Biblical* basis for that kind of preaching—which means we must know *how* it is done. We should therefore list the "how" references on our worksheet. However, since we already are told by the command in our study passage what we are to exhort ("the Word"), it is not *really* necessary to amplify the "what" aspect unless we just plainly want to know more. And since we already have a fairly good number of references on "preaching," it is unlikely that a search of the "to whom" verses will reveal anything startling. But, it could be worthwhile to run down those "to whom" references in the concordance listings to see the main "whoms" of the exhortation. When we do that, it is quickly seen that exhortation is to the brethren, to the people, and to the gainsayers . . . or, in other words, to everybody. That verifies our decision *not* to list the "to whom" verses in this particular study. That only leaves the "by whom" category. When we look at those two references in the concordance listing, we see that both of them speak of exhortation "by the Lord." And that is equivalent to a "how," so we can list those along with those "how" verses on the worksheet.

advocate
1Jo 2: 1 *a'* with the Father, Jesus Christ *3875*

beseech See also BESEECHING: BESOUGHT.

M'r 7:32 *b'* him to put his hand upon him. *3870*
Lu 8:28 high? I *b'* thee, torment me not. *1189*
     9:38 I *b'* thee, look upon my son: "
Ac 21:39 I *b'* thee, suffer me to speak unto "
    26: 3 I *b'* thee to hear me patiently. "
Ro 12: 1 I *b'* you therefore, brethren, by *3870*
    15:30 Now I *b'* you, brethren, for the "
    16:17 Now I *b'* you, brethren, mark "
1Co 1:10 Now I *b'* you, brethren, by the *3870*
     4:16 Wherefore I *b'* you, be ye followers "
    16:15 I *b'* you, brethren, (ye know the "
2Co 2: 8 Wherefore I *b'* you that ye would "
     5:20 as though God did *b'* you by us: * "
     6: 1 him, *b'* you also that ye receive * "
    10: 1 I Paul myself *b'* you by the * "
     2 I *b'* you, that I may not be bold *1189*
Ga 4:12 Brethren, I *b'* you. be as I am; "

Eph 4: 1 *b'* you that ye walk worthy of the *3870*
Ph'p 4: 2 I *b'* Euodias, and *b'* Syntyche, * "
1Th 4: 1 we *b'* you, brethren, and exhort *2065*
    10 but we *b'* you, brethren, that ye *3870*
     5:12 And we *b'* you, brethren, to know *2065*
2Th 2: 1 Now we *b'* you, brethren, by the "
Ph'm 9 for love's sake I rather *b'* thee, *3870*
    10 I *b'* thee for my son Onesimus. "
Heb 13:19 But I *b'* you the rather to do this,* "
    22 I *b'* you, brethren, suffer the * "
1Pe 2:11 beloved, I *b'* you as strangers " "
2Jo 5 now I *b'* thee, lady, not as though *2065*
beseeching
M't 8: 5 unto him a centurion, *b'* him, *3870*
M'r 1:40 there came a leper to him, *b'* him, "
Lu 7: 3 *b'* him that he would come and *2065*

comfort See also COMFORTABLE; COMFORTED;
COMFORTETH; COMFORTLESS; COMFORTS.

M't	9:22 Daughter, be of good c'; thy faith	*2293
M'r	10:49 of good c', rise; he calleth thee.	* "
Lu	8:48 Daughter, be of good c': thy faith*	"
Joh	11:19 to Martha and Mary, to c' them	*3888
Ac	9:31 and in the c' of the Holy Ghost,	3874
Ro	15: 4 patience and c' of the scriptures	"
1Co	14: 3 and exhortation, and c'.	3889
2Co	1: 3 of mercies, and the God of all c';	3874
	4 that we may be able to c' them	3870
	4 by the c' wherewith we ourselves	3874
	2: 7 to forgive him, and c' him, lest	3870
	7: 4 I am filled with c', I am exceeding	3874
	13 we were comforted in your c':	"
	13:11 Be perfect, be of good c', be of	*5870
Eph	6:22 and that he might c' your hearts.	"
Ph'p	2: 1 if any c' of love, if any fellowship	*3890
	19 that I also may be of good c',	2174
Col	4: 8 your estate, and c' your hearts;	3870
	11 which have been a c' unto me.	3931
1Th	3: 2 to c' you concerning your faith:	3870
	4:18 c' one another with these words.	"
	5:11 c' yourselves together, and edify	* "
	14 c' the feebleminded, support the	*3888
2Th	2:17 C' your hearts, and stablish you	3870

comfortable

gSo	14:17 my lord the king shall now be c'.	4496
Zec	1:13 with good words and c' words.	5150

comforted See also COMFORTEDST.

M't	2:18 would not be c', because they	3870
	5: 4 that mourn: for they shall be c'.	"
Lu	16:25 but now he is c', and thou art	"
Joh	11:31 in the house, and c' her, when	*3888
Ac	16:40 the brethren, they c' them, and	3870
	20:12 alive, and were not a little c'.	"
Ro	1:12 that I may be c' together with you.	4837
1Co	14:31 may learn, and all may be c'.	3870
2Co	1: 4 wherewith we ourselves are c'	"
	6 or whether we be c', it is for your	"
	7: 6 down, c' us by the coming of Titus;	"
	7 wherewith he was c' in you,	"
	13 we were c' in your comfort: yea,	"
Col	2: 2 That their hearts might be c',	"
1Th	2:11 ye know how we exhorted and c'	*3888
	3: 7 we were c' over you in all our	3870

comfortedst

Isa	12: 1 is turned away, and thou c' me.	*5162

comforter See also COMFORTERS.

Ec	4: 1 oppressed, and they had no c';	5162
	1 was power; but they had no c'.	"
La	1: 9 down wonderfully: she had no c'.	5162
	16 the c' that should relieve my soul	"
Joh	14:16 and he shall give you another C',	3875
	26 the C', which is the Holy Ghost,	"
	15:26 But when the C' is come, whom I	"
	16: 7 the C' will not come unto you; but	"

comforters

2Sa	10: 3 that he hath sent c' unto thee?	5162
1Ch	19: 3 he hath sent c' unto thee? are not	"
Job	16: 2 miserable c' are ye all.	"
Ps	69:20 none; and for c', but I found none.	"
Na	3: 7 whence shall I seek c' for thee?	"

comforteth

Job	29:25 as one that c' the mourners.	5162
Isa	51:12 I, even I, am he that c' you:	"
	66:13 As one whom his mother c', so will	"
2Co	1: 4 Who c' us in all our tribulation,	3870
	7: 6 that c' those that are cast down,	"

consolation See also CONSOLATIONS.

Jer	16: 7 give them the cup of c' to drink	8575
Lu	2:25 waiting for the c' of Israel:	3874
	6:24 for ye have received your c'.	"
Ac	4:36 being interpreted, The son of c',) *	"
	15:31 had read, they rejoiced for the c'.	"

Ro 15: 5 the God of patience and *c* grant   * "
2Co 1: 5 in us, so our *c* also aboundeth   * "
       6 it is for your *c* and salvation,   * "
       6 we be comforted, it is for your *c*   * "
       7 so shall ye be also of the *c*.   * "
     7: 7 but by the *c* wherewith he was   * "
Ph'p 2: 1 any *c* in Christ, if any comfort   * "
2Th 2:16 given us everlasting *c* and good   * "
Ph'm   7 we have great joy and *c* in thy   * "
Heb 6:18 we might have a strong *c*, who   * "

desired See also DESIREDST.

M't 13:17 righteous men have *d* to see those *1930*
     16: 1 *d* him that he would shew them *1905*
M'r 15: 6 one prisoner, whomsoever they *d*.* *154*
Lu 7:36 And one of the Pharisees *d* him *2065*
     9: 9 things? And he *d* to see him.   *2212*
    10:24 prophets and kings have *d* to see *2309*
    22:15 With desire I have *d* to eat this   *1937*
      31 Satan hath *d* to have you, that   *1809*
    23:25 into prison, whom they had *d*;   * *154*
Jo 12:21 *d* him, saying, Sir, we would see *2065*
Ac 3:14 the Just, and *d* a murderer to   * *154*
    7:46 *d* to find a tabernacle for the God * "
    8:31 And he *d* Philip that he would   *3870*
    9: 2 *d* of him letters to Damascus to * *154*
    12:20 their friend, *d* peace; because   * "
    13: 7 and *d* to hear the word of God.   *1934*
      21 afterward they *d* a king: and   * *154*
      28 yet *d* they Pilate that he should * "
    16:39 them out, and *d* them to depart *2065*
    18:20 When they *d* him to tarry longer * "
    25: 3 *d* favour against him, that he   * *154*
    28:14 and were *d* to tarry with them *3870*
1Co 16:12 Apollos, I greatly *d* him to come * "
2Co 8: 6 Insomuch that we *d* Titus, that * "
    12:18 I *d* Titus, and with him I sent * "
1Jo 5:15 the petitions that we *d* of him. * *154*

desiredst
De 18:16 According to all that thou *d* of the 7592
M't 18:32 all that debt, because thou *d* me:* *3870*

desires
Ps 37: 4 give thee the *d* of thine heart.   4862
   140: 8 Grant not, O Lord, the *d* of the   3970
Eph 2: 3 fulfilling the *d* of the flesh and of *2307*

desirest
Ps 51: 6 thou *d* truth in the inward parts: 2654
     16 For thou *d* not sacrifice; else   * "

desirous
Pr 23: 3 Be not *d* of his dainties: for they 183
Lu 23: 8 for he was *d* to see him a long   *2309*
Joh 16:19 they were *d* to ask him, and said   "
2Co 11:32 garrison, *d* to apprehend me: * "
Gal 5:26 Let us not be *d* of vain glory,   *2755*
1Th 2: 8 So being affectionately *d* of you, *2442*

intreat See also ENTREAT; INTREATED.

1Co 4:13 Being defamed, we *i*: we are   3870
Ph'p 4: 3 I *i* thee also, true yokefellow. *2065*
1Ti 5: 1 an elder, but *i* him as a father; *3870*

intreated See also ENTREATED.

Lu 15:28 came his father out, and *i* him.   3870
Heb12:19 *i* that the word should not be   3868
Jas 3:17 and easy to be *i*, full of mercy and 2138
intreateth See ENTREATETH.
intreaties
Pr 18:23 The poor useth *i*; but the rich   8469
intreaty See also INTREATIES.
2Co 8: 4 Praying us with much *i* that we   3874

We have now reduced the 30 potential references to eleven. But . . . we have not yet checked the other word

listings that are used in other parts of the New Testament. These we had already noted were of two kinds: the "begging" kind of exhortation and the "helping" kind of exhortation. Obviously, *both* kinds should be used in preaching the Word. So, we have to limit the "exhort." That is, a limit of the "how" verses that would provide some additional information on the mechanics of proper exhortation with the Word of God.

And once again, it is best to retain an organized approach to this research by keeping the search within the "kind" of exhortation. That is, we should search through those listings that are parallel in use: "beseech," "desire," and "intreat" should be taken together and "comfort" and "consolation" together. Then, when we find references that may be applicable to the "how" of exhortation, we can note them on our worksheet under the proper "kind" of "how." That means that on the worksheet proper, or on another piece of scratch paper, we must note the English word that is used in the passage. In this case there seems to be some four references under "beseech," none under "desire," and two under "intreat." And under "comfort," there appear to be about eleven possible references, with three more under "consolation." The main worksheet should now look like this:

preach the word	#2980 - Mk. 2:2; Acts 8:25; 11:19; 14:25; Acts 16:6
	#2097 - Acts 8:4; 15:35
preach - Rom. 10:8 I Cor. 2:4; Tit. 1:3 Acts 10:42; Rom. 10:15	#2605 - Acts 13:5; 15:36; 17:13
	# 189 - Heb. 4:2
word - John 5:24; 8:31; 17:17	
be instant in season out of season **instant** - **season** - Mk. 6:21; Lk. 22:6 **season** - Phil. 4:10	

reprove - John 16:8; Eph. 5:11; Jn. 3:20;
　　　　　Eph. 5:13; I Cor. 14:24; I Tim. 5:1;
　　　　　Titus 1:13; 2:15; 1:9;　Jas. 2:9

rebuke - stronger word: examples only - poss. Jude 9

exhort - how to:
　　　　　I Th. 2:3; 4:1; II Th. 3:12; I Th. 2:11;
　　　　　I Tim. 4:13; Tit. 2:15; Ro. 12:8; I Cor.
　　　　　14:3; Acts 11:23; 15:32; I Pet. 5:12

"beseech" - Rom. 12:1; I Cor. 1:10; II Cor. 5:20; 10:1
"intreat" - I Tim. 5:1; II Cor. 8:4
"comfort" - II Cor. 1:4; 7:6; I Cor. 14:31; Eph. 6:22;
　　　　　4:8; I Th. 3:2; 4:18; 5:11; II Th. 2:17
"consolation" - II Cor. 1:5, 6; II Th. 2:16

Obviously, there is a lot of information to be studied, but our objective here is only to locate *potential* references. We will examine each reference in its own context later. But for now, we must continue with the location process for the remainder of our study passage in II Timothy.

WITH ALL LONGSUFFERING AND DOCTRINE

The next major "line" in our study passage is the phrase "with all longsuffering and doctrine." That explains the technique that we are to use when preaching the word by means of reproving, rebuking, and exhorting (see original worksheet, page 116). This technique has two basic parts to it, "longsuffering" and "doctrine." We are told to "reprove, rebuke, exhort *with* all longsuffering and doctrine." Therefore, our research will be limited to locating those verses that show *how* to be longsuffering, and *how* to use doctrine when we are preaching the Word through reproof, rebuke, and exhortation.

The word for longsuffering, number 3115, is also
translated
"patience" in
the Scriptures,

longsuffering
Ex 34: 6 merciful and gracious, *l*. and *750,639
Nu 14:18 Lord is *l*. and of great mercy, * " "
Ps 86:15 *l*. and plenteous in mercy and * " "
Jer 15:15 take me not away in thy *l*:
Ro 2: 4 goodness and forbearance and *l*; *3115*
　　9:22 endured with much *l* the vessels　"

137

2Co   6:   6 by *l*, by kindness, by the Holy   "
Ga   5: 22 of the Spirit is love, joy, peace, *l*,   "
Eph   4:   2 with *l*, forbearing one another in   "
Col   1: 11 all patience and *l* with joyfulness;   "
      3: 12 humbleness of mind, meekness, *l*;   "
1Ti   1: 16 Christ might shew forth all *l*,   "
2Ti   3: 10 of life, purpose, faith, *l*, charity,   "
      4:   2 exhort with all *l* and doctrine.   "
1Pe   3: 20 the *l* of God waited in the days of   "
2Pe   3:   9 but is *l* to us-ward, not willing   *3114*
      3: 15 the *l* of our Lord is salvation;   *3115*

patience
M't 18: 26 Lord, have *p* with me, and I will   *3114*
     29 Have *p* with me, and I will pay   "
Lu   8: 15 it, and bring forth fruit with *p*.   *5281*
     21: 19 In your *p* possess ye your souls.   "
Ro   5:   3 that tribulation worketh *p*';   "
          4 And *p*', experience; and experience,"
      8: 25 not, then do we with *p*' wait for it.   "
     15:   4 *p* and comfort of the scriptures   "
          5 Now the God of *p* and consolation   "
2Co   6:   4 the ministers of God, in much *p*', in"
     12: 12 were wrought among you in all *p*',   "
Col   1: 11 unto all *p* and longsuffering with   "
1Th   1:   3 and *p* of hope in our Lord Jesus   "
2Th   1:   4 for your *p* and faith in all your   "
1Ti   6: 11 godliness, faith, love, *p*, meekness."
2Ti   3: 10 faith, longsuffering, charity, *p*,   "
Tit   2:   2 sound in faith, in charity, in *p*.   "
Heb   6: 12 faith and *p* inherit the promises.   *3115*
     10: 36 For ye have need of *p*', that, after   *5281*
     12:   1 let us run with *p*' the race that is   "
Jas   1:   3 the trying of your faith worketh *p*'.   "
          4 But let *p*' have her perfect work,   "
      5:   7 and hath long *p*' for it, until he   **3114*
         10 of suffering affliction, and of *p*'.   *3115*
         11 Ye have heard of the *p*' of Job,   *5281*
2Pe   1:   6 temperance *p*'; and to *p*' godliness;"
Re   1:   9 the kingdom and *p*' of Jesus Christ,"
      2:   2 works, and thy labour, and thy *p*',   "
          3 hast *p*', and for my name's sake   "
         19 faith, and thy *p*', and thy works;   "
      3: 10 thou hast kept the word of my *p*',   "
     13: 10 it the *p* and the faith of the saints."
     14: 12 Here is the *p* of the saints: here   "

patient
Ec   7:   8 *p*' in spirit is better than the proud **750**
Ro   2:   7 by *p*' continuance in well doing   **5281*
     12: 12 in hope; *p*' in tribulation;   *5278*
1Th   5: 14 the weak, be *p*' toward all men.   **3114*
2Th   3:   5 and into the *p*' waiting for Christ.**5281*
1Ti   3:   3 *p*', not a brawler, not covetous;   **1933*
2Ti   2: 24 gentle unto all men, apt to teach, *p*',**420*
Jas   5:   7 Be *p*' therefore, brethren, unto the*3114*
          8 Be ye also *p*'; stablish your hearts:"

patiently
Ps   37:   7 in the Lord, and wait *p*' for him: **2342**
     40:   1 I waited *p*' for the Lord; and he   **6960**
Ac   26:   3 I beseech thee to hear me *p*'.   *3116*
Heb   6: 15 And so, after he had *p*' endured,   *3114*
1Pe   2: 20 for your faults, ye shall take it *p*'? *5278*
         20 ye take it *p*', this as acceptable with"

and as should now be known necessitates our research under that word heading also. Our research is limited, remember, to those verses that show *how* to be longsuffering. And since there are two words, our worksheet should record the verses under the appropriate category. Under "longsuffering," there seem to be only three verse references that relate to the "how" of longsuffering: II Cor. 6:6, Eph. 4:2, and Col. 1:11. Under the "patience" category, there also appear to be three: I Thes. 5:14 and Jas. 5:7, 8. These verses all use the word "by" or "with" in connecting longsuffering to the rest of the phrase, thereby indicating to us that there may be some "how to" information within the context of the reference cited. We do not *know* if that will be the case yet, but we have a good *indication.* Therefore, we should record these passages on our main worksheet.

"Doctrine" is the other mechanic necessary for the preacher to use when he is exhorting, etc. And once again, we are only looking for those parallel references that help explain *how* to "doctrinize." As we have already discovered, "doctrine" means "teaching" and the action form of that word is "teach." We are now looking for those verses that show how to preach, re-

```
doctrine  See also DOCTRINES.
De  32: 2 My d' shall drop as the rain.        3948
Job 11: 4 My d' is pure, and I am clean in      "
Pr   4: 2 I give you good d', forsake ye not    "
Isa 28: 9 shall he make to understand d' ?    *8052
    29:24 that murmured shall learn d'.       ‡3948
Jer 10: 8 the stock is a d' of vanities.      *4148
M't  7:28 people were astonished at his d':  *1322
    16:12 of the d' of the Pharisees and of  *  "
    22:33 they were astonished at his d'.    *  "
M'r  1:22 they were astonished at his d':    *  "
    27 what new d' is this? for with         *  "
     4: 2 and said unto them in his d',       *  "
    11:18 people was astonished at his d'.    *  "
    12:38 he said unto them in his d',        *  "
Lu   4:32 they were astonished at his d':     *  "
Joh  7:16 My d' is not mine, but his that     *  "
    17 he shall know of the d', whether       *  "
    18:19 of his disciples, and of his d'.    *  "
Ac   2:42 in the apostles' d' and fellowship,*  "
     5:28 filled Jerusalem with your d',      *  "
    13:12 astonished at the d' of the Lord.   *  "
    17:19 what this new d', whereof thou      *  "
Ro   6:17 form of d' which was delivered      *  "
    6:17 offences contrary to the d' which      "
1Co 14: 6 or by prophesying, or by d' ?       *  "
    26 of you hath a psalm, hath a d',        *  "
Eph  4:14 about with every wind of d',        1819
1Ti  1: 3 some that they teach no other d',     "
    10 that is contrary to sound d';         1819
     4: 6 up in words of faith and of good d',"
    13 to reading, to exhortation, to d'.    *  "
    16 unto thyself, and unto the d';        *  "
    5:17 who labour in the word and d',      *  "
     6: 1 God and his d' be not blasphemed.  *  "
     3 to the d' which is according to       *  "
2Ti  3:10 thou hast fully known my d',       *  "
    16 is profitable for d', for reproof,    *  "
     4: 2 with all longsuffering and d'.     *1322
     3 they will not endure sound d';       1819
Tit  1: 9 able by sound d' both to exhort       "
     2: 1 things which become sound d':        "
     7 in d' shewing uncorruptness,           "
    10 adorn the d' of God our Saviour        "
Heb  6: 1 leaving the principles of the d'   ‡3056
     2 Of the d' of baptisms, and of        *1322
2Jo  9 abideth not in the d' of Christ,      *  "
     9 that abideth in the d' of Christ,     *  "
    10 bring not this d', receive him not    *  "
Re   2:14 that hold the d' of Balaam, who    *  "
    15 hold the d' of the Nicolaitanes,      *  "
    24 as many as have not this d',          *  "
doctrines
M't 15: 9 for d' the commandments of men.    1819
M'r  7: 7 for d' the commandments of men.       "
Col  2:22 the commandments and d' of men ?    "
1Ti  4: 1 seducing spirits, and d' of devils;  "
Heb 13: 9 about with divers and strange d'.  *1322
```

prove, rebuke, and exhort by means of teaching the Word of God. And as was the case in previous research, we find several verses that seem to contain such "how to" information. But, since this seems to be a key element in the overall teaching of the II Timothy passage, we would do well to take the time to check each reference in its own context to make sure that we do not miss any important points. This is not the time to do that, however. We need only to jot down those references that appear to be parallel. In this case, they seem to be: Jn. 7:16-17; Rom. 6:17; I Tim. 1:3, 10; 4:13, 16; 6:3; II Tim. 3:16; Titus 1:9; 2:1, 7, 10. These thirteen references may be satisfactory, but a quick check under the "teach" listing in the concordance shows that there are a large number of references using our word number, so we should be consistent enough to research those listings as well.

teach
```
M't  5:19 but whosoever shall do and t' them, 1321
     11: 1 to t' and to preach in their cities.   "
     28:19 Go ye therefore, and t' all nations,*3100
M'r  4: 1 began again to t' by the sea side:  1321
      6: 2 he began to t' in the synagogue.      "
        34 he began to t' them many things.      "
      8:31 he began to t' them, that the Son of "
Lu  11: 1 teach us to him, Lord, t' us to pray.
     12:12 Holy Ghost shall t' you in the same  "
Joh  7:35 the Gentiles, and t' the Gent.'es?     "
      9:34 born in sins, and dost thou t' us?     "
     14:26 he shall t' all things, and bring*"
Ac   1: 1 that Jesus began both to do and t',   "
      4:18 at all nor t' in the name of Jesus.    "
      5:28 that ye should not t' in this name?    "
        42 ceased not to t' and preach Jesus     "
     16:21 t' customs, which are not lawful  *2605
1Co  4:17 I t' every where in every church.   1321
     11:14 Doth not even nature itself t' you.    "
     14:19 by my voice I might t' others also,*2727
1Ti  1: 3 some that they t' no other doctrine,2085
      2:12 But I suffer not a woman to t', nor 1321
      3: 2 given to hospitality, apt to t';     1317
      4:11 These things command and t'.      1321
      6: 2 benefit. These things t' and exhort."
         3 If any man t' otherwise, and      *2085
2Ti  2: 2 who shall be able to t' others also. 1321
        24 but be gentle unto all men, apt to t',1317
Tit  2: 4 t' the young women to be sober,  *4994
Heb  5:12 ye have need that one t' you again 1321
      8:11 not t' every man his neighbour,      "
1Jo  2:27 ye need not that any man t' you:      "
Re   2:20 to t' and to seduce my servants to *  "
```

teacher See also TEACHERS.
```
1Ch 25: 8 as the great, the t' as the scholar.  995
Hab  2:18 the molten image, and a t' of lies. 3384
Joh  3: 2 that thou art a t' come from God: 1320
Ro   2:20 a t' of babes, which hast the form    "
1Ti  2: 7 a t' of the Gentiles in faith and     "
2Ti  1:11 an apostle, and a t' of the Gentiles. "
```

teachers
```
Ac  13: 1 at Antioch certain prophets and t';1320
1Co 12:28 secondarily prophets, thirdly t,     "
        29 are all prophets? are all t'? are all "
Eph  4:11 and some, pastors and t';            "
1Ti  1: 7 Desiring to be t' of the law;      3547
2Ti  4: 3 shall they heap to themselves t,  1320
Tit  2: 3 to much wine, t' of good things;  2567
Heb  5:12 when for the time ye ought to be t',1320
2Pe  2: 1 there shall be false t' among you,  5572
```

It is always necessary in this kind of study to remind oneself *to stick to the thesis of the study passage.* The temptation to look up "that neat verse" is always popping up, but the careful student is controlled by the objective research job at hand. We have already established, that "doctrine" is a technique for preaching the word. And we have already established that we

teachest
Ps 94:12 O Lord, and t' him out of thy law; 3925
M't 22:16 true, and t' the way of God in truth, *1321*
M'r 12:14 men, but t' the way of God in truth:"
Lu 20:21 know that thou sayest and t' rightly,"
        21 of any, but t' the way of God truly: "
Ac 21:21 that thou t' all the Jews which are "
Ro   2:21 Thou therefore which t' another, "
        21 t' thou not thyself? thou that "

teacheth
Ac 21:28 man, that t' all men every where *1321*
Ro 12: 7 or he that t', on teaching; "
1Co 2:13 the words which man's wisdom t', *1318*
        13 but which the Holy Ghost t'; "
Gal 6: 6 unto him that t' in all good things. *2727*
1Jo 2:27 as the same anointing t' you of all *1321*

teaching
2Ch 15: 3 without a t' priest, and without 3384
Jer 32:33 them, rising up early and t' them, 3925
M't 4:23 all Galilee, t' in their synagogues, *1321*
        9:35 and villages, t' in their synagogues,"
        15: 9 t' for doctrines the commandments "
        21:23 people came unto him as he was t', "
        26:55 sat daily with you t' in the temple, "
        28:20 T' them to observe all things "
M'r 6: 6 he went round about the villages, t'."
        7: 7 t' for doctrines the commandments "
       14:49 was daily with you in the temple t', "
Lu   5:17 pass on a certain day, as he was t', "
       13:10 he was t' in one of the synagogues "
        22 through the cities and villages, t', "
       21:37 day time he was t' in the temple; "
        23: 5 the people, t' throughout all Jewry,"
Ac   5:25 in the temple, and t' the people. "
       15:35 t' and preaching the word of the "
       18:11 t' the word of God among them. "
       28:31 t' those things which concern the "
Ro 12: 7 or he that teacheth, on t'; *1319*
Col 1:28 and t' every man in all wisdom; *1321*
        3:16 t' and admonishing one another "
Tit 1:11 t' things which they ought not, for "
        2:12 T' us that, denying ungodliness *＊3811*

are only interested in the "how to" information within the supportformation within the supporting words. Therefore, we should keep the same limits *each* time we search a listing so that we will be consistent in our information gathering. In this case, of the many references under the "teach" heading, only some thirteen additional references seem to apply within the "how to" framework that has been established. They are Matt. 5:19; Acts 5:42; I Cor. 4:17; I Tim. 1:3; 4:11; 6:2; II Tim. 2:2;, Lk. 20:21; Acts 21:28; I Cor. 2:13; Acts 15:35; 18:11; Col. 1:28. These verses should be listed on the main worksheet under "doctrine." (NOTE: It would be quite valuable for you to check out each of these references on the example from Strong's concordance. That would help you get a feel for the thinking process required in choosing the verses.) The worksheet should now look like this:

| preach the word | #2980 - Mk. 2:2; Acts 8:25; 11:19; 14:25; Acts 16:6 |
| | #2097 - Acts 8:4; 15:35 |

preach - Rom. 10:8   #2605 - Acts 13:5; 15:36;
  I Cor. 2:4; Tit. 1:3   17:13
  Acts 10:42; Rom. 10:15   # 189 - Heb. 4:2

word - John 5:24; 8:31;
          17:17

be instant in season out of season
  instant -
  season - Mk. 6:21; Lk. 22:6   **season** - Phil. 4:10

reprove - John 16:8; Eph. 5:11; Jn. 3:20;
          Eph. 5:13; I Tim. 5:1; Titus 1:13; 2:15;1:9;
          I Cor. 14:24; Jas. 2:9

rebuke - stronger word: examples only - poss. Jude 9

exhort - how to: I Th. 2:3; 4:1; II Th. 3:12;
          I Th. 2:11; I Tim. 4:13; Tit. 2:15;
          Rom. 12:8; I Cor. 14:3; Acts 11:23;
          15:32; I Pet. 5:12

  "beseech"- Rom. 12:1; I Cor. 1:10; II Cor. 5:20;
          10:1
  "intreat"- I Tim. 5:1; II Cor. 8:4
  "comfort"- II Cor. 1:4; 7:6; I Cor. 14:31;
          Eph. 6:22; 4:8; I Th. 3:2; 4:18; 5:11;
          II Th. 2:17
  "consolation"- II Cor. 1:5-6; II Th. 2:16

with all longsuffering and doctrine
  longsuffering - II Cor. 6:6; Eph. 4:2; Col. 1:11;
          I Th. 5:14; Jas. 5:7-8
  doctrine - Jn. 7:16-17; Rom. 6:17; I Tim. 1:3, 10;
          4:13, 16; 6:3; II Tim. 3:16; Tit. 1:9;
          2:1, 7, 10

"teach" - Mt. 5:19; Acts 5:42; I Cor. 4:17;
 I Tim. 1:3; 4:11; 6:2; II Tim. 2:2;
 Lk. 20:21; Acts 21:28; I Cor. 2:13;
 Acts 15:35; 18:11; Col. 1:28
NOTE: Just in case you are wondering why the verses are not in book order, you should know that they are listed (for the most part) as they appear in descending order under the heading in Strong's concordance.

Now is about the time that everybody is ready for a coffee break. The study is somewhat involved, and there is a great temptation to say, "I've got so much stuff now I'll never use it all." Please suppress that temptation. Whether it is "used" in some formal presentation or not, it *will* be used by the Holy Spirit in the life that "hides" the Word in its heart (Psa. 119:11). But . . . and this is the main "but," we can never be too thorough in our *study.* We can try to present too much to the hearers, but we must be sure that we have researched the Word of God carefully enough to insure accuracy in our teaching. Remember, God's Word itself warns us that we will be considered the "least in the kingdom of heaven" if we teach men to break even the least of the commandments (Matt. 5:19). God counts His Word too valuable to be trifled with; indeed, He has magnified it beyond His very name (Psa. 138:2). *Therefore,* we must "study to show" ourselves approved unto God . . . not men.

These last three chapters have contained a vast amount of detail and have been pretty rough to follow. However, if you have stuck with it thus far, you are "over the hump." Everything learned so far will be used over and over again in the more complex kinds of study. You will not have to learn a new technique for every new approach to research. Relieved? Good! Now read the next chapter and finish the job.

11

EXAMINE THE VERSES

Perhaps the best way to begin an earnest study of this phase is to preview the various parts before we start. There are four simple guidelines necessary to insure a very accurate and fulfilling study. As we go through the examples for each step, it should become clear how they are related. If you feel unsure about the procedure, go back to the appropriate section in that last chapter and reread the discussion. That should help.

Make A New Worksheet

This step may not be necessary after you have become proficient in the analysis of verses, but it is wise to be careful at the beginning to keep the information as organized as possible. Since we have already developed the "visual" outline of our study passage in chapter eight, we do not have to repeat that work here. The main purpose in making this new worksheet is that we must now record the main points of the parallel verses and, later on, organize them into categories. However, the concordance only gave a very small portion of the verses and we can seldom learn the real intent of a passage merely by noting the phrase in the concordance. Therefore, we must examine each *potential* reference, in its own context, to see if it does have *actual* bearing on our study passage. And since there is such a great amount of possible information, it is best to make a new worksheet which will help us organize the data.

Any worksheet should do two things: make the complex simple and assist the visualizing of the subject. As we have already seen, it is very easy to lose the perspective of the overall teaching among the small bits of information. The very first worksheet we made has served as the visual model for the study passage and should still be used as the basis for this new worksheet. Remember, we are not now finding new material, nor are we going to develop a new thesis. We are merely trying to find amplifying and clarifying information for the framework that has already been established by the Holy Spirit. So, our new sheet would be "different" from our main worksheet only in the additional space allowed between the points. And since we do not know in advance how many verses will have to be organized on the final outline, it is best *not* to structure the entire worksheet at first. In other words, we start the new worksheet merely by entering the first major part of our study passage on a blank sheet of paper. In this case "preach the word."

preach the word
preach

xxxxxx .... The verses should be listed in a vertical column under the key word to which they pertain. The main point of each verse should be recorded immediately to the right of each verse.

xxxxxx ....

xxxxxx ....

Work Through The Entire Study Outline

The best place to start is at the beginning. It is very difficult to improve on the word progression that has been chosen by the mind of God, so it is always best—at least during this study procedure, to start at the beginning of the passage and work straight through to the end. The temptation is always strong to outline each section while we are studying it. Unfortunately, that procedure is not best. The *whole* passage contains the message, not merely part of it. Therefore, we *must* continue to relate each individual piece of information to the whole passage. The best way to avoid improper organization of data in this type of study is to finish the entire research process *before* trying to outline and organize.

Cross Out The Verses That Do Not Apply

There will be some references on the main worksheet that are not applicable to the study passage. As we have already noted, the concordance does not give us enough information to determine if the reference actually relates to the thesis of our study section, only that it *might* apply. Therefore, we must now disregard any passage of Scripture that does not positively enhance the understanding of the study passage. We are not trying to relate every possible thought or word (there is a constant pressure to do so), but we are only trying to find what additional information the Scriptures have which will help us obey the Word of God as it is presented in the specific section of study. Do not "feel bad" when it seems that a reference does not have any bearing, or does not add any real clarity. Cross it out. There will be more than enough information for proper understanding. Do not obscure the truth with too many irrelevant facts.

Record The Main Point Of Each Applicable Verse

Many of the references discovered in the "seek out" stage of our research *will* be worth including in the final outline. That means that there must be some way for us to relate the various points together. The best way to guard against confusion is to jot down the main thought of each reference on the new worksheet. Remember, we will be working straight through the entire study passage and will be unable to retain all of the information in our heads. Therefore, it is necessary to record the information as we find it so that we may be able to sort it out later. It is best to develop the new worksheet as we progress through the study so that enough room will be maintained for the new information. We already have the visual format established from the initial worksheet. Now, as we work through the passage, we can record the main thought of each parallel reference on the new worksheet using the original format. That way we will be less likely to stray from the Biblical message and will be less likely to make an error in our later outlining.

One additional thought here: an effort should be made to keep the worksheet notes as brief as possible. We are trying to discover *only* the supporting and clarifying information within the parallel references. We are not trying to perform a study on them. That means that we should keep the thoughts of those parallel references in line with the specific points within the study passage. We are looking for the piece of information which is most relevant to the particular thought expressed by the phrase under study. We are not trying to explain what the parallel verse means. Therefore, we should record, as briefly as possible, the main point of the verse. Usually, one or two words will be sufficient. Sometimes it is best to copy out a key phrase of the verse, but more often it is better to generate a word or phrase in our own words that expresses the thought clearly.

These three guidelines should be remembered as a unit when actually performing the work. We broke them apart in order to understand the purpose for each requirement, but they really are parts of a single step. It should be noted that part of this process involves crossing out the verses that we will find do not really apply to our study after all. Obviously, there are no verses on the

new worksheet to cross off, so we will have to use our
old worksheet in conjunction with this step. (Many passages for our study will not be as complex as the one we
are now doing and will not require the new worksheet.
However, it is worthwhile to cover many possible problems in an instructional experience.)

Note: You will need to use your Bible for the remainder
of this section. All of the text and each of the examples assume that you are looking at a copy of
the King James Version for each of the references.
Please get your Bible before you proceed.

PREACH THE WORD

Well, let's begin. A check of the main worksheet under the key word "preach," reveals five main verses
which we had found using the same key word. There are
several other verses that use other words which we are
going to check, but it is usually best to check these verses
which use the same word as the study verse first. So we
must look up the verses in their own context and read
each passage in its entirety. We cannot take a chance.
We must be *sure* that the possible application is an actual application.

preach the word	#2980 - Mk. 2:2;
14:25; Acts 16:6	Acts 8:25; 11:19;
	#2097 - Acts 8:4; 15:35
preach - Rom. 10:8	#2605 - Acts 13:5; 15:36;
I Cor. 2:4; Titus 1:3	17:13
Acts 10:42; Rom. 10:15	#189 - Heb. 4:2

Four of these passages seem to have an actual bearing on our study thesis. Romans 10:8 speaks of the
"word of faith" and is amplified in verses 9 and 10.
Most Christians should recognize these verses as familiar

149

instruction to the unsaved world. I Corinthians 2:4 is an excellent contrast to Romans 10:8 in that it warns against "man's wisdom" for the preacher. Titus 1:3 observes God "manifested His word through preaching." Acts 10:42 is merely another command to preach and does not provide any new information. Romans 10:15 is in the same context with 10:8.

Now we must record the main point of each of these verses on the new worksheet. Since our effort is toward making our work understandable, we must try to make the notation as brief and concise as possible. The Romans passage deals with faith and the gospel, the Corinthians passage with man's wisdom, and the Titus passage with the necessity of manifesting His Word through preaching. The worksheet should look something like this:

> **preach the word**
> **preach**
> Romans 10:8-15 - faith/gospel
> I Cor. 2:4 - man's wisdom
> Titus 1:3 - preaching necessary

Now all we have to do is sort through the remaining verses under "preach" and we will be on our way. Back to the main worksheet.

preach the word	#2980 - Mk. 2:2; Acts 8:25; 11:19; 14:25; Acts 16:6
	#2097 - Acts 8:4; 15:35
preach - Rom. 10:8	#2605 - Acts 13:5; 15:36;
I Cor. 2:4; Tit. 1:3	17:13
Acts 10:42; Rom. 10:15	# 189 - Heb. 4:2

The distinction here is that these verses use different words for "preach." We must know the difference, and we must be sure that they are true parallel words before we can use them in our study. The best way to shorten the work is to read each verse first to see if it does apply;

then if it does, check out the difference. Each verse that is not clearly a positive help to our understanding of the study thesis ("preach the word") should *not* be used. The objective is better understanding, not lots of neat verses.

Reading through each of this first group of verses does not reveal any new or enlightening information. Each verse gives an example of preaching the Word, but there is nothing which would give us additional insight into the thesis of the II Timothy study passage. Therefore, we would cross out each of those verses on our old worksheet.

preach the word	#2980 - Mk. 2:2; Acts 8:25; 11:19; 14:25; Acts 16:6
	#2097 - Acts 8:4; 15:35
preach - Rom. 10:8	#2605 - Acts 13:5; 15:36;
I Cor. 2:4; Tit. 1:3	17:13
Acts 10:42; Rom. 10:15	# 189 - Heb. 4:2 .

The next two verses are quite similar, with the possible exception of Acts 15:35. That verse connects "teaching" with "preaching" and also notes that it was done "with many others also." Since there does seem to be a parallel thought in that verse—especially since the II Timothy passage talks about "longsuffering" and "doctrine," we should record that verse on the new worksheet. It may not be worth including on the final outline, but we must not make up our minds yet. Therefore, cross out Acts 8:4 and enter Acts 15:35 on the new worksheet with a notation such as "teaching/with others." We should also make a note of the different word used in that verse, number 2097.

Of the three references, Acts 13:5; 15:36; 17:13, there are none that provide any real additional insight to our study. When we were looking them up in the concordance, all we were able to see was the phrase "preach the word." We could not take the chance that we would miss some important information, so we recorded them on our worksheet. Now we can see that they are not necessary for the purpose of our study in II Timothy. We would cross them out on our main worksheet.

Hebrews 4:2, however, does seem to apply. We have already discovered a "faith/gospel" verse in Romans 10:8. This verse in Hebrews has both of those elements and seems to tell why the gospel preaching did not work. We should add that verse to our new worksheet which now should look something like this:

---

preach
Rom. 10:8-15 - faith/gospel
I Cor. 2:4 - not man's wisdom
Titus 1:3 - preaching necessary
Acts 15:35 - teaching/with others #2097
Heb. 4:2 - why not work #189

The old worksheet should look like this:

---

preach the word   #2980 - Mk. 2:2; Acts 8:25; 11:19; 14:25; Acts 16:6
                              #2097 - Acts 8:4; 15:35

preach - Rom. 10:8   #2605 - Acts 13:5; 15:36;
  I Cor. 2:4; Tit. 1:3   17:13
  Acts 10:42; Rom. 10:15   # 189 - Heb. 4:2

word - John 5:24; 8:31;
  17:17

That exercise is a fairly good example of the kind of work that is ahead of us. And, it is also fairly representative of the ratio of eliminated verses. That is, we started with 16 possible verses to look up and wound up with 6 that actually applied. Usually the verses that use other Greek or Hebrew words are not as applicable as those verses that use the same word as the study passage. In this case, four of the same-word verses (Rom. 10:8, 15; I Cor. 2:4; and Tit. 1:3) were usable, but only two out of the other eleven were found to be worth recording. That ratio tends to be fairly common in this kind of study.

The main worksheet example also shows us the three verses that we had selected as being representative of the "word" concept. Since they were selected out of a large number of references in the concordance, it is likely that all of them will apply. And indeed, that is the case. John 5:24 tells how important the word is to salvation, John 8:31 shows that the word is necessary for discipleship, and John 17:17 explains that the word is vital for sanctification. So, once again, we would jot those references down on the new worksheet along with a brief notation of their main point.

---

preach the word
  preach
    Rom. 10:8-15 - faith/gospel
    I Cor. 2:4 - not man's wisdom
    Titus 1:3 - preaching necessary
    Acts 15:35 - teaching/with others #2097
    Heb. 4:2 - why not work # 189

  word
    John 5:24 - salvation
    John 8:31 - discipleship
    John 17:17 - sanctification

BE INSTANT IN SEASON, OUT OF SEASON

The next section on our old worksheet reveals only three verses that need to be checked out.

---

be instant in season out of season
  instant -
  season - Mk. 6:21; Lk. 22:6   **season** - Phil. 4:10

The "instant" term was not sufficiently used in the Scripture to add anything to our study passage, but we should quickly check the word definition worksheet (page 109) to refresh our memory.

The three verses under "season" are really in two separate categories. Both Mark and Luke show other uses of the "in season" concept, but merely give us Scriptural examples of the word use. They do not give us any better understanding of "preaching the word," but they do help clarify the way Paul wanted Timothy to preach the Word. So, we *could* use these references in our final outline. However, when the only information to be gained is a word use example, it is often best simply to cite the other English words used in the other references, rather than the references themselves.

This last reference, however, does have some pertinent information. Our II Timothy passage tells us to "preach the word" when it is "convenient" and when it is "out of season." Philippians 4:10 translated that phrase "lacked opportunity" and uses the word in a passage that shows how Paul himself was able to minister to his responsibilities even when it was "out of season." That example is worth our observing and-should be recorded on the new worksheet.

During this second section of the study passage, we have eliminated two verses, verified the word usage of the one term, and found a good example to use for another. The old worksheet would have the verses crossed out which we eliminated,

be instant in season out of season
instant -
season - Mk. 6:21; Lk. 22:6   **season** - Phil. 4:10

and the new worksheet would have the information about the verified English words and the new example reference.

be instant in season out of season
    instant - be present
    in season - convenient, opportunity
    out season - Phil. 4:10 - example

REPROVE, REBUKE, EXHORT

This next section, the one that contains the three "how to" words for preaching, is going to involve a lot of reference checking. But remember, we found that many of the previous references were not applicable after all, so the size of the job should not discourage us.

reprove - John 16:8; Eph. 5:11; Jn. 3:20;
              Eph. 5:13; I Tim. 5:1; Titus 1:13; 2:15; 1:9;
              I Cor. 14:24; Jas. 2:9

There is no "quick" way of going through a number of references like this, but it does seem to make it a little more systematic if we try to look up those references that are in the same book rather than following them in the order of their appearance on the worksheet as we have done previously. At any rate, the two references in John do not speak directly about "reproving with the word." However, they both use the word in such a manner that it is easy to see that "reproof" is a negative term. That is, when we are "reproved" we are being fussed at or made to feel very uneasy. John 16:8 shows what the Holy Spirit reproves, but John 3:20 only gives an example of the unbeliever hiding from the "reproof" of light. Probably, that last reference is unnecessary for our study, but John 16:8 does show the three things about which the Holy Spirit "reproves," and would, therefore, be well worth our noting on the new worksheet.

The two references in Ephesians give us some good information. Ephesians 5:11 tells us what to reprove: "the

155

unfruitful works of darkness.'' Ephesians 5:13 teaches that ''the light'' is the instrument for reproof. However, ''the light'' is a figurative term, and unless we know what ''the light'' is, we have no right to use that illustration. That means that we must determine the *Scriptural* definition for that figure of speech *before* we can teach about it. Maybe you think you know what it means, and maybe you are right . . . maybe. If you incorrectly use the Scripture, you come under the judgment of Matthew 5:19. Are you willing to take that chance?

Pardon the sober injection there, but we can *never* be too careful with God's Word. In this case, we are not sure what ''the light'' is, and we have not had the opportunity to study out that concept. Therefore, we should disregard that reference until and unless we have determined, Scripturally, what ''the light'' means. So, we should cross out Ephesians 5:13 on the main worksheet, and add Ephesians 5:11 to the new worksheet along with the notation concerning its main point.

The verse in I Timothy 5 provides a limitation to reproving activity and might be worth our noting on the worksheet. It does not seem to directly relate to the activity of ''reproving with the word'' and, therefore, might not be applicable to the thesis of our study passage. However, we must be sure of any data that relate to the study thesis, and the only way to do that is to work through the entire outline before we decide what relates to what. Therefore, it would be wise to record I Timothy 5:1 on the new worksheet along with the notation that it contains a limitation for rebuking.

The verses in Titus all provide some good insight into the concept of our study passage. Remember, we are trying to find out ''how to reprove'' with the Word of God. Titus 1:9 instructs us to use ''sound doctrine'' to ''convince the gainsayers.'' (By the way, both the word ''convince'' and the word ''rebuke'' are translations of our study word. We had determined that in our ''seek out'' process.) Titus 1:13 tells us to ''rebuke them sharply,'' and Titus 2:15 says to ''rebuke with all authority.''

However, Titus 2:15 is a summary verse. That is, it tells us to rebuke "these things." What things? The things that are spoken about in the context of the verse. When we read back in the context (as we discussed on pages 88-89) it seems to deal with several topics. Verse one of chapter two ties in very nicely with the reference in Titus 1:9 about rebuking "by sound doctrine," so we can be fairly confident that the whole chapter relates to the way the preacher is to "reprove." We should list the entire chapter on our new worksheet along with some note to break it apart later ("Titus 2:1-15—what to speak—outline").

Neither one of these last two references (I Cor. 14:24; James 2:9) provides any direct tie to our study thesis, although they do show the effect of reproving. We are only trying to gain Scriptural insight into the II Timothy passage that we are currently studying. With that limitation, these passages do not apply.

The old worksheet should now look like this:

> **reprove** - John 16:8; Eph. 5:11; Jn. 3:20;
>   Eph. 5:13; I Tim. 5:1; Titus 1:13; 2:15; 1:9;
>   I Cor. 14:24; Jas. 2:9

The new worksheet should have this new information:

> **reprove**
>   John 16:8 - sin, righteousness, judgment
>   Eph. 5:11 - unfruitful works of darkness
>   I Tim. 5:1 - limitation/elder
>   Titus 1:9 - sound doctrine
>   Titus 1:13 - sharply
>   Titus 2:1-15 - what to speak: outline

The section of our study passage that deals with "rebuke" only has one verse to check. We had previously determined that all of the other verses using this term were simply examples of the action of "rebuking" and were not directly connected with our study thesis. We had noted on our old worksheet that "rebuke" was a stronger word than "reproof" and had cited Jude 9 as a possible reference with further insight in it. The instructions in that passage, however, do not seem to be very clear—at least as to their relationship to the rebuking preacher. So, it is better not to include that reference in our final outline, unless and until we have carefully studied the instruction in Jude.

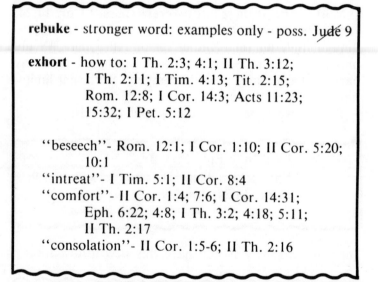

rebuke - stronger word: examples only - poss. Jude 9

exhort - how to: I Th. 2:3; 4:1; II Th. 3:12;
I Th. 2:11; I Tim. 4:13; Tit. 2:15;
Rom. 12:8; I Cor. 14:3; Acts 11:23;
15:32; I Pet. 5:12

"beseech"- Rom. 12:1; I Cor. 1:10; II Cor. 5:20;
10:1
"intreat"- I Tim. 5:1; II Cor. 8:4
"comfort"- II Cor. 1:4; 7:6; I Cor. 14:31;
Eph. 6:22; 4:8; I Th. 3:2; 4:18; 5:11;
II Th. 2:17
"consolation"- II Cor. 1:5-6; II Th. 2:16

This next section contains a large number of references dealing with the subject of exhortation. When we were doing the research on this in chapter ten, we found that many of the references amplified and explained the "how to" idea even in the short phrases listed in the concordance. It is likely, although not always so, that the concept which yields the most parallel information during research is to be more heavily taught or more heavily used than other, less emphasized concepts. In this case, the preacher of the Word is told to "reprove, rebuke, exhort." The "reproving" ministry is amplified by some six parallel passages, the "rebuking" ministry is not amplified, and this "exhorting" ministry seems to have a whole host of parallel instruction. Perhaps we will find this portion of the preacher's work to be the most frequently necessary, or the most often stressed. The only way to find out is to look up the verses.

The two verses in II Thessalonians chapter two are located at both ends of a rather thorough explanation on how to exhort. Paul is explaining how he ministered to these folks, what he said to them, and what he did while he was with them. The information is certainly worthwhile recording on the new worksheet and should be logged in such a way that we will remember to do a more careful breakdown of this passage when we come to the final outlining process. We did the same thing for Titus 2:1-15 when we were examining the verses under "reprove." Remember?

I Thessalonians 4:1 does not seem to have any direct bearing on our study thesis, even though it does note that the exhorting was "by the Lord." We would cross out this reference on the old worksheet.

The same thing is true of II Thessalonians 3:12. The passage contains some instruction on the thing that is to be exhorted about (not working), but it does not give any additional light on *how* the preacher is to exhort. We would cross out this reference on the old worksheet also.

The I Timothy and Titus references, however, seem to be parallel to our study thesis. I Timothy 4:13 is a command to exhort, and Titus 2:15 is tied in with another of our key words, "reprove." We had already determined that the entire second chapter of Titus was an instruction on what was involved with the "reproof" ministry, and we can now understand that it is also applicable for the exhortation ministry as well. Therefore, both of these references would be entered on the new worksheet, making some special notation to tie in Titus 2:15 to the earlier use under "reprove."

These next five references (Acts 11:23; 15:32; Rom. 12:8; I Cor. 14:3; I Pet. 5:12) all seem to be giving some specific example of the actual exhortation of some person or some thing. Although this information is quite valuable in understanding the complete concept of such a ministry, it is irrelevant to the immediate subject that we are studying. Remember, we are not trying to perform a doctrinal study on any of these terms—as necessary as that may be. That kind of study is much more involved and exacting than we are prepared to do at this point. However, we are interested in finding those additional Scriptures which will help us understand how to "preach the Word" (our study thesis) by exhortation. Of all these references, only Acts 15:32 has a "how to" phrase. That verse notes that Judas and Silas "exhorted the brethren with many words . . . ." Since we already know that the II Timothy study passage limits exhortation to *the* Word, it is really not necessary to add the Acts 15 passage.

We have covered several verses now. A quick look at the worksheets will help solidify our progress.

The Old Worksheet

exhort - how to: I Th. 2:3; 4:1; II Th. 3:12;
I Th. 2:11; I Tim. 4:13; Tit. 2:15;
Rom. 12:8; I Cor. 14:3; Acts 11:23;
15:32; I Pet. 5:12

The New Worksheet

rebuke - strongest word, examples only

exhort
I Thess. 2:3-11 - example of: outline
I Tim. 4:13 - command
Titus 2:15 - what: see reprove

Now we come to the section of "exhort" where we have listed the other English words separately in a mini-subject study. When we were doing our earlier research, it was felt that each of these references may have held some profitable relationship to our study passage. So, we tried to organize the verses as systematically as possible—especially since the uses of the words seemed to indicate two different kinds of exhortation. It is always best to retain as much organization as possible in any study procedure, so we should plan to keep the word distinction and separation on the new worksheet.

The Old Worksheet

exhort - how to: I Th. 2:3; 4:1; II Th. 3:12;
    I Th. 2:11; I Tim. 4:13; Tit. 2:15;
    Rom. 12:8; I Cor. 14:3; Acts 11:23;
    15:32; I Pet. 5:12

"beseech"- Rom. 12:1; I Cor. 1:10; II Cor. 5:20;
    10:1
"intreat"- I Tim. 5:1; II Cor. 8:4
"comfort"- II Cor. 1:4; 7:6; I Cor. 14:31;
    Eph. 6:22; 4:8; I Th. 3:2; 4:18; 5:11;
    II Th. 2:17
"consolation"- II Cor. 1:5-6; II Th. 2:16

Both "beseech" and "intreat" carry the idea of begging for something. We had noted previously that this kind of ministry was inherent in the concept of "exhortation," especially when the preacher of the Word of God is trying to motivate Christian men and women to more fruitful service. Romans 12:1 and 2 are one of the more clear examples of this kind of ministry. Paul is "begging" or "exhorting" the Roman Christians to grow in their spiritual life and is calling on "the mercies of God" to remind the Christians of their position in the Lord. Paul's challenge and format for spiritual maturity are not incidental and must be obeyed. However,

161

the Holy Spirit of God will not force such obedience on
the heart, even though that obedience would be better
for the Christian. We must "present our bodies . . . ."
So, Paul "exhorts" us to do it. He "encourages" us. He
"begs" us. That is the kind of "preaching the word"
which is referred to in our study passage in II Timothy.

The second reference under this English word is parallel in its emphasis to the Romans passage. Paul is "begging" the Corinthian Christians to be unified in their
public testimony and church life. Obviously, such unity
requires the sincere commitment of each and every church
member to "live peaceably with all men" (Rom. 12:
16-18). Therefore, both of these references could be
used together as good examples of the "exhortation"
ministry of "begging" the Christian through the Word
of God. We should enter the verses on the new worksheet with a notation that would distinguish the message.
Something like: "Rom. 12:1-2 - Christian living; I Cor.
1:10 - unity."

Both II Corinthians 5:20 and 10:1 fail to add any additional light to the information that has been gained
from the previous references. Although both passages
do give an important teaching of their own, they do not
add to the concept of exhortation as it relates to our
study passage. We would cross out these references on
the old worksheet.

The same is true of the two verses listed under "intreat." Neither reference gives significant additional insight to our study passage, although II Corinthians 8:4
connects the idea of prayer to the action of "intreat." If
this is a new concept, it might be worthwhile to jot that
relationship down on the new worksheet; otherwise, the
references would be deleted.

The word "comfort" seems to be a common translation of our study word; and, if the number of references
that we have down on our old worksheet are any indication, it may well be the main idea of "exhortation." As
we check out these references, we should constantly
keep in mind that we are not looking for an in-depth

study of exhortation, but only for those references that will assist our understanding of how to exhort while preaching the Word.

I Corinthians 14:31 uses the word in connection with the idea of preaching, but does not add anything directly to our study thesis. II Corinthians 1:4 does show the chain by which comfort (exhortation) is connected through us to the Heavenly Father. That verse would be worth noting. However, both II Corinthians 7:6 and Ephesians 6:22 do not provide any special wisdom to our work here, so they should be crossed out. The second chapter of Colossians seems to outline the purpose of "exhortation" and also seems to parallel the so-called "chain of comfort" that we saw back in II Corinthians 1:4. We should note that relationship on our new worksheet. The verse in chapter four of Colossians, however, is not necessary to our study.

The Thessalonian references contain some information for us—all except I Thessalonians 3:2. That verse is very similar to a few of the others we have seen, providing only an example of comfort. We would not need to include that reference. However, both I Thessalonians 4:18 and 5:11 show one of the major sources of comfort, the promised return of our Saviour! And, both verses end in a command to "comfort" each other with that teaching. We should note those verses on the new worksheet, along with II Thessalonians 2:17 which implies the "comfort" contained in the "everlasting consolation and good hope through grace." That reference also ties in the purpose of such comfort and could well be parallel to the passage in Colossians 2:2. It would be worthwhile, then, to note that relationship on the new worksheet.

Often in studies like this, the Holy Spirit will help us to see patterns in the verses which we will use later when we try to outline the material. We should learn to be sensitive to such possible relationships during our research. Seldom is the pattern clear until the last stages. However, if we have not been alert to the possibility or the hint of parallel thoughts during the research stages, we will have a more difficult time during the actual outlining. In this case, I Thessalonians 4:18, 5:11, and II Thessalonians 2:17 all relate to the comfort found in the promise of the Second Coming. We should note that on the worksheet. II Thessalonians 2:17 *also* relates to the purpose of comfort in a similar vein to Colossians 2:2. We should record that fact.

This last heading contains two verses, one of which is not applicable to our study. II Thessalonians 2:16 (which, by the way, we saw in connection with 2:17) does not add any special insight to our study passage. However, II Corinthians 1:5 and 6 do explain why "comfort" is valuable and provide more information about the purpose of such a ministry. Since we have already established a "purpose" category with II Thessalonians 2:17 and Colossians 2:2, we should place this passage along with them.

Well! We did manage to get through all those verses easily enough, and we are much the richer for it. But, since we examined a wealth of information, we should glance over the way our worksheet is progressing—just to refresh our memory.

The New Worksheet

exhort
    I Thess. 2:3-11 - example of: outline
    I Tim. 4:13 - command
    Titus 2:15 - what: see reprove
beseech
    Rom. 12:1, 2 - example
    I Cor. 1:10 - example
comfort
    II Cor. 1:4 - chain of comfort
    Col. 2:2 - purpose

    I Thess. 4:18 - 2nd coming   **consolation**
    I Thess. 5:11 - 2nd coming   II Cor. 1:5, 6 -
    II Thess. 2:17 - purpose   purpose

WITH ALL LONGSUFFERING AND DOCTRINE

It does not take a brilliant student to recognize the progress that is being made. We have come a long way from our first reading of II Timothy 4:1-5. Even though we can see a pattern beginning to develop on the new worksheet, and even though the Holy Spirit has already given some exciting glimpses of the truths in this passage, we will really be rewarded when we put it all together a little later. However, right now we have to finish this last segment of the passage.

The Old Worksheet

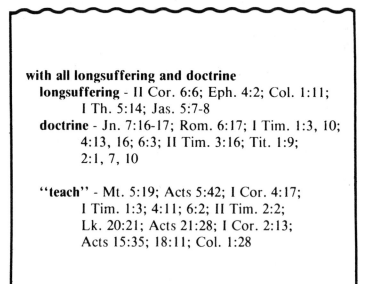

with all longsuffering and doctrine
   longsuffering - II Cor. 6:6; Eph. 4:2; Col. 1:11;
      I Th. 5:14; Jas. 5:7-8
   doctrine - Jn. 7:16-17; Rom. 6:17; I Tim. 1:3, 10;
      4:13, 16; 6:3; II Tim. 3:16; Tit. 1:9;
      2:1, 7, 10

   "teach" - Mt. 5:19; Acts 5:42; I Cor. 4:17;
      I Tim. 1:3; 4:11; 6:2; II Tim. 2:2;
      Lk. 20:21; Acts 21:28; I Cor. 2:13;
      Acts 15:35; 18:11; Col. 1:28

During our research for verses with some additional information about longsuffering, we found five passages that held that possibility in the concordance. The first reference, however, does not seem to do much more than list longsuffering as one of the things we ought to use (II Cor. 6:6). Both Ephesians 4:2 and Colossians 1:11 speak of "walking worthy" through longsuffering. However, neither one seems to give much specific information about longsuffering preaching. We could pick up the point in Ephesians about "forbearing one another in love," or the point in Colossians about being "strengthened with all might," but those points really relate to a more detailed study of the teaching on longsuffering—we are not doing that here. So, we would not use either of these passages in this study.

However, I Thessalonians 5:14 does seem to parallel the "preaching" theme of II Timothy. It contains the admonition to "be patient toward all men" and gives that admonition at the end of a list of preaching instructions. James notes that our "patience" is to be based on the fact of the nearing return of the Lord, but does not directly relate that "patience" to the work of preaching as would be necessary for our use here. Of all these five passages, only I Thessalonians 5:14 provides direct parallel information. That reference we would record on our new worksheet.

This next concept, "doctrine," has a rather large number of verses which could be applicable to our study passage. When we were doing the research, we found that the word "teach" was also used to translate the same Greek word, so we tried to keep "doctrine" and "teach" separate on our main worksheet to help us organize the information better. We should keep that same separation on the new worksheet to prevent confusion.

Our study passage in II Timothy has told us to "reprove, rebuke, exhort *with* all longsuffering and doctrine." We must now find out what doctrine is, and if necessary, why it is so important to use doctrine. However, not all doctrine is *good* doctrine. But once again, it is not the scope of this kind of study to find out the difference between correct and incorrect doctrine. It is necessary to find out *why* "doctrine" is the *way* Paul commanded Timothy to "reprove, rebuke, and exhort."

John 7:16 and 17 give an exciting promise, but do not tell us "why" teaching is necessary. Romans 6:17 discusses obedience to teaching, but, again, does not amplify the "why" aspect. I Timothy 1:3, however, gives us some insight. We are first given the command to "teach no other doctrine," and then told why: "Fables, and endless genealogies" minister questions. That passage would be worth recording on the new worksheet. Not so with 1:10, however. It discusses a number of things that are "contrary to sound doctrine," but it does not discuss why.

I Timothy 4:13 contains a command to teach and is in the same context as verse 16 which tells us why the command was given. That reason may need some further study, but we are only interested in verifying whether the verse applies to our study passage. And indeed, both of the verses in I Timothy 4 are applicable, but not I Timothy 6:3. That section describes the kind of people who will not listen to sound teaching. That is worth knowing, but it does not directly apply to our study passage. Remember, we are not trying to do a deep study on every subject raised by our study passage. We are only trying to clarify the teaching *of* the study passage. Out of those eight verses, only three are applicable.

The message in II Timothy 3:16 is well known to many conservative Christians. It is to the doctrine of inspiration what John 3:16 is to the doctrine of salvation. No doubt, dozens of sermons have been preached from this text; and, quite probably, you have heard one or two yourself. So, there is not much point in trying to elaborate on the inspiration concept of the verse. However, there is a very strong application in the passage to our study thesis. Scripture is profitable "for doctrine . . . ." And, that "doctrine" is to be used "that the man of God may be perfect, throughly furnished unto all good works." We are given two points to tie in to our study outline. The "teaching" mode commanded by Paul for the various kinds of preaching is most profitable when Scripture is the thing taught. Secondarily, the purpose of such Scriptural teaching is to make the man of God complete and perfectly equipped for every kind of good work. Obviously, that passage needs to be included in our final outline and might even need some additional clarification itself. We should make some notation on

our new worksheet that will remind us to check out the
words in the verses:
  "II Timothy 3:16,17 - teach Scripture/for perfection
  (check words)"
The next four references under the "doctrine" heading are also valuable to us. Titus 1:9 gives us a reason
for teaching. Verses 7-10 of Titus chapter two provide
an example of how we are to teach. The first verse of
Titus, chapter two, gives a list of the things which Paul
wants Titus to know about sound doctrine, and we are
not interested at this point in such material. However,
the passage from verse seven through verse ten does provide some excellent information about the way that the
"preacher" should "teach." We should make that notation on our new worksheet along with the other references.

The next section of verses contains passages that we
selected because they seemed to help explain the "teaching" concept of our study passage. Everyone of them
use the English word "teach" in some form or other,
and we have isolated them on our old worksheet for organizational purposes. It is always best to follow the
same structure throughout any given study to assist the
retention of information. So, we should keep the "teach"
verses separate on the new worksheet, yet not so separate
that we separate the "teach" verses from the "doctrine"
point of our overall outline. Each section of our worksheet should help us visualize the relationship between
the points of the study passage. That is why we have in-
dented the minor points under the major "precepts" of
II Timothy 4:2. Now, on the new worksheet, we are developing the sub-points under the minor points. That is,
we are reading each of the verses to determine what additional information is available to help clarify and amplify the message of our study passage. Right now, we
are trying to find out why Paul told Timothy to use
"doctrine" when he was "reproving, rebuking, exhorting." So, the "teach" verses should be related *under* the
"doctrine" part of our study.

The words of the Lord in Matthew 5:17-19 are some of the most beautiful and most sobering in all Scripture. On the one hand they give us the promise that the Word of God is eternal and absolutely accurate, and on the other hand they give us warning against improper teaching of that Word. The Lord bases that warning on the absolute truth of the Word which He verifies in verses 17 and 18, and then gives the stunning warning that we will be relegated to the "least in the kingdom of heaven" if we teach other men to break even "the least of these commandments." Whenever the Scripture specifies a negative limitation concerning the concept we are studying, we would be very wise to record it—and teach it to others. In this case, although the verse does not directly explain why we are to teach, it does tell us to be very careful with our teaching. And since the warning is predicated on the fact of the accuracy of the Word of God, it would tie in very well with the teaching which we discovered in II Timothy 3:16. The notation on the new worksheet should be something like this:

"Matthew 5:17-19 - warning (comp. II Tim. 3:16)"

The last time we had a string of verses to check out, we tried to look them up in Bible book order rather than in the order that they appeared on our main worksheet. That is purely for convenience sake and is not necessary, merely easier. One caution should be observed: it is easy to miss one reference, especially if there are very many. Get in the habit of double-checking your work as you go along. That should prevent any major errors. At any rate, the four passages in Acts (3:42; 15:35; 18:11; 21:28) all give some example of teaching and preaching. However, they do not add any specific clarity to the thesis of our study passage and can be deleted from our final outline.

The same is true of I Corinthians 4:17. That verse is just another example of the ministry of teaching in the early church. It does not amplify our study thesis. But I Corinthians 2:12 and 13 do provide parallel information. In fact, it almost seems to be a restatement of II

Timothy 3:16 and Matthew 5:17-19. All three of these passages talk about the importance of teaching the Word of God and do provide excellent insight into the reasons for using the Word. There is also a parallel to verse four of the same chapter which we had discovered earlier pertaining to the "preach" concept of our study passage. So, on our new worksheet we would make a notation something like this:

"I Corinthians 2:13 - teach Scripture (comp. II Tim. 3:16 and I Cor. 2:4)"

Each of the verses in I Timothy (1:3;4:11;6:2) seem to be giving some information about the kinds of things that are to be taught by sound teaching. That is valuable information. Indeed, it is vital information. But, we are not trying to develop that thesis now. (Maybe that song is getting old to you, but we must never forget the scope of our study. The teachings of the Bible are *so* interesting, it is almost painful to ignore, even temporarily, a portion of it. However, if we are to be able to understand a passage, we must keep our study limited to the thesis of the passage that we are studying.) Therefore, we would not record those three verses on our new worksheet.

II Timothy 2:2 is the "marching order" verse for teachers. Groups like the Navigators, who specialize in a teaching ministry, use this verse as the basis for their operation. Our study passage is in the same book (II Timothy) and should be easily related to this command. Remember, Paul told Timothy to "preach the word, reprove, rebuke, exhort, with all longsuffering and *doctrine.*" Doctrine is teaching. Teaching is done by teachers. Teachers are to teach other teachers to teach! That is why the command was given in II Timothy 4:3 to do all the preaching, rebuking, and exhorting with . . . teaching. Our new worksheet should record:

"II Timothy 2:2 - teach teachers"

Luke 20:21 does not give any particularly new insight to our study passage, so we can delete that reference. But, Colossians 1:28 seems to parallel the last part of

II Timothy 3:16 that talks about being "throughly furnished" and "perfect." We should record the Colossians passage along with a reminder to compare it to the II Timothy reference.

"Colossians 1:28 - perfection (comp. II Tim. 3:16)"

A quick review would be profitable here. We have finished this stage, but it is always good to re-check our progress. One of the most effective learning techniques is repetition. By reviewing our work while we are still involved with it, we are reinforcing what we are learning while it is still fresh in our minds.

The section of the old worksheet with which we have been working now looks like this:

with all longsuffering and doctrine
    longsuffering - II Cor. 6:6; Eph. 4:2; Col. 1:11;
        I Th. 5:14; Jas. 5:7-8
    doctrine - Jn. 7:16-17; Rom. 6:17; I Tim. 1:3, 10;
        4:13, 16; 6:3; II Tim. 3:16; Tit. 1:9;
        2:1, 7, 10

    "teach" - Mt. 5:19; Acts 5:42; I Cor. 4:17;
        I Tim. 1:3; 4:11; 6:2; II Tim. 2:2;
        Lk. 20:21; Acts 21:28; I Cor. 2:13;
        Acts 15:35; 18:11; Col. 1:28

The section of the new worksheet which we have been developing now looks like this:

      with all longsuffering and doctrine
        longsuffering
         I Thess. 5:14 - toward all men

doctrine
I Tim. 1:3 - teaching clarifies
I Tim. 4:13-16 - teaching saves
II Tim. 3:16, 17 - teach Scriptures/
for perfection (check words)
Titus 1:9 - to convince
Titus 2:7-10 - example

teach
Matt. 5:17-19 - warning (comp. II Tim. 3:16)
I Cor. 2:13 - teach Scripture (comp. II Tim.
3:16 and I Cor. 2:4)
II Tim. 2:2 - teach teachers
Col. 1:28 - perfection (comp. II Tim. 3:16)

Our new worksheet is now completed with a brief "topic" recorded for each verse, all under the appropriate relationship to the main structure of the passage. We have covered a lot of material, and our worksheet is really two sheets.

The New Worksheet

preach the word
preach
Rom. 10:8-15 - faith/gospel
I Cor. 2:4 - not man's wisdom
Titus 1:3 - preaching necessary
Acts 15:35 - teaching/with others #2097
Heb. 4:2 - why not work # 189

word
John 5:24 - salvation
John 8:31 - discipleship
John 17:17 - sanctification

be instant in season out of season
  instant - be present
  in season - convenient, opportunity
  out season - Phil. 4:10 - example

reprove
  John 16:8 - sin, righteousness, judgment
  Eph. 5:11 - unfruitful works of darkness
  I Tim. 5:1 - limitation/elder
  Titus 1:9 - sound doctrine
  Titus 1:13 - sharply
  Titus 2:1-15 - what to speak: outline

rebuke - strongest word, examples only

exhort
  I Thess. 2:3-11 - example of: outline
  I Tim. 4:13 - command
  Titus 2:15 - what: see reprove
  beseech
   Rom. 12:1, 2 - example
   I Cor. 1:10 - example
  comfort
   II Cor. 1:4 - chain of comfort
   Col. 2:2 - purpose
   I Thess. 4:18 - 2nd coming
   I Thess. 5:11 - 2nd coming
   II Thess. 2:17 - purpose
  consolation
   II Cor. 1:5, 6 - purpose

with all longsuffering and doctrine
  longsuffering
   I Thess. 5:14 - toward all men

doctrine
I Tim. 1:3 - teaching clarifies
I Tim. 4:13-16 - teaching saves
II Tim. 3:16, 17 - teach Scriptures/
  for perfection (check words)
Titus 1:9 - to convince
Titus 2:7-10 - example

teach
Matt. 5:17-19 - warning (comp. II Tim. 3:16)
I Cor. 2:13 - teach Scripture (comp. II Tim.
  3:16 and I Cor. 2:4)
II Tim. 2:2 - teach teachers
Col. 1:28 - perfection (comp. II Tim. 3:16)

Well! We have finished . . . the verse check. All that remains to be done is to sort out the verses into categories and then to organize the categories into a final outline. That will not be difficult. In fact, if you want to quit now, you are missing the greatest joy of the whole job. The "glimmer" of light that is beginning to shine on our minds at this point will be brought into brilliant beauty when we organize the material of God's Word into the clarity of the truth. Please stay with it through the end of the job.

12

SET IN ORDER
MANY PROVERBS

This is the place where all the work pays off. Nothing is more satisfying to a child of God than being fed from His Word. And when you sort out the ingredients yourself, the meal is doubly rewarding!

This chapter will cover the entire "set in order" process from a purely conceptual viewpoint. There is a good chance of some questions being raised this way, but it is worthwhile having some feel for the events to come before we actually get down into the mechanics of the operation. The principles covered in this chapter will be repeated in detail in the following chapters and will become clearer as we go on.

In chapter two we went through the exegesis of the "Bible Study Guide" verses in Ecclesiastes 12:9-10 and Isaiah 28:9-10. Those two passages gave us a framework that can be applied to *any* type of study, whether simple or complex. We have followed the Ecclesiastes framework as the main technique for the research and development of unknown (to us) truth. The first two steps, "give good heed," and "seek out" are the research steps. This last step, "set in order many proverbs," is the development step. The Isaiah passage ties in with and mixes in to the Ecclesiastes framework by giving us the direction to follow in both the research and the development. We are told to build "knowledge" and "doctrine" by first finding the "precepts" and then finding the "lines," neither of which will be found in one single spot in the Scriptures.

That simple-to-complex procedure which the Lord provided for us through Isaiah is recognized by every scientist, philosopher, teacher, or whatever, to be an absolute necessity for the discovery and presentation of information. So it should not be a real surprise to find that the Creator of all things would explain how best to understand His creation . . . or His Word. However, the "Isaiah Framework" is especially meaningful in this development step. So far, we have used that framework only as an overall guideline in finding the relationship of the sub-points of the passage to the major thesis. Now, we need to bring that framework into full focus while we try to put together all of the information that we have found so far.

The mechanics of this step are not too difficult, but they do require some patience and attention to detail. It is necessary to read each verse that has been listed on the worksheet so that we can discover the proper relationship of the information to the structure of the study passage. The problem is somewhat complicated by the multitude of verses. However, if we follow the formula given to us by the Holy Spirit through Isaiah, it is much easier. We have been told to look for the "precepts". . . the basic commandments, first; then to look for the "lines" . . . the supporting points, next. Therefore, we should approach each section of our study passage with that criteria, looking first for those verses which provide some "basic commandment" for the section, then for those verses which support or amplify.

All of this sounds relatively easy, but we must remember that the overall framework of the study passage has been structured by this same "Isaiah formula." That is, we are not at liberty to change the relationship of the "precepts" and "lines" which belong to the study passage itself, but only to discover the various relationships *within* each "precept" and "line." The Isaiah formula is applicable to both perspectives. We have already used it initially to determine the main thesis and its supporting points, now we will use it to determine how the verses of additional information relate to the individual thoughts of the II Timothy passage.

ORGANIZE THE VERSES

Categorize The Verses We have already had opportunity to go through this kind of process in the "seek out" procedure. During the examination of "exhort," it became necessary to sort out the kinds of verses within the word uses to determine which verses applied to the study thesis. The same basic process will apply now. We must put the verses into similar categories in order that we might be able to determine how the categories relate to the study passage.

The notation that has been made on the worksheet about the main thought of each parallel reference will be the key for organization. During the time that each verse is read and cataloged, some general impressions will be gained about the relationship of the various pieces of the puzzle. Those impressions will come into focus a little better as each section of the study passage is examined for sub-points. If proper limitations have been applied during the several steps prior to this point, there should be little difficulty in organizing the verses into catagories under a specific section of the study passage. The main point to remember in this process is to keep the organizing within the framework of the section being examined. In other words, do not relate a verse in one "precept" or "line" to a similar category in another "precept" or "line." Keep the categories of verses *within* the same section of the new worksheet as they were recorded earlier on the main worksheet.

177

Pinpoint The Relationships

After the entire study passage has been gone through and "categorized" under each section, it is necessary to pinpoint the best relationship for each category to the section within which it is located. However, we must relate the entire organizational process to the main thesis of the study passage. As has already been stressed, we are not trying to develop a composite doctrinal survey for every subject discussed by the study passage. Nor are we trying to use the study passage as a springboard to launch some personal vendetta against the evils of some idea. *We are bound* to the study thesis alone. It is not possible in this kind of study to answer every question or explore every possible avenue. We must keep our study limited to the thought and message provided by the immediate context of the study passage.

That means that we must constantly ask ourselves where the category fits in relation to the study thesis. Of course, each category must fit within the section of the study outline where it was found, but each category must also relate to the main thesis. If we have done our homework through the previous steps, there will be very little information that will not fit these two criteria. However, there will be occasions where some verses, when placed into categories, simply do not relate to the main thesis. When that is the case, the category must not be used. Nothing, no "neat thought" or "great verse" should be used in such a manner that it must be forced into the flow of the message from the study passage. Never force God's Word to fit your categories!

By the way, it may be necessary to make another worksheet for this organizational step. The one that we have been using for the reading, notation, and category steps, will not likely provide enough room for rearranging the categories into the proper relationships. If the study passage is not very complex, then it is a good technique to number the categories in order of their importance on the old worksheet, not making a new worksheet until coming to the final outlining stage. With practice, a Bible

178

student will be able to develop an outline rather rapidly, but to start with, it is best to be cautious. Remember, this is God's Word we are dealing with. We can never be too careful!

DEVELOP THE OUTLINE

Use Complete Sentences

This is the stage where it all comes together. We began with a coherent thought in the Scriptures, took it apart into dozens of little pieces, dug around in the Treasury for other valuables, and now are going to put it back together. The additional "things, new and old" (Matt. 13:52) will make the rebuilt passage much more valuable—providing we are careful enough to build it in such a manner that we can use it again and again. The best way to do that is to make this final outline in sentence form. Every point, both major and minor, should be recorded by the use of complete sentences. The sentences do not have to be "zingers" with some great insight of philosophical wisdom, nor do they have to begin with the same letter of the alphabet or follow some rhyme scheme. But, they do have to make sense!

There are many books written on homiletics (the art of preaching) and "outlineology" (that's bound to be the Latin term for "how to outline"). So, if there is a need to make the outline more professional, the resources are easily available. But for most Bible study, it is not necessary to make the type of permanent record that would please a homiletics or English professor. It *is* necessary to make the record so that an ordinary human being can pick up the work six months or six years later and understand what has been said. There is so much information and insight gained from this type of Bible study, that it is a shame to depend merely on the memory of the Bible student. Most people are aware that the memory is not always the most reliable source of information. It just makes good sense, then, to insure that all of the hard work done to get insight from the Scriptures is pre-

179

served in such a fashion that it can be retrieved and re-vived quickly.

Read Through The Entire Outline

After the outline is finished, a careful student will read through the entire outline to check its ac-curacy. Nothing is quite as disap-pointing as finding out that an incorrect reference has been placed on the final outline inadvertently—especially when it is discovered in front of an audience! It is there-fore wise to check each reference, reading it in the Bible, to make sure it is correct. That is not wasted time. Not only will it insure accuracy, but it will reinforce the in-formation already learned. However, the main help that this checking process will provide is a "feeling" for the message of the study passage.

Check For The Flow Of The Message

It almost seems incorrect to use such a subjective term to describe the objective study of the Bible. However, the ministry of the Holy Spirit of God does take place through the Word of God in our "hearts." Obviously, the "heart" of the spiritual nature of man is not the physical organ. But, it is not precisely clear in the Scrip-ture what the "heart" really is. Probably, it corresponds most closely to our instantaneous thinking response—our reaction to a situation. The conscious brain can be, and often is, controlled by our will in such a manner that we say and do things that we know to be incorrect. Our sudden response, almost an involuntary response, is often the truest indication of what we are really like (Matt. 15:17-20).

Paul wrestled with that terrible problem in the passage we studied back in chapter six of this book. He noted that our flesh seems to have a "heart" of its own, and that it is in constant conflict with the new "heart" that God has given to the born-again Christian. Paul wound up that section in Romans 7:15-24 with an awful cry: "Oh wretched man that I am! Who shall deliver me from the body of this death?" If the Scripture had ended there, we would all be in great trouble. But, praise the Lord, the remedy is given in chapter eight of Romans. The gist of that whole chapter is that we can be directed by the Holy Spirit of God, and that we can discover the absolute confidence of God's care, provision, protection, and perfect will in our lives. We are most privileged!

Well, back to the point. When we have taken the time to dig into the one place where the Holy Spirit gets His instruction (read John 14:15-18, 26; 15:26; 16:7-15), we will find that He will minister in His special way to our "hearts" so that we will "feel right" about the work we have done. Please do not misunderstand what is being said. The Holy Spirit does not give "goose bumps" or special trances, etc., etc., but He does give the peace of God — He does give the assurance of righteousness — He does give the blessings of truth. Oh yes, sometimes "goose bumps" do come. Sometimes tears flow. Sometimes the Word is so exciting that you giggle and laugh for several minutes. Whatever emotion happens as a result of the ministry of the Holy Spirit, is *not* the "feeling" that God expects us to follow as some "sign" of truth. To the contrary, He tells us to "stir up your pure *minds* by the way of remembrance . . ." (II Pet. 3:1) and to "be transformed by the renewing of your *mind* . . ." (Rom. 12:2). Paul prays for us that we "might be filled with the *knowledge* of his will in all *wisdom* and *understanding*" (Col. 1:9). Over and over again the Scriptures stress the use of our minds—our intellect instead of our emotions in determining truth.

All of that has been said simply to bring a necessary note of caution to our Bible study. We have all been trained to let our emotions rule our "hearts" in nearly every facet of our life. It takes a real effort to subdue the emotions and come under the control of the spirit. And it takes a real effort to suppress emotional "leanings" while trying to discover the truth of God's Word. But if we are able, through the power of the Holy Spirit, to control our emotions during the research and organization of our study, the Holy Spirit will bless us through our emotions when we read through the final outline. That is the "feeling" that we will gain when we view the truth

181

of God's Word with a deeper insight than we had before we began the study. That is the point where the "heart" begins to "rejoice with joy unspeakable and full of glory" (I Pet. 1:8).

That general overview expresses a lot of work! But, you know what? It is not hard work. It really is not even "smart" work. One of the most remarkable things about Bible study is that we have been given the mind of the Lord Jesus Himself for that very purpose. You don't believe that . . . ? Read I Corinthians 2:13-16. God wants every one of His children to *know* what His Word says. All we have to do is "study to shew thyself approved. . . ." Isn't that great?! All right, read chapter thirteen.

13

CATEGORIZE THE VERSES

This step in our work, although not difficult to do, is difficult to explain. Once a student becomes used to the kind of work being done, the actual time involved is relatively minor. However, it does require rather careful attention on the part of a new student to gain a feeling for the job. If organizing was accomplished by following a strict set of rules, it would be easy. Unfortunately, there are so many small factors involved that it is almost impossible to list them. Yet, anyone who wants to understand the things of God's Word can acquire the skills necessary. In fact, we have a direct promise from the lips of the Lord Jesus Christ Himself to that effect in John 7:17, "If any man will do his will, he *shall* know of the doctrine." We can understand, we can find truth, and we can increase in our knowledge of the Word (Eph. 1:17-19; Phil. 1:9-11; Col. 1:9-12).

Locate The Same Theme

Although there is no "cut-and-dried" method of developing categories, there are a few general guidelines that will help. One fairly obvious step is to try to find the same theme or thesis in other verses. It stands to reason that if two verses are talking about the same thing, they would be in the same category. Since this is so obvious, it is often wise to try this approach first.

Locate Verses With Similar Themes

Then, if no verses are found that have the same theme, we can look for passages that discuss similar or related themes. This distinction is somewhat difficult to draw, mainly because there is a built-in similarity to the passages already. Since we have already selected the verses as having a bearing on one common point, they will all be "similar." However, it is necessary to think *within* the framework of the specific section of the overall study passage and try to locate those verses which discuss related topics within that section.

Locate Contrasting Themes

Sometimes, the passages that have been provided by the Scriptural research will be related by contrasting their ideas. That is, one verse will present the positive side of the issue, another will present the negative side. One of the best ways to understand truth is to understand its limitations. We need to know what something is *not,* as well as what it *is.* Frequently, the Scriptures will fall into this type of relationship.

Reread The Verses

Even though we have gone through each passage already, it is almost impossible to remember what was covered in a given reference. It is best to reread the verses when categorizing them so that fewer mistakes will be made. The more frequently we read the words of God, the more clearly we will be enlightened by the Holy Spirit. It will be imperative to reread each verse during the final outlining phase, but it may be helpful to do so even during this step. If the topic listed on the worksheet is clear enough to bring to mind the content of the verse, it is probably not necessary to reread the verse before placing it into a category. If there is any doubt, or if the content of the verse is not clear in the mind, read it.

Check The Context

As we have already discovered, the context is critical in any Bible study. We should have been doing this all along, and the likelihood of finding some startling new insight is slim. However, every study is somewhat involved and it is possible to overlook a key point. Usually this happens when the context has not been adequately explored. The *indicator* for such a possibility is *confusion*. If the passage or topic listed on the worksheet does not seem to "fit" anywhere, chances are a mistake has been made. That is the time to check the context of the passage (read pages 88-89 if you need a reminder).

Work Through The Entire Study Outline

As we have been doing all along, we should continue to complete the entire study passage before we proceed to a new step. Each process in the study procedure is to be a *partial* revealer of truth. Only when we have gone through *all* of the steps will we be sure that we have done everything required by Ecclesiastes 12:9-10 and Isaiah 28:9-10. Therefore, during each step we must be careful not to lose the flow of the message in the study passage. The only way to insure that is to work through the passage, from start to finish, each time we use a different approach. If that is done, two things will be the result: one, we will be less likely to make an error in using some verse that does not apply, and two, we will be reinforcing the message of the study passage in our own minds. The overall result of those two factors will be a very well-prepared piece of truth and an indelible impression of that truth on the mind of the student.

A REVIEW seems in order now. We have covered the steps for bringing our study worksheet into a form from which we can better relate the details. There are several parts, and it is beneficial to have a fairly good picture of them before we actually work through an example.

1. Locate the same theme.
2. Locate verses with similar themes.
3. Locate contrasting themes.
   a. Reread the verse if necessary.
   b. Check the context if necessary.
4. Work through the entire study outline.

We have been working through II Timothy 4:2. So far, we have researched the verses in the concordance, checked those verses in their context, and eliminated those verses that did not seem to apply. What we have now is a two-page worksheet that contains those passages of Scripture most likely to provide parallel information for our better understanding of the study passage. One of the points that has been made all along in this study is that it is very difficult to relate the big picture of the study passage to the small pieces of which it is made. Or, put more simply, it is hard to know what verse *really* applies to the main thesis, and what verse is merely interesting.

These steps will help narrow down the amount of passages about as much as the other steps have. When we read through the concordance listings, we eliminated many passages that were obviously unrelated. Then, when we actually read through the verses and their context, we were able to see other passages that were not applicable. Now, as we try to organize the verses into categories we will find that there are verses that do not provide as much insight as we thought they did at first. We will be able to trim our worksheet to the essential material from which will come a final outline.

PREACH THE WORD

Under this point, which is our main thesis, we had broken out two main sub-points: "preach" and "word." We had chosen five passages under "preach" and three under "word" as representative of the message of the thesis. Our first job is to put these verses into categories, combining whatever verses we can into the same category.

At first glance there does not seem to be much similarity in these topic notations on the worksheet. But, by this time we have probably forgotten why we chose a particular topic for any given verse. So, we should take the time to reread each verse to refresh our memory. In that way we can relate the passages more clearly.

> **preach**
> Rom. 10:8-15 - faith/gospel
> I Cor. 2:4 - not man's wisdom
> Tit. 1:3 - preaching necessary
> Acts 15:35 - teaching/with others #2097
> Heb. 4:2 - why not work #189

Remember, the limiting factor in every portion of this study is the main thesis. Every verse, every subject, every sub-point *must* relate to the main thesis *first,* then relate to the subject, sub-point or whatever within which it is found. Therefore, when we reread the verses, we must re-ask the question, "Does this relate to the thesis?" If it does not help, if it does not *really* provide some insight into the message of the study passage, then we must not use it.

A good example of that problem is Romans 10:8 to 15. Although that passage does deal with "preaching the word," and although it is an excellent gospel passage and example, it does not give any real *new* insight into the "how" or "why" aspect of the thesis. Therefore, we would eliminate that category from consideration.

I Corinthians 2:4, however, is important. It tells us that this preaching is not to be based on man's wisdom, but in the power of the Holy Spirit. There are a couple of words in that text that need to be examined later, but we can be confident that this verse is necessary for our study.

The same is true of Titus 1:3. The context establishes the subject of verse three and tells us that the Lord Himself decided that preaching the Word was the means He would use to get out His truth. Both I Corinthians 2:4 and Titus 1:3 should be identified as important separate categories for our final outline.

However, Acts 15:35 and Hebrews 4:2, while both interesting passages, do not give us any new or incisive information about our thesis. They would not be valuable for a teaching outline as it would relate to "preaching the word." Therefore, we would delete those two references from our worksheet.

Out of the first five references, only two were found to be significant enough to bear directly to the thesis. And, both of these are independent of each other and cannot be combined into one category. Furthermore, the original topic notation we had made about each verse is accurate. Therefore, we can leave the work as it is, merely making a check mark (✓) next to the two verses on our worksheet. It may be necessary yet to make another worksheet for this stage, but it would simplify things if we can keep our work to a minimum.

> **word**
> John 5:24 - salvation
> John 8:31 - discipleship
> John 17:17 - sanctification

These next three verses were selected out of a whole host of possibilities because they were representative of the "why" aspect of preaching the word. It is likely that each of these will apply, since we were so selective to begin with. What we must do here is determine if the verses are *necessary* to the thesis and, at the same time, determine if they may be combined into a similar category. Again, a quick review of the verses in their context would be helpful.

Once that is done, it is fairly easy to see that each of the references has valuable information. The main point of each verse is an explanation of what the Word does. Or, looked at another way, they explain why the preaching of the Word is so important. When we think back to the reference we just examined in Titus 1:3, we can recall that we were told that preaching was necessary — that the Lord Himself decided to use that medium to get out His truth. Now, through these three references, we are told three of the reasons for that decision. First, the Word produces salvation. Second, it maintains discipleship, and third, it is the instrument of sanctification. Each reference is worth putting into a final outline, and, while each discusses a different aspect, they all are "reasons" for preaching the Word. Therefore, we should make one category out of all three of these verses, but retain each of them.

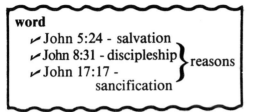

The best way to make that kind of notation on our worksheet is to bracket the three references, and put a notation to the right of the bracket about the category topic.

BE INSTANT IN SEASON OUT OF SEASON

This point does not offer much work. We have already eliminated any references for "instant" and for "in season" because there were no additional Scriptures that dealt with the concept of preaching. The one reference we selected in Philippians was selected because it translated our "out of season" word by another English phrase that seemed to be easier to understand. Our objective for this study (or for any study for that matter) is to make the Bible teaching as clear as possible. In this case, although the reference does not deal with preaching, the translation is helpful to our understanding of the message in our study passage. Therefore, we should retain this reference as a Scriptural example of the meaning of our study phrase, "out of season." A check mark (✓) on the worksheet is sufficient.

REPROVE, REBUKE, EXHORT

These three "action" words contain several passages which need to be correlated. But, we must remember that each passage *must* be related to the thesis or our study passage and then to the sub-point under which it was originally researched. All three of these sub-points tell us *how* to preach the Word. Or, more accurately, what technique to use when preaching the Word. We are, therefore, not looking for *what* to say. We must confine our choices to those references that help explain what the actions of "reprove, rebuke, exhort" are like . . . or, that tell us when we are supposed to reprove, rebuke, or exhort.

```
reprove
    John 16:8 - sin, righteousness,
                judgment
    Eph. 5:11 - unfruitful works of
                darkness
    I Tim. 5:1 - limitation/elder
    Tit. 1:9 -   sound doctrine
    Tit. 1:13 -  sharply
    Tit. 2:1-15 - what to speak: outline
```

Once again, the first glance does not give any immediate suggestion about similar categories. The verses all seem to have independent thoughts about reproving, so we must refer to the Scriptural context to help establish the point.

This first passage, John 16:7-11, is difficult to pinpoint. On the one hand, it does not directly relate to the thesis of II Timothy 4. But, on the other hand, it does give us an excellent insight into the ministry of reproving. We are not interested in *what* to say, but we are interested in *how* to reprove. This passage tells us that the Holy Spirit reproves in three specific areas: sin, righteousness, and judgment. We could use this passage to draw a broad reference for the ministry of reproving since the Holy Spirit is the author of the Word of God. However, the categories are *so* broad, that it would be difficult to explain their relationship to our study thesis without greater study of the John passage. Therefore, we should not use this passage.

The Ephesians reference, however, tells us when to reprove. Furthermore, it also gives us the reason for the reproof of the "unfruitful works of darkness." We should include this passage in our outline and make the additional notation that this is a "when" category. On our worksheet, we should check the reference ($\checkmark$) and add the category title: "when."

I Timothy 5:1 does not do much for our study thesis.

It does have a limitation and may be valuable as a warning to us. The information, while part of the truth about the reproving ministry, is not necessary to understanding how to reprove while preaching the Word. If our conscience would not let us delete that passage, then we should check it (✓) along with a notation that it might not be easy to parallel to the thesis. A student has to develop his own shorthand system for these things. A symbol like ≠, (not parallel or equal), or even a simple question mark (?) could be used. The point is, whenever we "hate" to delete a reference, but are unsure of its application, we should mark our worksheet in such a manner that we will remember our concern when we come to the final outlining procedure.

Both of the verses in Titus chapter one, along with the intervening context, provide some definitive information for our study. However, we did not identify the main point in Titus 1:9 during our earlier research. The verse does tie in with our thesis directly through the "faithful word" and through the "sound doctrine" to which this person is "holding fast." But the focus of this passage is on the purpose of the reproving aspect of such ministry. Here our word is translated "convince," and we are told that the object is to convince the "gainsayers." There then follows, in verses ten through twelve, an explanation of the statement in verse nine. The explanation is verified in verse thirteen and summarized with an even clearer command, "rebuke them sharply." That command is followed by its purpose, "that they may be sound in the faith." So, the whole passage is an excellent text to help us understand *who* to reprove, *how* to reprove, and the *purpose* of reproof. We should bracket those two references on our worksheet and note the three points: "who, how, purpose," out to the right of the bracket.

Earlier, we had felt it necessary to list Titus 2:1-15 as providing in-depth material for our study of both "reprove" and "exhort" (verse 15). However, in rereading the passage, we can see that the main point of the passage is to give a list of the kinds of things that are to be taught through the different medium. In fact, the last verse gives the command to "speak, and exhort, and rebuke with all authority." Although there is much valuable information here, it does not apply to the "how," "when," "who," or "purpose" categories with which we have been dealing. . .except for verse 15. That verse has one "how" phrase: "rebuke with all authority." That verse should be noted on our worksheet.

This little section has produced several categories almost by itself. We must make sure that we get these impressions down on our worksheet before we lose them. The first verse that applied was Ephesians 5:11. We initially felt that it gave us a "when" to rebuke, but after reading Titus 1:9-13, it seems to fall in the same general category as the "who" of Titus 1:9. That questionable verse in I Timothy 5:1 would also fit easily into that category. So, we should make some columns or tabulations that would tie those three verses together. Titus 1:13 and 2:15 both fit into a "how" category, and Titus 1:13 also stands alone as a "purpose" category. That section of the worksheet might look like this:

reprove		who/what
John 16:8 -	sin, righteousness, judgment	Eph. 5:11
✔Eph. 5:11 -	unfruitful works of darkness	Titus 1:9
⑦ ✔I Tim. 5:1 -	limitation/elder	I Tim. 5:1
✔Tit. 1:9 -	sound doctrine	**how**
✔Tit. 1:13 -	sharply	Titus 1:13
Tit. 2:1-15 -	what to speak: outline	Titus 2:15
		purpose
		Titus 1:13

THE "REBUKE" SECTION was not found to have any verses in the Bible that dealt directly with preaching the Word. We did find several examples that helped us establish the fact that "rebuke" was a stronger word than "reprove." If it is felt necessary to use a reference or two in the final outline, it will only take a minute to go back to the concordance, read quickly through the listings, and find examples that will assist our illustration of the distinctions between the two words. Once again, remember that we are not trying to teach about rebuking. We are only trying to establish how to "preach the word" while using the technique of rebuking. If the Scriptures do not provide any specific information about that technique as it relates to preaching, then we must not develop that point beyond the necessary clarification of the word meaning.

exhort
> I Thess. 2:3-11 - example of:
> outline
> I Tim. 4:13 - command
> Titus 2:15 - what: see reprove

beseech
> Rom. 12:1, 2 - example
> I Cor. 1:10 - example

comfort
> II Cor. 1:4 - chain of comfort
> Col. 2:2 - purpose
> I Thess. 4:18 - 2nd coming
> I Thess. 5:11 - 2nd coming
> II Thess. 2:17 - purpose

consolation
> II Cor. 1:5, 6 - purpose

There are more verses in the "exhort" section than any other in our study. When we were doing the research for this point, we found many passages that seemed to tie in with the major theme of our study passage, indicating that this kind of preaching was to be used quite frequently. Therefore, we must be all the more careful as we try to categorize these passages.

The first passage contains a good bit of data. It is information that is valuable to our study because it tells us *how* Paul exhorted. However, since it is rather lengthy, we must sort out the information into some sub-categories before it can be usable for outline purposes. The first thing that strikes the reader of this section in I Thessalonians two is that it is structured in a positive/negative relationship. Verse three tells us how *not* to exhort, then verse four explains how it was done properly. Verses five and six give further negatives that are offset by the correct behavior in verses seven through eleven. Verse twelve finally gives the purpose of all of these actions as the encouragement to "walk worthy of God . . . ."

The main thrust of the first contrasting relationship is that we are to please God, not men. The second section explains how to speak and how to behave while exhorting the believers. It may well become necessary to do some word studies in this passage before we can use it in our final outline. But for now, we can merely list the main sub-categories on our worksheet.

I Timothy 4:13 is a command to exhort, but does not provide any relevant information about the act of exhortation. We would not use this verse in our final outline.

We have already noted Titus 2:15 in our study under "reprove." The same instruction about how to reprove, also applies to the concept of exhortation. We should make a note about the "how" category on our worksheet along with the "authority" sub-point.

The beautiful passage in Romans twelve, as instructive and valuable as it is, does not give any direct bearing on the technique of exhortation. We should not use *any* passage in our final outline unless it is directly applicable to our study thesis. This passage does not "fit" the flow of the message in II Timothy 4:2. We must not use it.

The same thing is true of the words of I Corinthians 1:10. Although they give good information about *what* to exhort, they do not give any explanation on *how* to exhort.

II Corinthians 1:4-6, however, contains much information that relates to our study concept. There are two

194

different English words used: "comfort" and "consolation." We had already noted on our worksheet that verses three and four describe a "chain of comfort." That is, God comforts others with the same comfort which we use. That is very important to know in relation to the instruction that we have been given in II Timothy. We are not to "exhort" through our own made-up devices, but we are to use the same comfort that God has given us. Verses five and six explain that we go through various "sufferings" and "afflictions" so that we can comfort others. In other words, exhortation is not merely an academic technique but an acquired skill! (Read Romans 5:3-5 and I Peter 4:12-19.) We should make a notation on our worksheet that would distinguish between the "chain" in verses three and four and the "acquired skill" of verses five and six.

The passage in Colossians two, while not easily summarized, does give us a "purpose" for the ministry of exhortation. We had already noted that on our worksheet, so we would only have to check (✓) the reference. We will study it in depth when we come back to pinpoint the relationship of the various categories.

Neither I Thessalonians 4:8 or 5:11 give us any direct information about the technique of exhortation. They do tell us that we are to comfort one another with the thought of the second coming of the Lord, but we are not trying to develop a study on the subjects for exhortation. We should not use these verses in our final outline.

II Thessalonians 2:17, however, does seem to give a purpose of exhortation—at least that is one way of looking at the verse. When we read the verse from the beginning of the sentence in verse sixteen, we find that "The Lord Jesus Christ" is the subject of the two verbs in verse seventeen. We should read it this way: "Now our Lord Jesus Christ . . . (verse 16 gives information about the Lord) comfort your hearts, and stablish you. . . ."

In other words, verse seventeen is merely asking the Lord to perform His special comforting ministry *and* His special "stablishing" work in our lives. We should not

195

use this verse. Even though it may apply, (the literal reading) the natural reading of the verses would not permit our use for an application to II Timothy 4:2.

These verses under the "exhort" section have been reduced to four passages that have been subdivided into several sub-points. However, all of the passages will fit easily into two main categories: "how" and "purpose." We should make adequate notations on our worksheet so that we will be able to pinpoint the relationships later. This portion of our worksheet should look like this:

```
exhort                    how
  ✓I Thess. 2:3-11 - example of: outline
     please God     speak      behave      purpose
        2:3 4          5 8        9 11          12
  I Tim. 4:13 - command
  ✓Titus 2:15 - what: see reprove
                     how: authority
     beseech
        Rom. 12:1-2 - example
        I Cor. 1:10 - example
     comfort
        ✓II Cor. 1:4 - chain of comfort
                 (3-4) acquired skill (5-6) -how
        ✓Col. 2:2 - purpose
        I Thess. 4:18 - 2nd coming
        I Thess. 5:11 - 2nd coming
        II Thess. 2:17 - purpose
     consolation
        II Cor. 1:5-6 - purpose
```

WITH ALL LONGSUFFERING AND DOCTRINE

```
longsuffering
  I Thess. 5:14 - toward all men
```

In our earlier research, this was the only verse that we felt had direct import to our study thesis. Actually, it is a general command—sort of a "catch-all" command to the church at Thessalonica. The application to our study thesis is merely the extent of "longsuffering." We would use this verse in that manner.

---

doctrine
I Tim. 1:3 - teaching clarifies
I Tim. 4:13-16 - teaching saves
II Tim. 3:16, 17 - teach Scriptures/
  for perfection (check words)
Titus 1:9 - to convince
Titus 2:7-10 - example

teach
Matt. 5:17-19 - warning (comp. II Tim. 3:16)
I Cor. 2:13 - teach Scripture (comp. II Tim.
  3:16 and I Cor. 2:4)
II Tim. 2:2 - teach teachers
Col. 1:28 - perfection (comp. II Tim. 3:16)

This section contains information about why "doctrine" is so important. Our study thesis told us to "preach the word." We were given three techniques to use while preaching, and now we are told to use those techniques "with all longsuffering and doctrine." Once again, we are not trying to find out *what* to teach, but only what "doctrine" *is* and *why* "doctrine" is so *necessary*.

The verses that we have selected earlier must now be categorized. I Timothy 1:3 and 4 note that "doctrine" produces a "godly edifying" in contrast to the "fables and endless genealogies, which minister questions. . . ." We had noted on our worksheet that this verse taught us that "teaching clarifies." That is an adequate point, but it is only the point of one passage. We are trying to develop broader categories to house several verses. In this case, the category would probably be "the importance of," or something like that.

And the same category would fit the passage in chapter four. Paul gives a command to "give attendance . . . to doctrine" in verse thirteen and then tells us why that is so important in verse sixteen. Since we had already noted the sub-point of what the verses themselves are teaching, we need only to make another note on our worksheet that will identify this passage with the "importance" category.

However, II Timothy 3:16-17, as important a verse as it is, does not relate to the importance of teaching, or to the reasons for teaching. What it does tell us is that we must use the Scriptures when we teach. The question is: shall we use this verse in our final outline? Ordinarily, when a passage does not relate directly to the kinds of information needed to clarify the study passage, we would not include it. In this case, the emphasis is so parallel to our thesis ("preach the word") that it would be difficult not to include it . . . especially since we have noted several other passages that tie back to the concept of inspiration. So, the best thing to do is keep the reference, making a "special" category for it.

The Titus 1:9 passage gives another sub-point in the "importance" category. Since we have already noted that on our worksheet previously, all we have to do now is make the proper record of the category.

Chapter two of Titus contains some interesting information about the way "doctrine" should be used. Verse seven demands that it be done sincerely, and verse eight explains that it must done in such a way that those who are "of the contrary part may be ashamed, having no evil thing to say of you." Verse nine begins a new sentence directed to "servants." They are told to work hard and do a good job so "that they may adorn the doctrine of God our Saviour in all things." The passage seems to break down into two categories: verses seven and eight are "how" verses, and verses nine and ten are "purpose" verses. We should make such notations on our worksheet.

Matthew 5:17-19 contains one of the sternest warnings

198

in Scripture about the teaching ministry. We have been told to use doctrine, or teaching, to preach the Word. Here, the Lord Jesus tells us that we had better be careful when we teach! No matter what we do, God's Word is inviolate. And if we break even one of the most insignificant commandments and teach others to do likewise, we will be relegated to the "least in the kingdom of heaven." This type of warning should always be included in a study outline when we are dealing with a methodological concept.

The passage in I Corinthians 2:13 has a good explanation of why we are to teach the Word of God. Further, it explains that we are not to use the wisdom of men in our teaching and are to be very careful, "comparing spiritual things with spiritual."

Earlier, we had noted that we should compare that verse with the similar teaching in verse four of the same chapter along with the basic instruction in II Timothy 3:16. It is becoming apparent that one of the major points in this study will be the teaching about teaching! This "how to" category seems to be getting a workout in this section.

Paul's instruction to Timothy about the teaching of teachers in II Timothy 2:2 not only explains the formula for perpetuation of sound doctrine, but also gives us another passage that verifies the importance of the *method* of teaching when we "preach the word."

Colossians 1:28 contains another emphasis on the importance of teaching, along with the qualifier, "in all wisdom." It also directs us to the purpose of such teaching. Our worksheet should note the tie-in to II Timothy 3:16 and the tie in to the "how" category.

We have found each of these references to be worth retaining in our study and have been able to separate them into some common categories. Since there are several passages, it might be good to make a tabular notation of the appropriate categories somewhere on the worksheet. Usually, the left-hand margin is open and can be used for that purpose.

199

	doctrine
importance	✓I Tim. 1:3 - teaching clari-
I Tim. 1:3	fies -**importance**
I Tim. 4:13-16	✓I Tim. 4:13-16 - teaching
Titus 1:9	saves - **importance**
II Tim. 2:2	✓II Tim. 3:16-17 - teach
	Scripture/for perfection
	(check words)
how	✓Titus 1:9 - to convince -
Titus 2:7-8	**importance**
I Cor. 2:13	✓ Titus 2:7-10 - example (7,8 **how**)
Col. 1:28	(9, 10 **purpose**)
purpose	teach
Col. 1:28	✓Matt. 5:17-19 - warning
Titus 2:9-10	(comp. II Tim. 3:16)
	✓I Cor. 2:13 - teach Scrip-
warn	ture (comp. II Tim. 3:16
Matt. 5:17-19	& I Cor. 2:4) **how**
	✓II Tim. 2:2 - teach teachers
Scripture	**importance**
II Tim. 3:16-17	✓Col. 1:28 - perfection
	(comp. II Tim. 3:16)
	how, purpose

Having categorized the various verses, we must now
go back through the worksheet and pinpoint the relationships between those verses. The next chapter describes that process in detail.

14

PINPOINT THE RELATIONSHIPS

After the entire worksheet has been organized into categories, it is necessary to go back through the study and pinpoint the relationship of the various categories. As was the case during earlier steps, the Holy Spirit will have already "suggested" some relationship to us while we were developing the categories. However, we must now concentrate on this procedure in order that we might "set in order many proverbs." Remember, one of the overall guidelines given to us by the Scripture is the building process of "precept upon precept, precept upon precept, line upon line, line upon line, here a little, and there a little." That process is a process of simple to complex, of easily identifiable items to difficult-to-see items. We have followed that overall procedure all the way through our study and have been gaining good perspective all along. In this portion of our study, we began by locating the easily identifiable categories of our parallel verses. Now we must determine the less obvious relationship between those categories.

Review Each Section In Order

This point does not need too much elaboration. We have followed this mechanism all throughout our study. The main reason for this is that it helps us to keep the message of the study passage in the proper perspective. The words, the word order, and the word flow are never incidental in God's Word. We must be careful that we never lose sight of what the study passage is saying. Everything, from the word study sheet, the verse study worksheet, to the final outline must follow that order of thought which is presented by the writer of the Scripture.

Examine The Categories First

We have already gone through the verses fairly carefully in an effort to develop major categories under each section of our study passage. Now, we should start with those categories and try to pinpoint the relationship between each category. We must not try to relate the verses themselves yet; only the category.

Establish The Order Of Importance

The objective is to establish the order of importance for the various categories under each section of the study passage. But, that is easier said than done. If we have been paying attention to the bits and pieces of information that we have been seeing, there should be a fairly good "feel" for the general thrust of the study passage by this time. The problem is that the "feeling" is subjective, not objective.

As we have discussed earlier, the Holy Spirit of God has His main function in our "hearts" as we are studying the Word which He inspired. We are required to suppress our "feelings" when the objective directions of the Word are available. But when we come to an area of study that is not "cut-and-dried," we can expect the Holy Spirit to direct us to the truth . . . providing we have followed the objective directions previously. This is the case here. If we have been following the Biblical procedures up to this point, we will have gained an internal sensitivity to the thesis, concepts, and purposes of the study passage. These "feelings" for the message are the working of the Holy Spirit on our mind through the instrumentality of the Word of God. To sharpen those impressions into the clear "proverbs" needed to teach others, we can follow two fairly simple steps.

ALWAYS RELATE TO THE MAIN THESIS. The very first point in our study process was to establish the main thesis of the study passage. All during the research phase we used that thesis to help "weed out" those phrases in the concordance which would not amplify the study. When we were trying to separate out the verses that were actually valid material for our study, we did not use the main thesis as directly because we were trying to discover which verses dealt directly with a sub-point under the main thesis. Now we need to bring the main thesis back consciously into the study process.

Every category which we have developed must relate to the message of our study passage. If it does not, we cannot use it. We are never at liberty to "force" the Scriptures. The Holy Spirit is anxious for us to understand His Word, and He will be doing everything He can to help us learn the truth. That means that He will *not* direct us into some area that is not part of the message. Back during the stage of verse research, it was easy to "like" a verse and put it down on our worksheet. Sometimes the verses contain very exciting information that had not been realized before. Inevitably, such verses are recorded on the worksheet because they are so interesting. However, now that we are trying to finalize the relationship of the various bits of information to the truth contained in our study passage, the Holy Spirit will unsettle our "hearts" whenever we are about to misuse or misapply His Word. Those categories that do not "feel right" should not be used.

AVOID GOING TOO DEEP into a minor point. This principle is another way of looking at the problem of non-applicable categories. However, even though we are sensitive enough to avoid using verses that do not apply to the main thesis, it is always tempting to develop a relatively minor point beyond the depth necessary for adequate clarity. The objective in this kind of study is to amplify and clarify the message of the study passage. We are not engaged on a doctrinal quest. Therefore, we must limit the *amount* of information in our study to that information which directly pertains to the message of the study passage. That which is merely interesting should be avoided.

Follow The Same Pattern Upon whatever pattern of priorities you decide, and there are many, you should be consistent throughout the entire study outline. It may be difficult to decide on what order or system to follow, and it may be best to look at several areas of the outline before making the decision. But once a format has been actualized, it is normally best to follow that format for the entire worksheet. There are several kinds of patterns.

SIMPLE TO COMPLEX is always easy to use. That is the basic application of Isaiah 28:9-10. Many of the passages in the Bible are written this way, and it is often advisable to set the priorities of the various categories in this order. That is, the simplest point would be presented first, followed by the next simple, and so on.

BIG TO LITTLE is another way of looking at priorities. This is especially true when dealing with abstract concepts that are difficult to understand. It makes the job easier when we build the concept from the big, basic points, through the medium-sized ideas, to the smallest fillers that round out the overall concept. This approach is basically the same as simple-to-complex.

NEGATIVE TO POSITIVE, or vice versa, may well be a good format for some passages. Often the Scripture deals with contrasting ideas in order to express the true concept more precisely. Sometimes, the concept must be expressed by defining its limitations as well as its capabilities. If such seems to be the case in a given study passage, then it is wise to follow this kind of priority format throughout.

There is an endless list of ways to form relationships,

and it would be pointless to describe many more. A serious student of the Scripture will soon develop a good awareness of this procedure and will be able to accomplish this job very quickly. However, it may be worthwhile to show a few of the more common kinds of relationships that will be found at some time.

1. Comparison and contrast
2. Cause and effect
3. Means and end
4. Question and answer
5. Need and remedy

There are dozens more, each one being demanded by the peculiar set of circumstances which are developed within the study itself. The more a student works with the Scripture, the more this step becomes a part of the student's "second nature." It may seem somewhat technical at first, but it is nothing more than allowing the Holy Spirit to congeal the impressions He has been giving all during the study process. We need to be aware of the various mechanics and technical procedures in order to be a more effective tool in the hands of the Holy Spirit. However, we must not become so "technical" that we do not allow the Holy Spirit to guide our minds.

Examine The Verses Next

After we have determined in what order to place the categories, we should try to place each verse within a category in a proper order. There will always be some categories with several verses, and we need to examine their content for a key to their priority. Usually, the work that we have just finished will be adequate for this step. If there is a mental blank about the verse content, then it is necessary to check the verse in its context.

Establish The Sub-Points

One objective at this level is to find out which of the verses in a given category are more important than others. Sometimes, we will discover that one verse is really not necessary to our study after all. The other objective is to determine what verse order will present the truth of the category in the most effective manner.

205

Once again, we should constantly relate our thinking back to the main thesis of the study passage. With that information as a background, we can go through our worksheet now and complete this phase.

PREACH THE WORD

preach
Rom. 10:8 - faith/gospel
✓ I Cor. 2:4 - not man's wisdom
✓ Titus 1:3 - preaching necessary
Acts 15:35 - teaching/with others
#2097
Heb. 4:2 - why not work #189

word
✓ John 5:24 - salvation
✓ John 8:31 - discipleship ⎬ reasons
✓ John 17:17 - sanctifi-
cation

be instant in season out of season
instant - be present
in season - convenient,
opportunity
✓ **out season** -Phil. 4:10 - example

There are only two verses for our consideration under "preach." There are three under "word," and only one under the section about being "instant." Obviously, our categories and verse relationships are going to be rather limited. When the amount of work is small, or the worksheet itself affords ample working room, it is best to number the various points right on the worksheet itself. And in order to make the numbering system more visible, we should circle the number. We will then be able to use the existing worksheet and at the same time keep a visual perspective to the whole passage.

In this initial section, we were unable to combine I Corinthians 1:4 and Titus 1:3 into one category because they each dealt with a different aspect of preaching. Therefore, we merely need to determine which of the two verses is either the most important or the first

206

in logical order. Since we are dealing directly with the main thesis and since we are really asking the question, "why preach the word," we would probably place the most direct answer to that question in the first order. Titus 1:3 tells us that preaching is necessary. That verse should be number one. Since there is only one verse left, it would be number two.

Under the "word" section, there are three verses. We had determined earlier that they were all under the one category of "reasons." Therefore, we will just subdivide that category in the order of the importance of the verses. John 5:24, the "salvation" reason, certainly comes as the number one priority. However, both John 8:31 and John 17:17 are equally important. In fact, they may well be so interwoven that it would be difficult to tell them apart. When that kind of situation happens, it is usually best to present them in book or chapter order. The reason for that is, simply, the ease of location or presentation. So, the "word" verses would be in 1, 2, 3 order, just as we have them on our worksheet.

The section on being "instant in season, out of season" is not hard to categorize at all. There is only one verse with which to deal. For all practical purposes, we will pass over that section for now. Later, we will come back to it when we make our final outline.

Our worksheet is beginning to look like this:

The New Worksheet

preach the word
  preach
    Rom. 10:8-15 - faith/gospel
    ✓ I Cor. 2:4 - not man's wisdom ②
    ✓ Titus 1:3 - preaching necessary ①
    Acts 15:35 - teaching/with others #2097
    Heb. 4:2 - why not work # 189
  word
    ✓ John 5:24 - salvation   ① ⎫
    ✓ John 8:31 - discipleship ② ⎬ reasons
    ✓ John 17:17 - sanctification ③ ⎭

> **be instant in season out of season**
> **instant** - be present
> **in season** - convenient, opportunity
> ✔ **out season** - Phil. 4:10 - example

REPROVE, REBUKE, EXHORT

> **reprove**   **who/what**
>   John 16:8 - sin, righteousness,   Eph. 5:11
>   judgment   Titus 1:9
>   ✔Eph. 5:11 - unfruitful works of   I Tim. 5:1
>   darkness   **how**
> (?) ✔ I Tim. 5:1 - limitation/elder   Titus 1:13
>   ✔Tit. 1:9 -   ~~sound doctrine~~   Titus 2:15
>   ✔Tit. 1:13 -   sharply   **purpose**
>   Tit. 2:1-15 - what to speak: outline   Titus 1:13
> **rebuke** - strongest word, examples only

In this section, there are three major categories. We had tabulated the verses under each of the categories over on the right-hand side of our worksheet, in order to facilitate the very thing we are going to do now. Our objective is to determine which of the categories is the most important, or which is the most necessary from a logical standpoint. In this case, all three are important, and it would be very difficult to decide on one or the other as being more important. So, we try to determine which is first in a logical sequence.

The general guidelines we discussed earlier (page 204-205) stressed "simple-to-complex" as one of the easier patterns to follow. In this case, it does seem simpler to know "who/what" before we know "how" and to know "how" before we know the "purpose." It could be argued that "how" is necessary before "who," but our main thesis seems to demand that we tie in the "who/what" before we discuss the "how." Anyway, if there is a question about some relationship, it should settle itself when we make the final outline. If a doubt exists, make a decision and proceed. The Holy Spirit will "guide you into all truth."

After numbering the categories, we must subdivide the categories themselves. And since we have used numbers for the categories, we should use letters for the subdivision of the verses. Under category number one, we have three verses. Ephesians 5:11 tells us about the "unfruitful works of darkness." Titus 1:9 talks about the "gainsayer," and I Timothy 5:1 gives us "limitation/elder," according to our worksheet. Our memory should help us now. We know that we are dealing with the section of our study passage that discusses how to preach the Word by reproof. Our worksheet only notes, "unfruitful works of darkness" next to Ephesians 5:11. But, our memory tells us that the verse said something about not fellowshipping with the "unfruitful works of darkness," but rather to reprove them. And, our mind seems to remember that Titus 1:9 talked about "convincing the gainsayer." So, following the general pattern of simple-to-complex, it seems that Ephesians 5:11 ought to go first since it has a more clearly stated principle, Titus 1:9 following as an outgrowth of Ephesians 5:11. We would put an "*a*" next to Ephesians 5:11, and a "*b*" next to Titus 1:9.

I Timothy 5:1 is another story. The more we try to figure out how that verse works into the other two verses, the less it fits. Therefore, we should not use it. Remember, we felt uneasy about that verse earlier—even put a question mark next to it. Whenever a verse does not "feel right,'" do not use it. We should draw a line through that verse in the tabular column under "who/what" on our worksheet.

The "how" category only has two verses, Titus 1:13 and 2:15. We have a notation on our worksheet about 1:13, but nothing about 2:15. That verse was at the end of the long passage in chapter two that we decided was too involved for our study. But (praise the Lord for memory) our mind recalls—or should I say more cor-

rectly—the Holy Spirit brings to our remembrance that
Titus 2:15 said we were to reprove "with all authority."
That "authority" idea seems to take priority over the
"sharply" idea of Titus 1:13. So we would label Titus
1:13, "*b*," and Titus 1:15, "*a*."

"Rebuke" does not have any more work for us now,
so we should quickly check our worksheet.

> **reprove**
>   John 16:8 - sin, righteousness,
>   judgment
> ✔Eph. 5:11 - unfruitful works of
>   darkness
> (?) ✔I Tim. 5:1 - limitation/elder
> ✔Tit. 1:9   sound doctrine
> ✔Tit. 1:13 - sharply
>   Tit. 2:1-15 - what to speak: outline
>
> ① **who/what**
> ⓐ Eph. 5:11
> ⓑ Titus 1:9
>   I Tim. 5:1
> ② **how**
> ⓑ Titus 1:13
> ⓐ Titus 2:15
> ③ **purpose**
>   Titus 1:13

EXHORT

This next section is more complex than what we have
done so far.

> **exhort**   **how**
> ✔I Thess. 2:3-11 - example of: outline
>
> | please God | speak | behave | purpose |
> |---|---|---|---|
> | 2:3-4 | 5-8 | 9-11 | 12 |
>
>   I Tim. 4:13 - command
> ✔Titus 2:15 - what: see reprove
>   **how:** authority
> **beseech**
>   Rom. 12:1-2 - example
>   I Cor. 1:10 - example

comfort
   ✓ II Cor. 1:4 - chain of comfort
         (3-4) acquired skill (5-6) -**how**
   ✓ Col. 2:2 - **purpose**
    I Thess. 4:18 - 2nd coming
    I Thess. 5:11 - 2nd coming
    II Thess. 2:17 - **purpose**
consolation
    II Cor. 1:5-6 - **purpose**

To begin with, one of the passages (I Thess. 2:3-11) is a lengthy section that we had broken down into several sub-points. Also, the major categories are spread out all over the page, making it difficult to connect the references visually. That may seem like a minor point, but visual comprehension is important. That is why so much has been said about keeping the worksheet neat and in order. If we have difficulty reading our own work, we will have difficulty organizing it into a teachable format. We must be constantly aware of every piece of information as we develop the final product.

We had established two major categories: "how" and "purpose." The "how" category is by far the largest, including the lengthy passage in I Thessalonians. The first thing to do is to determine which of the two major categories is most important. We have already been placing the other "purpose" categories last in the other sections, so we should follow that same order here. Anyway it is fairly obvious that the many "how" passages require first attention.

But since there are so many "how" verses, it might be wise to divide that category into one or two other categories. In this case, the lengthy Thessalonian passage is a "how" *example,* the II Corinthians 1:4 passage is a "how" theory, and the Titus 2:15 reference has a "how" *mechanic.* When we compare the Titus passage to the other two Scriptures, it does not seem to be of the same "quality." That is, it is not of the same importance or depth as either of the other two "how" passages, so we would be wise to leave it out of this section. However, the II Corinthians reference seems to fit in front of the Thessalonians reference in order for us to have a clear understanding of the "how" category. If we are going to follow our simple-to-complex formula, it makes good sense to understand the "theory" before the working "example." Therefore, we would label II Corinthians 1:4 as number one and I Thessalonians as number two. We should also record that number one is "how-theory" and number two is "how-example." The "purpose" category would become number three.

It now becomes necessary to label the subdivisions in each category. We had already divided the several verses in the Thessalonians passage and had placed their titles in a short heading off to the right-hand side of our worksheet. All we have to do now is decide in what order to place the four headings. The last heading, verse twelve, was a "purpose" verse. Even though it goes with the context of the Thessalonians passage, we should put it in the same category as the other "purpose" verse, Colossians 2:2. And, since it will probably not have the same force as the major verse in Colossians, we ought to label it *"3 b."* That requires us to go back to the Colossians reference and label it *"3 a."*

The other three sub-headings for the Thessalonians passage are broken down in the order in which they are given in the passage itself. That is, verses three and four precede verses five through eight, and so on. We have entitled the first section, "please God," the second, "speak," and the last, "behave." That order seems to be quite adequate both from an importance standpoint, and a logical standpoint. Therefore, we would label the "please God" division, *"a,"* the "speak" division, *"b,"* and the "behave" division, *"c."*

There are only two sub-divisions in the II Corinthians passage, and they also follow a logical numerical order. It makes good sense that the "chain of comfort" division in verses three and four would precede the "acquired skill'' division of verses five and six. So, we would put the appropriate "*a*" and "*b*" on the worksheet which now looks like this:

```
exhort                    ②how - example
   ✔I Thess. 2:3-11 - example of: outline
   ⓐ please God  ⓑ speak  ⓒ behave  ③ purpose
      2:3-4         5-8      9-11      b    12
   I Tim. 4:13 - command
   ✔Titus 2:15 - what: see reprove
                       how: authority
beseech
      Rom. 12:1-2 - example
      I Cor. 1:10 - example
comfort
   ✔II Cor. 1:4 - chain of comfort ⓐ        theory
            ⓑ(3-4) acquired skill (5-6) - how ①
   ✔Col. 2:2 - purpose ③
      I Thess. 4:18 - 2nd coming
      I Thess. 5:11 - 2nd coming
      II Thess. 2:17 - purpose
consolation
      II Cor. 1:5-6 - purpose
```

WITH ALL LONGSUFFERING AND DOCTRINE
This is another section with a lot of work in it. But we have done most of the sorting out already.

```
with all longsuffering and doctrine

                    longsuffering
                        ✔I Thess. 5:14 - toward all
                        men - extent

                    doctrine
importance              ✔I Tim. 1:3 - teaching clari-
I Tim. 1:3              fies - importance
```

```
I Tim. 4:13-16            ✓I Tim. 4:13-16 - teaching
Titus 1:9                  saves - importance
II Tim. 2:2               ✓II Tim. 3:16-17 - teach
                           Scripture/for perfection
how                        (check words)
Titus 2:7-8              ✓Titus 1:9 - to convince -
I Cor. 2:13                importance
Col. 1:28               ✓Titus 2:7-10 - example (7,8 how)
                           (9, 10 purpose)
purpose
Col. 1:28
Titus 2:9-10
                        teach
warn                    ✓Matt. 5:17-19 - warning
Matt. 5:17-19             (comp. II Tim. 3:16)
                        ✓I Cor. 2:13 - teach Scrip-
                          ture (comp. II Tim. 3:16
                          & I Cor. 2:4) how
                        ✓II Tim. 2:2 - teach teachers -
Scripture                 importance
II Tim. 3:16-17         ✓Col. 1:28 - perfection
                          (comp. II Tim. 3:16)
                          how, purpose
```

The "longsuffering" section only has one reference in it and does not require our attention now. But the "doctrine" section does. Fortunately, we have already tabulated the verses into category columns on the left-hand margin. All we have to do immediately is figure out in what order to put them.

It seems quite obvious that the "importance" category is the most important and should come first in the logical sequence. The "how" category is more necessary than the "purpose" category, so we would probably place the "how" category as number two. But, what do we do with the "warn" and "Scripture" categories? Our memory should help us out here. We can recall that Matthew 5:17-19 contains instruction against teaching men to break even one of the least commandments, and that II Timothy 3:16-17 is the verse that tells us to use Scripture when we teach because it is inspired. Both of those verses, although unique to themselves, are really special thoughts within the "how" category. So, we can subjugate them to the number two category and then try to determine which of those two verses is "a" and which is "b." Probably the "Scripture" verse would be more important than the "warn" verse, if only because the "warn" verse warns because Scripture is inspired. II Timothy 3:16-17 should be labeled "2a," and Matthew 5:17-19 should be labeled "*2b*."

We now have three major categories instead of five. Number one is the "importance" category, number two is "how," and number three is "purpose." That being decided, we have to examine the verses within the various categories to assign an order for their relationships. The four verses within the "importance" category are all adequately labeled on our worksheet. They appear as follows:

> I Timothy 1:3 - teaching clarifies
> I Timothy 4:13-16 - teaching saves
> Titus 1:9 - to convince
> II Timothy 2:2 - teach teachers

Once again, we should follow the same kind of priority progression that we have been using all along. In this case, we have two yardsticks to use: "how important is it," and "what point is the least complex." When we read the notations on our worksheet, it seems that "teaching saves" is the most important point and should be point "*a*." The fact that "teaching clarifies" would probably take priority over the purpose of "convincing," and the work of "teaching teachers" is normally the hardest and most complex job of all. Therefore, we should follow that order for now. If we find out later that we have not made a correct judgment, we can correct easily enough.

The "how" category lists three references which appear on the worksheet in this order.

215

Titus 2:7-10 - example (7-8-how) (9-10-purpose)
I Cor. 2:13 - teach Scripture (comp. II Tim. 3:16
   and I Cor. 2:4
Col. 1:28 - perfection (comp. II Tim. 3:16)

Without making recourse to the suggested comparison verses, the order is readily apparent. It is necessary to know that we must "teach Scripture" before we can follow an "example," and we surely must have an "example" before we could understand how to teach "perfection." Therefore, the notations for "*a*," "*b*," and "*c*" priority should follow that order.

The "purpose" category only has two verses in it. The Colossians reference has already been used under the "how" category and placed in last priority. Until we are able to think through the finer points of these relationships during our final outlining process, it is best to keep the same pattern within a given section. Therefore, we would place Colossians 1:18 as "*b*" priority and Titus 2:9, 10 as the "*a*" priority. Our worksheet for this section now looks like this:

---

doctrine

importance ①
b I Tim. 1:3
a I Tim. 4:13-16
c Titus 1:9
d II Tim. 2:2

✓ I Tim. 1:3 - teaching clarifies -**importance**
✓ I Tim. 4:13-16 - teaching
saves - **importance**
✓ II Tim. 3:16-17 - teach
Scripture/for perfection
(check words)
✓ Titus 1:9 - to convince -
importance
✓ Titus 2:7-10 - example (7,8 **how**)
(9, 10 **purpose**)

how ②
b Titus 2:7-8
a I Cor. 2:13
c Col. 1:28

purpose ③
b Col. 1:28
a Titus 2:9-10

teach
~ Matt. 5:17-19 - **warning**
~ I Cor. 2:13 - teach Scrip-
(comp. II Tim. 3:16)

warn (2b)   ture (comp. II Tim. 3:16
Matt. 5:17-19   & I Cor. 2:4) **how**
~ II Tim. 2:2 - teach teachers

Scripture (2a)   **importance**
II Tim. 3:16-17   ~ Col. 1:28 - perfection
(comp. II Tim. 3:16)
how, purpose

Isn't the Lord marvelous? One of the most exciting things about this kind of study is the way it all begins to come together. Whenever anyone starts to study the Scriptures in depth, the first impression is always one of vagueness. But, as we begin to follow the Biblical formulas for learning truth, as we patiently work through God's Word, we begin to sense more and more that the Holy Spirit is really directing our study and helping us to *know* what the Word says. We have just about finished. Already we are sensing the message of our study passage in a much more magnificent way than we had at the start, but we must congeal the thoughts into "many proverbs." We must complete the job of the "wise preacher" spoken about in Ecclesiastes and make the truths of God's Word usable. All right, let's finish the job.

15

THE FINAL OUTLINE

This portion of the study process must be done as soon after the organizational stage as possible. The Holy Spirit works with us most keenly when we are studying or considering His Word, so we should be the most able to make righteous judgments when the Word is still fresh in our minds. Frequently, a study will require a prolonged interruption. If that is necessary, then it is wise either to review the organizational work or wait until enough time is available to complete the final outline immediately afterwards.

The objective of this step is to put the information which has been so carefully exegeted in some form of permanent record that can be retrieved and used time and time again. Although this kind of study is enjoyable, it would be both unnecessary and unproductive to repeat the process on the same material. Therefore, it becomes a matter of good stewardship to insure that the work performed and the information gained can be used effectively for the Lord's glory (Col. 3:17 and I Cor. 10:31).

In order to make the final outline as effective as possible, it is necessary to follow some basic steps of organization. There are as many ways to outline as there are purposes for outlining, and it would be impossible to develop an exhaustive study of those ways. However, there are a few simple procedures that will assist any student in making a final product that is both usable and valuable.

Check The Main Points First

The outline is a peculiar form of a sales presentation. There is an overall objective; there are main points that demonstrate the value of the overall objective; and there are supporting points that enhance the clarity of each main point. The outline is peculiar in that it is designed most often for the salesman, not the buyer. That is, the person who is going to do the telling needs to have some organized reminder of the most orderly and effective way to tell the story. That means that the outline needs to be structured in such a way that the main points are easily read and remembered. Here are several suggestions that will help.

LOOK FOR RELATIONSHIPS between the main points. Often the key elements of an outline will be in a question/answer relationship. Sometimes the main points will follow each other in a sequential pattern, and other times they will present themselves as a contrast. Whatever the design, each thought development has an overall pattern that can be expressed easily. The knowledge that has been gained in the preparatory study will provide more than adequate background for discovering these relationships.

LOOK FOR THE CENTRAL THEME of the outline. More than likely this will be the "main thesis" of the specific study passage. However, there are times when that "thesis" is too limited to express the overall thought of the information within the scope of the outline. If that is the case, then it is the job of the student to express the central theme in the main points of the outline. Care should be taken to tie the central theme to the individual points of the outline.

Keep Similar Grammatical Structure

It is always best to use complete sentences for every point on the outline. It is imperative that complete sentences be used for the main points of the outline. While the information of a study is fresh in the student's mind, it is easy to coin a short phrase that expresses the thought of a point adequately. However, when such a phrase is all that remains of the thought at a much later date, it is very difficult to recall the reasoning behind the choice of words. Besides that, if such a terse phrase is read by one who has not done the preparatory study, the phrase is almost always meaningless. It may seem repetitive to structure each point in the same basic way, but it will make the outline far more usable.

Work Each Main Point

Once the relationships of the main points have been established, the supporting information within each main point may be organized. The bulk of the work for this part has already been done in the preparatory study. However, there are two procedural principles that should be observed.

RECHECK THE CATEGORY RELATIONSHIPS. Care should be taken at this point to insure that the various categories within a main point still flow in the same order as initially developed. Sometimes, after the student has organized the central theme and structure of the main points, the original order of categories within a given point may not seem to be as applicable. A review of the order is always valuable and will frequently produce new insight.

FIND THE CENTRAL THEME of the categories within a main point and structure each sub-point around that theme. Normally, this theme will be readily apparent in the thought of the main point. The student must always express the thought of any given point in such a manner that it easily relates to the central message of the outline. However, some material may require a different grammatical structure or different phrasing than the main point under which they fall. When that is true, it should be easy to find the different theme or key phrase that is necessary.

Work Through The Entire Outline

Once again, it is vital that the entire outline be structured from beginning to end. The student of the Scriptures must always be careful that the human element be filtered through the Word of God as much as possible. By consistently working through the study process in the same order as the Scriptural message, the possibility of human error is reduced.

Review Outline For Readability

After the outline has been formulated, it is always worthwhile to review the entire work for its general clarity and readability. The whole purpose in studying portions of God's Word is to enable the student to become knowledgeable in the truth of that portion, and then to enable that student to help others less knowledgeable to understand the teaching of that passage as well. If the final product of the study is not clear, then the job is not well done. If the outline does not provide an adequate base for further teaching, then much of the work will be wasted.

Perhaps the best check that can be done at this point is to read the outline aloud, omitting the verse references unless they have been incorporated into the sentence structure. If the outline has been properly prepared, the verbalizing of the points will produce a pleasant and understandable story. If this exercise leaves a stilted and incomplete feeling, the chances are excellent that the outline is not properly done. If that is the case, rework the outline in those areas that need attention.

Determine How To Use Study

Knowledge without use is sterile! A foolish person does not care to learn anything. A careless person does not use what knowledge is available, and a selfish person keeps knowledge from others. But, "the tongue of the wise useth knowledge aright" (Proverbs 15:2). The diligent Bible student is always anxious to use the information that the Holy Spirit has provided for the glory of the matchless name of our Lord Jesus Christ.

However, not all of the Bible may be used in the same manner. It is necessary to make good discernment in the dissemination of the study. Solomon told all of God's people, "to everything there is a season, and a time to every purpose under the heaven . . . a time to keep silence, and a time to speak . . ." (Eccl. 3:1, 7). Sometimes the best application of knowledge is to our own lives, privately. Other times we will find that our professional lives are benefited. And, frequently we will find that it is necessary to teach or preach the information to others. Whatever the case, every study should be used . . . and may be used many times in many ways.

A quick summary of these points would be valuable before we actually complete our outline.

1. Check the main points first.
    a. Look for relationships between the main points.
    b. Look for the central theme of the outline.
2. Keep similar grammatical structure.
3. Work each main point.
    a. Recheck the category relationships.
    b. Find the central theme of the categories.
4. Work through the entire outline.
5. Review the outline for readability.
6. Determine how to use the study.

Very well, with this information fresh on our minds, we should now proceed to finalizing our work.

Check The Main Points First

Before we can organize our outline into sentence form, we must gain a good perspective on the overall message. We have done much study, and that study will now render its first observable dividend as we try to tie in the central theme of our study. The main points are:

1. Preach the word
2. Be instant in season out of season
3. Reprove, rebuke, exhort
4. With all longsuffering and doctrine

It should be obvious that each of these main points is in the form of a command except the instruction of point "4," "with all longsuffering and doctrine." Our sentence structure for these commands will not have to vary too much from the Biblical format, but we should couch them in such a manner that each point will be understandable by itself.

However, before we try to structure the sentences for the main points, we should verbalize the central theme of the outline. That theme, or title, should be reflected in the wording of each main point. It is not necessary to repeat the theme, only to structure the sentences so that it is clear that the theme is discussed. In this case, we have a clear tie to the main thesis, "preach the word." But, we need to identify *who* is to preach.

In the contextual setting of our study passage, we had already determined that this entire section was a serious "charge" (II Tim. 4:1) because of the inspiration of the Scriptures (II Tim. 3:16-17). We also know from the third and fourth verses of our study passage that the contrasting error, the incorrect kind of preaching, is equated with "teachers" who are tickling the ears of those who do not want to hear truth.

The "who" of this section seems to be anyone who is responsible for teaching the Scriptures. Therefore, our central theme could be, *The Responsibility of a Teacher of the Scriptures.* We could shorten it to *The Teacher's Responsibility,* or *Teaching the Scriptures Correctly,* or something like that. The point here is simply that this section of Scripture deals with what a teacher is supposed to do when they use the Word of God. That theme should be reflected in each of the sentences we use to state the main points.

It is possible, once a student has become proficient in this procedure, to go into the outlining of the category information without actually having written out the sentences for the main points. That is, once a central theme or title has been developed, the proficient student would develop the sentence structure for each main point as

224

it came up in the study process, rather than all at once. However, until proficiency is obtained, it is best to structure the main points of the outline *before* working through the category information.

Keep Similar Grammatical Structure
Since our theme involves a teacher, that idea should be incorporated into each main point. Each main point should be structured as a complete sentence which is grammatically similar to every other main point. Since most of the main points are commands, we should follow that format, supplying an adequate grammatical complement for each command.

1. The teacher must preach the Word.
2. The teacher should always be ready to preach.
3. The teacher should use the techniques of reproving, rebuking, and exhorting.
4. The teacher must always be longsuffering and use the teaching format.

By phrasing each main point in a complete sentence, and by using some of the general information already gained from the study, we are able to develop a readable message even from these few sentences. Some of the sentences use the same wording as in the Scripture passage. Others are amplified in such a way that the meaning of the Scriptural words is more readily apparent. The objective is to structure the sentences so that the one who is going to use the outline will be able to get the main thrust of the point in one quick sentence. All our study procedure up to this stage is behind our reasoning. It is easy to make summary statements based upon the overall impressions gained from the research.

Work Each Main Point
After we have made the initial effort to establish the grammatical structure and relationship of the main points, we must begin to develop the specific information within each main point. And as has been the practice all along, we will work through the entire outline from start to finish.

THE TEACHER MUST PREACH THE WORD

We will now be working with the two pages of notes and categories previously developed and with a new outline worksheet that will develop as we go along.

---

preach the word
  preach
    Rom. 10:8-15 - faith/gospel
    ✔ I Cor. 2:4 - not man's wisdom ✔ ②
    ✔ Titus 1:3 - preaching necessary ✔ ①
    Acts 15:35 - teaching/with others #2097
    Heb. 4:2 - why not work # 189

  word
    ✔ John 5.24 - salvation   ①
    ✔ John 8:31 - discipleship   ② } reasons
    ✔ John 17:17 - sanctification   ③

Our notesheet reveals two categories within the "preach" section and three categories within the "word" section. Both of those sub-sections must relate verbally to the wording of the main point. That is, the "preach" categories and the "word" categories must be so structured that they harmonize verbally with the thought that "The teacher must preach the word."

As was mentioned earlier, it is always best to use complete sentences for each point of the outline. If we commit ourselves to that procedure, we will avoid the temptation to reduce the thought to a short phrase, thereby eliminating future questions about the meaning. In this case, the two sections, "preach" and "word," could be structured as independent points of equal value, as parallel points of equal value, or as parallel points of unequal value. These options are nearly always available in every major point. However, we must try to structure each section in the way that will positively enhance the information within the section.

Our main point is: *The teacher must preach the Word.* As was the case during our research, we have to ask the "Why" question. We have already answered that through our research, and the answers are waiting there on our notesheet in their proper order. Now we must structure sentences that express the answers verbally so that the user of the outline will know at a glance what those answers are.

THE RESPONSIBILITY OF A TEACHER OF THE SCRIPTURES

I. The teacher must preach the word.
   A. He must preach because it is necessary.   Titus 1:3
   B. He must not preach man's wisdom. I Cor. 2:4
   C. He must preach the Word of God because:
      1. It is necessary for salvation.   John 5:24
      2. It is necessary for discipleship. John 8:31
      3. It is necessary for sanctification. John 17:17

This first section was not very difficult to organize because each sub-point was fairly obvious. Each of the thoughts under "preach" were independently equal, so we structured each one that way. Each of the three thoughts under "word" were equal among themselves, but were not equal to the points under "preach." However, all three of these thoughts made up the reason for using the Word of God, and therefore, were structured as sub-points under a more parallel relationship to the "preach" points.

It is difficult to explain specific criteria for this process because so many variables can be present. However, if we have been observing the accumulation of data all during our study process, the structuring of the categories will not seem strange at all. Perhaps, if we continue, the vagueness will clear up.

THE TEACHER MUST ALWAYS BE READY TO PREACH

be instant in season out of season
  instant - be present
  in season - convenient, opportunity
  ✓**out season** - Phil. 4:10 - example

There is so little information here, that it seems awkward to place it as a main point even though we have treated it as one all along. When we glance at our notesheet, we can readily see that this point has not produced any depth of information, and that it is mainly an explanation of how the teacher is to be in relationship to his responsibility to preach. In other words, this information should be treated as a sub-point to the first command, "preach the word." Therefore, we would list this as point "*D*" under Roman numeral "*I*".

THE RESPONSIBILITY OF A TEACHER OF THE SCRIPTURES

I. The teacher must preach the word.
  A. He must preach because it is
     necessary.   Titus 1:3
  B. He must not preach man's wisdom.   I Cor. 2:4
  C. He must preach the Word of God because:
     1. It is necessary for salvation.   John 5:24
     2. It is necessary for discipleship.   John 8:31
     3. It is necessary for sanctification. John 17:17
  D. He must always be ready to preach.
     1. When he feels like preaching.
     2. When he does not feel like preaching.

We have changed the wording to conform to the same grammatical structure of our point and have placed the two contrasting ideas as sub-points for maximum clarity. Since the Scripture reference, Philippians 4:10, was cited only to provide a linguistic example for the idea of "out of season," it is not necessary to place that reference on the final outline.

THE TEACHER MUST USE THE TECHNIQUES OF REPROVING, REBUKING, AND EXHORTING

This section is a little more complex in that there is a wealth of information for two of these techniques and very little for the third. Each of these techniques is also parallel to the other and should probably be treated as a main point in its own right. It seems like the best thing to do is reword our main point in a more general fashion, then make each of the techniques as equal points of that general statement. (This would be very similar to the way we treated the "word" section in the previous point.) Our main point and subsequent parallel points might look like this.

II. The Teacher must use appropriate techniques when preaching.
   A. He should reprove when necessary.
   B. He should rebuke when necessary.
   C. He should exhort when necessary.

The idea of "appropriate techniques" and the "when necessary" qualification given to each of the techniques came out of the treatment given each of the points in Scripture. We know from our research that the teacher will not use all three of the kinds of preaching at once. Nor will the teacher use any one of the techniques all the time. Therefore, "the teacher must use appropriate techniques when preaching," and he must use the appropriate technique "when necessary."

Now, we may examine the category information.

```
reprove                                    ① who/what
    John 16:8 - sin, righteousness,       ⓐ Eph. 5:11
                    judgment               ⓑ Titus 1:9
  ✔Eph. 5:11 - unfruitful works of
                    darkness               ② how
 ⟨?⟩ ✔I Tim. 5:1 - limitation/elder       ⓑ Titus 1:13
     ✔Tit. 1:9 -   sound doctrine ⎫       ⓐ Titus 2:15
     ✔Tit. 1:13 -  sharply         ⎬ gainsayer   purpose
        Tit. 2:1-15 -what to speak: outline ③ Titus 1:13
```

In the "reprove" section we have three categories: "who/what," "how," and "purpose." We have already established a good order for them, so all that remains is for us to structure the sentences that express each thought accurately. The outline should reflect the information of each verse and the relationship of that specific verse to the overall point:

```
II. The teacher must use appropriate techniques
    when preaching.
    A. He should reprove when necessary.
       1. The unfruitful works of
          darkness require it.            Eph. 5:11
       2. The convincing of the gain-
          sayer requires it.              Titus 1:9
       3. The Scriptures provide
          instruction for the method
          of reproof.
          a. It must be with all authority. Titus 2:15
          b. It must be sharp.             Titus 1:13
       4. The purpose is to make sound
          in the faith.                   Titus 1:13
```

Again, we find that the categories do not express themselves as precisely parallel or equal in value. The two sub-points under the "who/what" category help explain parallel reasons for the necessity of reproof, and the two sub-points under the "how" category give a composite picture of the method or manner in which reproof should be conducted. The "purpose" category stands as an independent and equal point to the others. By structuring the sentences so that they can answer the natural question generated by the major point, the one who uses the outline can quickly relate each thought back to the flow of the message. Back to the worksheet.

> **rebuke** - strongest word, examples only

There is virtually no information on our notesheet about this part of our study passage. Yet it is a fairly major point. We must not overlook the thought, nor must we leave to pure memory the information that has been uncovered. Our notesheet makes the observation that "rebuke" is the strongest of all three terms. That should be recorded on our outline. The notesheet also observes that the Scripture does not provide any direct information about rebuking with the word, but does provide examples of rebuke. We have not listed any of these examples, but it would make our outline clearer if we were to have at least one familiar passage to demonstrate the strength of the word, "rebuke." That means that we need to check the Strong's concordance again quickly and locate at least one passage that can be used.

However, when we read the listings, a new insight begins to dawn as we consider the contrast of the terms. Each of the

rebuke See also REBUKED; REBUKES; REBUK-
ETH; REBUKING; UNREBUKABLE.
M'r 8:32 took him, and began to r' him.   ··
Lu 17: 3 trespass against thee, r' him; and ··
    19:39 unto him, Master, r' thy disciples. ··
Ph'p 2:15 the sons of God, without r', in the* *298*
1Ti 5: 1 R' not an elder, but intreat him as *1969*
    20 Them that sin r' before all, that *1651*
2Ti 4: 2 r', exhort with all longsuffering *2008*
Tit 1:13 Wherefore r' them sharply, that *1651*
    2:15 exhort, and r' with all authority. * ··
Jude 9 but said, The Lord r' thee.   *2008*
Re 3:19 many as I love, I r' and chasten: *1651*

rebuked

M't 8:26 and *r*' the winds and the sea; and *2008*
17:18 And Jesus *r*' the devil; and he "
19:13 pray: and the disciples *r*' them. "
20:31 the multitude *r*' them, because they' "
M'r 1:25 And Jesus *r*' him, saying, Hold thy "
4:39 he arose, and *r*' the wind, and said "
8:33 he *r*' Peter, saying, Get thee behind "
9:25 he *r*' the foul spirit, saying unto "
10:13 his disciples *r*' those that brought "
Lu 4:35 And Jesus *r*' him, saying, Hold thy "
· 39 and *r*' the fever; and it left her; "
8:24 he arose, and *r*' the wind and the "
9:42 Jesus *r*' the unclean spirit, and "
55 he turned, and *r*' them, and said, "
18:15 his disciples saw it, they *r*' them. "
39 they which went before *r*' him, "
23:40 But the other answering *r*' him, * "
Heb12: 5 nor faint when thou art *r*' of him:*1651
2Pe 2:16 But was *r*' for his iniquity: the *2192,1649*

references seem to portray the Lord Jesus rebuking some single person or demon rather than rebuking a crowd or congregation. That makes a distinction that had escaped our earlier research, and a distinction that is well worth noting on our final outline.

There are a few references that indicate the disciples rebuked more than one person at a time (Matthew 19:13; 20:31; Mark 10:13; 18:15, etc.), but even in those instances there is no indication that it was in a formal meeting of some sort, but rather was an emotional outburst to a few people who were bothering them. A quick check of the passages involved confirms that Jesus was displeased at the outburst of the Apostles in such a public way, and that He Himself never rebuked except to one or two at a time. It would be well to have some concrete examples for our final outline. Mark 8:33 gives the Lord's rebuke of Peter; Mark 9:35 shows the Lord rebuking a demon; and Mark 10:13-14 shows the incorrect rebuke by the Apostles and the subsequent displeasure of the Lord. That portion of our outlines should now look like this:

B. He should rebuke when necessary.
  1. Rebuke is the strongest method of preaching.
  2. Rebuke is a more private method of preaching.
     a. The Lord rebuked Peter.   Mark 8:33
     b. The Lord rebuked a demon.   Mark 9:35
     c. The Apostles incorrectly rebuked a crowd.   Mark 10:13-14

The last of these three techniques contains a sizable amount of information.

---

exhort   ② how -example
 ✓I Thess. 2:3-11 - ~~example of:~~ outline
ⓐplease God   ⓑspeak   ⓒbehave   ③ᵇpurpose
   2:3-4   5-8   9-11   12
  I Tim. 4:13 - command
 ✓Titus 2:15 - ~~what: see reprove~~
                  ~~how: authority~~

  beseech
      Rom. 12:1-2 - example
      I Cor. 1:10 - example

  comfort   ⓐ
  ✓II Cor. 1:4 - chain of comfort   ①
          ⓑ (3-4) acquired skill (5-6) -**how**
  ✓Col. 2:2 - **purpose** ③ᵃ   -theory
      I Thess. 4:18 - 2nd coming
      I Thess. 5:11 - 2nd coming
      II Thess. 2:17 - **purpose**
  consolation
      II Cor. 1:5-6 - **purpose**

There are three categories: "How-theory," "How-example," and "Purpose." Both the theory and example sections have multiple sub-points, so we must make a careful analysis of the relationships as we develop the sentence structure. Since we have already established the order of importance, we must now word the sentences to reflect the development of a composite picture.

C. He should exhort when necessary.
  1. The Scriptures provide an adequate theory.
    a. There is a chain of
       exhortation.   II Cor. 1:3-4
    b. There is an acquired skill.   II Cor. 1:5-6

---

2. The Scriptures provide an adequate example.
   a. We are to please God always. I Thess. 2: 3-4
   b. We are to speak properly.   I Thess. 2:5-8
   c. We are to behave properly.   I Thess. 2:9-11
3. The Scriptures provide the purpose.
   a. The hearts should be knit together
      in love.   Col. 2:2
   b. The walk should be worthy
      of God.   II Thess. 2:12

In this case, each of the categories were parallel to each other, and each of the verses within the categories were parallel to each other. By structuring the three major categories so that they tied back to the Scripture, the points keep the reader of the outline conscious of the "responsibility" of the teacher.

THE TEACHER MUST ALWAYS BE LONG-SUFFERING AND USE THE TEACHING FORMAT

That sentence structure does not seem to follow the same pattern that we have been developing so far. When we first put that sentence down, we were trying to summarize the thought of main point. We have already had to break down another main point into three parallel sub-points in order to maintain the sense of the study message. The same thing seems to be true here. The last point stressed the *kinds* of preaching. This point stresses the *way* to preach those kinds of preaching. And since we should follow the same basic grammatical structure for the various parallel points, we should word this main point something like this.

III. The teacher should preach correctly.
   A. He should be longsuffering.
   B. He should use doctrine.

With that format in mind, we can examine the notesheet.

with all longsuffering and doctrine
        longsuffering
           ✓I Thess. 5:14 - toward all
           men - **extent**
        doctrine

importance ①   ✓I Tim. 1:3 - teaching clari-
b I Tim. 1:3   fies -**importance**
a I Tim. 4:13-16   ✓I Tim. 4:13-16 - teaching
c Titus 1:9   saves - **importance**
d II Tim. 2:2   ✓II Tim. 3:16-17 - teach
          Scripture/for perfection
how ②   (check words)
b Titus 2:7-8   ✓Titus 1:9 - to convince -
a I Cor. 2:13   **importance**
c Col. 1:28   ✓Titus 2:7-10 - example (7,8 **how**)
         (9, 10 **purpose**)
purpose ③   **teach**
b Col. 1:28   ✓Matt. 5:17-19 - **warning**
a Titus 2:9-10   ✓I Cor. 2:13 - teach Scrip-
        (comp. II Tim. 3:16)
warn ②*b*   ture (comp. II Tim. 3:16
Matt. 5:17-19   & I Cor. 2:4) **how**
        ✓II Tim. 2:2 - teach teachers
Scripture ②*a* **importance**
II Tim. 3:16-17 ✓Col. 1:28 - perfection
        (comp. II Tim. 3:16)
        how, purpose

There are three categories in the "doctrine" section: "Importance," "How," and "Purpose." Each of these three have several sub-points, all of which have been set in order during our previous work. The "longsuffering" section only has one Scripture reference, and the information of that reference can be easily incorporated into the wording of the outline sentence.

   A. He should be longsuffering
      to all men.   I Thess. 5:14

The "doctrine" section may take a little more thinking than that, but it is not at all difficult.

B. He should use doctrine.
  1. Because it is important.
    a. Teaching saves.   I Tim. 4:13-16
    b. Teaching clarifies.   I Tim. 1:3
    c. Teaching convinces.   Titus 1:9
    d. Teaching teaches other
       teachers.   II Tim. 2:2
  2. Because it is required.
    a. Teachers need the
       Scripture,   II Tim. 3:16-17
    b. Teachers are given examples.
      1) They compare spiritual
         things.   I Cor. 2:13
      2) They use sound speech.   Titus 2:7-8
      3) They teach with all wisdom. Col. 1:28
  3. Because it has a purpose.
    a. It will perfect God's people.   Col. 1:28
    b. It will adorn the doctrine
       of God.   Titus 2:9-10

It was necessary during that process to check the actual Scripture references on several points in order to pin down the main point of a specific verse. We found it necessary to change the "how" category to reflect the overall structure of the doctrine section. We had already noted on our worksheet that the verses containing the "warning" and the "Scripture" points were part of our "how" category as a separate main point parallel to "doctrine." That is, we could have given the "importance" reasons as 1, 2, 3, etc. under "He should use doctrine," then make the "how" category a "B" point with something like "He should use doctrine correctly" as the sentence structure. However, that would have required more restructuring of subsequent points, so it was better to keep our original idea.

Review The Outline For Readability

Now that the outline is put together, we must read through our work to make sure that we have not left anything unclear. If we have correctly phrased each sentence, the message of II Timothy 4:3-5 will come through very easily. If we have placed some thought out of its natural order, the outline will not "feel" right. It always seems strange to talk about "feeling" when the work is so "scientific." But we are dealing with the Word of God which must be passed through to our "hearts" by the work of the Holy Spirit. As we have discussed before, the Holy Spirit expects us to follow the instruction given in His Word concerning the procedures for study. After we have done that job, we can expect Him to assist the difficult areas through His ministry to our "hearts."

Our work up to this point has been predominately objective. That is, we have been as careful as we could be to use the wording of Scripture, the structure of the Scripture study passage, and the natural order of the verses within each area. Now we must read the outline, as though it were a paper or sermon, and see if it sounds right. And until practice has made a student proficient in this skill, it may be necessary to write out the outline in paragraph form. If that proves to be valuable, then there are three guidelines that should be followed:

1. Each Roman numeral should be a new paragraph.
2. Do not insert the verses into the paragraphs.
3. Leave out the repeated phrases of the sub-points.

These guidelines should become clear as we follow through the "reading" of our study outline.

THE RESPONSIBILITY OF A TEACHER OF THE SCRIPTURES

First, the teacher must preach the Word. He must preach because it is necessary, but he must not preach man's wisdom. The teacher must preach the

Word of God because it is necessary for salvation, discipleship, and sanctification. The teacher must always be ready to preach, when he feels like it and when he does not.

Second, the teacher must use appropriate techniques when preaching. He should reprove when necessary. The unfruitful works of darkness require reproof, as does the convincing of the gainsayer. The Scriptures provide instruction for the method of reproof. It must be with all authority, and done sharply. The purpose is to make sound in the faith.

The teacher should also rebuke when necessary. Rebuke is the strongest method of preaching and is more private. The Lord rebuked Peter and a demon, but was displeased when the Apostles incorrectly rebuked a crowd.

The teacher should also exhort. The Scriptures provide an adequate theory by explaining that there is a chain of exhortation and that exhortation is an acquired skill. The Scriptures also provide an example showing that we are to please God always, speak properly and behave properly. The purpose of exhortation is so that our hearts should be knit together in love and our walk worthy of God.

The teacher must also preach correctly. He must be longsuffering to all men, and he must use doctrine. That is because doctrine is important. Doctrine saves, clarifies, convinces, and teaches other teachers. Doctrine is also required. Teachers need the Scriptures, they must be careful, and follow the examples to compare spiritual things, use sound speech, and teach with all wisdom. Doctrine has a purpose in that it will perfect God's people and adorn the doctrine of God.

Other than being a little stilted, that reads fairly well. It makes sense, it flows logically from point to point, and it seems to amplify the message of the study passage adequately. When the outline "reads" that smoothly it is a good indication that the study process was done correctly. We can have confidence in the Scriptures, confidence in the work of the Holy Spirit, and confidence that we *know* the main truths of this passage of Scripture.

Determine How To Use The Study

However, that knowledge must be applied. We must use the information now for the Lord's glory, and that means that we must determine what ways and in what areas this information can be put to good use. There may be too much data there to be used as one single sermon—unless we reduce the content. And it might be difficult to teach that material to a Sunday school class—unless we made it into a series of lessons. Perhaps we could direct a Bible study group through the passage, but they need to understand how to research the Scriptures *before* they tackle anything like this.

So, we must try to analyze the values of this information and make an effort to use the information as the Lord provides the opportunity.

Always Apply Personally

Never study out a passage of Scripture and fail to examine your own life first.

And why beholdest thou the mote that is in thy brother's eye, but considerest not the beam that is in thine own eye? Or how wilt thou say to thy brother "Let me pull out the mote out of thine eye;" and behold, a beam is in thine own eye? Thou hypocrite, first cast out the beam out of thine own eye; and then shalt thou see clearly to cast out the mote out of thy brother's eye   (Matt. 7:3-5).

No teacher, no pastor, counselor, parent, or friend can give the truth of God effectively unless they have first examined their own private life for those "beams" that cloud their vision. Check the work done. Chances are that the Holy Spirit will have already brought conviction in the areas that need correction. If there is such a conviction, identify with it, confess it to the Lord, and

239

receive His cleansing "from all unrighteousness." Then examine the material for further application.

Always Apply Professionally
This study passage is directed mainly to preachers and teachers of the Word of God. If you fall into one of those two categories, you should have a field day with the material. But how does a housewife apply this data? Or, how does a construction worker, or an electronics engineer, or high school student apply this passage? The Bible tells us that "all Scripture is given by inspiration of God and *is* profitable for doctrine, for reproof, for correction, for instruction in righteousness." If those words mean anything, we can find pieces of information that will help us in our jobs as well. Read through the outline, looking specifically for verses or thoughts that apply to your work. You *will* find some.

Always Apply To Your Church
The local church assembly of believers is the ordained organization of the Lord Jesus Christ in this age. We are to be part of it, work in and through it, and give of ourselves, our talents, our money, and our time to it. Therefore, we should always examine every passage of Scripture that we study in light of how best to help, to teach, to correct, to improve the work and ministry of our local church. If you are in a leadership position in a church, then you have special responsibility and opportunity to do something with your new knowledge. If not, you still have the responsibility to share that knowledge with those that do have the oversight, if it becomes clear that they do not know, or are not aware of the information.

Always Apply To Teaching Situations
Everyone is a teacher of someone. Oh, you may not be a public teacher, or you may not be able to get up in front of people. But, you do teach your children, your friends, your neighbors, the kids down the block—whatever. Everyone is involved in a ministry to others: "For none of us liveth to himself, and no man dieth to himself" (Romans 14:7). There-

fore, any person who studies the Word of God, must examine that study for the application it has to the teaching situations available in his or her life. Check for skills or techniques that can be used, check for information *to* teach, and check for new areas *for* teaching.

File The Study

This last point may seem too obvious for discussion. Everybody knows that you are supposed to keep valuable information for future use. But . . . most of us put it in the family Bible, or in the bookcase along with the Sunday school stuff, or under the desk blotter, or some other place that we would never forget. If you have not yet found out that this does not work, please take the advice of one who has. It doesn't! Make some sort of file box for your Bible study work. If you are a Christian leader or teacher, you should have a filing cabinet and good filing system. If you are just beginning serious Bible study, you need to start with some small box or file folder that will be suitable for keeping your material together. It does not have to be elaborate or expensive—an old cardboard box will do to start. But it must be recognized as the *place* where you keep your Bible study information. As your file grows, you can become as sophisticated as you like or need. There is too much valuable information involved in this kind of study to let it become lost or misplaced. File your work!

All right. We have gone through a lot of material together, and the skills may be somewhat new to you. The next chapter will summarize the entire process. Read it through to help get the thoughts, and then you can refer to that one chapter later on if you need a refresher.

16

PENETRATING BIBLE STUDY SUMMARY

The past several chapters have painstakingly gone through a rather involved passage of Scripture. It is easy to get the impression that such a study would take a very long time. Actually, the normal work time is much less than expected. Depending on the proficiency of the student, the work time could be as little as two hours. Most beginning students require three to four hours for a comparable study, but the study need not be done all at once. Many passages are not as complex as the one just performed. The point is, the work involved is not too hard or too time consuming for any serious student. However, the procedure is fairly rigid and does require commitment from the student to follow through with the Biblical method. Short cuts, however tempting, will not help. Later, after the student has become proficient with this kind of work, he or she may find that it is possible to eliminate some duplication among worksheets. Initially, however, every new student of the Scriptures, or every student unfamiliar with this depth of study, should follow these outlines.

Purpose   This type of study is designed to increase the knowledge and the understanding of Bible passages. It can be used for virtually any length of passage, but must be limited to a single contextual structure. The objective is to search the rest of Scripture for those other passages that directly pertain to and increase the clarity of the passage. This method will allow for the inclusion of some small subject studies, but cannot be used to coordinate or integrate other theological studies. The Bible student is limited to the teaching of the passage under study.

Overview   This thought study is based on the two main Biblical instructions about study, Ecclesiastes 12:9-10 and Isaiah 28:9-10. The teaching of Isaiah is mainly that of the inductive study, and the teaching of Ecclesiastes is mainly procedural. Isaiah notes that the approach to study is twofold:

1. The student must first find the basic commandments or principles of the study.
2. The student must then find those less significant points that will fill out and complete the concept.

Isaiah also teaches that the entire process is governed by two general principles:

1. The study is a building process.
2. The study must be researched throughout the Bible.

The teaching of Ecclesiastes provides three main procedural mechanics:

1. The student must first pay close attention to the words of the text.
2. The student must next penetrate and examine the message of the text.
3. The student must then compose an ordered structure of the penetrated message that will be valuable for teaching and retention.

244

Procedure Caution should always be observed when working with the Word of God. No human being has the right to tamper with that Word, nor do we have the right to "interpret" it for ourselves. The Scriptures have given us the two perspectives with which we are to view Bible study. Therefore, we must use them. Any departure from the Scriptural methodology can only increase the chance that error will be introduced.

GIVE GOOD HEED

I. Isolate the total thought.
    A. Determine the contextual setting.
        1. Check back to the paragraph indicators.
        2. Check back to the chapter heading.
        3. Check back 10-15 verses.
    B. Read the entire contextual setting.
        1. Determine the main points of the contextual setting.
        2. Determine the most complete and least complex thought.
    C. Break down that thought to its major sub-points.
        1. Determine the parts of speech if necessary.
        2. Visualize the structure of the thought on paper.
II. Analyze the purpose and thesis of the thought.
    A. Find the independent clause.
        1. It will stand by itself as complete.
        2. It will clarify the other clauses in the thought.
    B. Find the dependent clauses.
        1. They will need more information to make them complete.
        2. They will add information to the independent clause.
    C. Finalize the visual relationship on paper.
        1. Place the main thesis at the top near the margin.
        2. Place the main sub-points in descending order as they appear in the study passage, indenting these main sub-points from the position of the main thesis.

3. Place the minor sub-points in descending order under their appropriate locations, indenting them still further from the main sub-points.

4. Place adequate verbal identification next to any point that may require some grammatical explanation.

III. Prepare the initial worksheet.

   A. Use ruled paper if possible.

   B. Structure with four vertical columns.

      1. Make a column for the key words.

      2. Make a column for the numerical code.

      3. Make a column for the word definition.

      4. Make a column for the other English words.

IV. Perform a word study on each key word.

   A. List the key words of the passage in the *word* column.

   B. Examine the concordance for the numerical codes.

      1. See the word study outline for assistance if necessary.

      2. List the numerical codes for every key word before going to the language dictionaries.

   C. Examine the appropriate language dictionary for definitions.

      1. Trace out the word history information.

      2. Analyze and summarize the word definition.

      3. Record the word definition in the *definition* column.

   D. Examine the language dictionary word listing for additional English words.

      1. Eliminate any words that would not convey the same sense as the usage in the study passage.

      2. Record applicable words in the *other words* column.

SEEK OUT

I. Locate the parallel Scripture passages.

   A. Prepare the verse study worksheet.

      1. Use ruled paper if possible.

2. Develop the worksheet while proceeding with the study.
3. Follow the visual format established during the initial structuring of the study passage.

B. Begin the research in the main concordance.
   1. Use the initial word study worksheet for reference.
   2. Locate the study word in the main concordance.
   3. Examine each word listing for parallel verses.
      a. Look for verses using the same numerical code.
      b. Look for verses discussing the same thesis.
      c. Look for verses using the same phrasing.
      d. Look for verses that answer the questions of the thesis.
      e. Eliminate any passage that does not apply.
   4. Examine the verses that use parallel numerical codes.
      a. Follow the same criteria as in I, B, 3 above.
      b. Eliminate any passage that does not directly apply.
   5. Examine the verses that use other English words.
      a. Use initial word study worksheet for reference.
      b. Locate the appropriate word in the main concordance.
      c. Use only those verses having the appropriate numerical code.
      d. Follow the same criteria as in I, B, 3 above.
   6. Record all those references that relate to the main thesis.
      a. List the verses in a vertical column under the appropriate key word.
      b. Maintain adequate spacing for visual organization.

II. Maintain constant awareness for variables in research procedure.

A. Some words may be used too many times for verse research.
   1. Locate the book or chapter with the maximum references.
   2. Select those references within that section that fit the criteria of I, B, 3 above.
B. Some words may be used too few times for parallel application.
   1. Locate all possible synonyms.
   2. Select those verses that may verify word usage or definition.

C. Some words may be used infrequently enough to justify a total examination of their subject.
   1. Sort out all references into their natural categories.
   2. List each category in a tabular column on the worksheet.
D. Some words may be used in two diverse ways.
   1. Organize the references under the English words.
   2. Keep visual separation and identification on the worksheet.
E. Some words may require substitutions of parallel translations.
   1. Refer to word study worksheet.
   2. Mentally substitute parallel English ideas into the verse wording.
   3. Record all necessary information.
F. Some verses may require parallel concordance studies.
   1. Unknown words must be verified.
   2. Unknown ideas must be verified or not used.
   3. Unknown figurative language must be verified or not used.

III. Prepare the main study worksheet.
   A. Use ruled paper if possible.
   B. Develop the worksheet while proceding with the study.

C. Follow the same visual format as the verse study worksheet.
IV. Check through the verses.
    A. Examine each verse in its own context in the Bible.
    B. Determine the actual application of each verse.
       1. It must apply to the thesis of the study passage.
       2. It must be eliminated from consideration if it does not apply.
       3. It must be recorded on the main worksheet if it is applicable.
    C. Determine the main point of every applicable verse.
       1. Record that main point on the main worksheet.
       2. Record the point as briefly as possible.
       3. Record the point immediately to the right of the verse reference.
    D. Record all references and information in a vertical column directly under the key word or phrase of the study passage.
    E. Work through the entire study outline.

SET IN ORDER MANY PROVERBS

I. Categorize the verses.
    A. Relate each verse to the main thesis initially.
    B. Relate each verse to the sub-point next.
    C. Locate those verses with the same theme.
       1. Use the main point information previously recorded.
       2. Use the information in the verse itself.
    D. Locate those verses with similar themes.
    E. Locate those verses with contrasting themes.
    F. Record each category on the main worksheet.
       1. Make each category heading as brief as possible.
       2. Make a tabular column for a multiple verse category.
    G. Work through the entire study outline.

II. Pinpoint the relationships.
  A. Review each section of the worksheet in order.
  B. Examine the categories first.
    1. Relate to the main thesis first.
    2. Relate to the sub-point next.
    3. Establish the order of importance.
    4. Label each category by numbering in respective order.
  C. Examine the verses within each category next.
    1. Relate to the main thesis first.
    2. Relate to the category next.
    3. Establish the order of importance.
  D. Eliminate any categories or sub-points that do not directly amplify or clarify the study passage.
    1. Look for new or incisive information.
    2. Avoid any verse or category that is too deep.
    3. Avoid repetitive and incidental information.
III. Prepare the final outline.
  A. Use another worksheet.
  B. Determine the central theme or heading of the outline.
    1. It may be the main thesis of the study passage.
    2. It may need to be restated to incorporate the total message.
  C. Check through the main points.
    1. Look for relationships between the main points.
    2. Allow the main thrust of the passage to become clear.
  D. Use consistent grammatical structure.
    1. The best form is complete sentences throughout.
    2. The sub-points may be dependent clauses to the main points.
    3. The wording should reflect the main thesis.
    4. The wording should also incorporate the teaching of the sub-points.
  E. Work through each main point in order.
    1. Recheck the category relationships.
    2. Determine the central theme of the categories.

    3. Structure the sentences to reflect the theme.

    4. Structure the sentences to reflect the relationships between the categories and sub-points.

  F. Work through the entire outline.

IV. Review the final outline for readability.

  A. Read the outline as though a narrative.

  B. Rewrite the outline in paragraph form if necessary.

  C. Determine the accuracy and teachability of the outline.

    1. It must flow smoothly.

    2. It must not generate unanswerable questions.

    3. It must be usable by someone other than the researcher.

V. Determine how to use the study.

  A. Always apply personally.

  B. Always apply professionally.

  C. Always apply to your local church.

  D. Always apply to teaching situations.

VI. File the study for future use.

These outlines are meant to be a quick overview and refresher for the developing student. They are not meant to take the place of the more detailed instruction and example within the previous chapters. A good student should have to refer to these outlines several times before he or she becomes familiar enough with the process to complete a study without a reminder.

God's Word is inexhaustible. The more we study it, the more we can appreciate the "depth of the riches both of the wisdom and knowledge of God! How unsearchable are his judgments, and his ways past finding out!" (Romans 11:33). However, the more we study, the more He reveals to us and the more excited we become to know more. One of the most delightful things about a child of God studying God's Word is that the child becomes so enthralled with the blessings of deeper understanding, that it seems to increase the desire to study. And, that deeper understanding produces a willingness—indeed, a desire to be more obedient to God's

Word. Such love, understanding, and effective Christian living was the prayer of the Apostle Paul for the church at Philippi:

And this I pray, that your love may abound yet more and more in knowledge and in all judgment; That ye may approve things that are excellent; that ye may be sincere and without offence till the day of Christ; Being filled with the fruits of righteousness, which are by Jesus Christ, unto the glory and praise of God (Phil. 1:9-11).

Structured
Bible Study

17

STUDY OF A CONCEPT

As delightful and informative as the study of a passage of Scripture can be, it still is not altogether satisfactory for trying to piece together the coherent teaching of God's Word on one lengthy subject or concept. Isaiah 28:9-10 has told us that we must build the teachings of the Bible inductively, and that we will not be able to find all of the teaching in one spot. Much of the New Testament *assumes* a knowledge of Old Testament doctrine on the part of the reader. And, much of the Old Testament is impossible to understand without the clarity and amplification of the New Testament writings. If we are able to become effective teachers, or leaders, or servants for the Lord, we *must* know the Word of God more thoroughly than we can through reading a commentary or listening in an academic classroom. We *must* have "searched the Scripture daily to see whether those things were so" (Acts 17:11).

As a matter of fact, if we develop a dependence on the writings of other men about the Word of God, we are little better off than the Mormons, the Moham- medans, the Christian Scientists, the Jehovah's Wit- nesses, or a host of other false religions who do just that. Every false teaching in the world today originates with man, not with God. Man often gets his "interpreta- tion" in the way of truth with the sanctimonious cry that he has the right to believe as "the Lord leads him." Although there is the responsibility of every Christian to recognize the difficulty of some Bible doctrines and to demonstrate true Christian liberty in those areas, there is no "right" to do anything with the Word of God ex- cept obey it. No child of God has any "academic free- dom" to believe whichever way he chooses. There is only one truth! Our job is to search the Scriptures—*the* truth (John 17:17)—and find out what God has said.

The problem lies in the fact that there are many good men on several different sides of the same issue. Are they all wrong? Are they all right? Is anyone right? How may I *know* which one, if any, is right? How may a sin- cere, willing-to-obey child of God sort through the claims of Christianity and *know* what is the truth? God's Word says it can be done, but it must be done by "precept upon line, here a little and there a little." In other words, if we are to be taught "knowledge" by the Lord, if we are to be made "to understand doctrine," we must have researched every single verse in the Bible that could pos- sibly relate to the question under consideration. We must have penetrated to the core of every passage that needs amplification. We must have organized *all* of the data into a complete, comprehensible body of "proverbs" that express *the* truth of the Word of God.

That is a tall order! But it is the order of Scripture, not a Bible professor. It is God's demand for our treat- ment of His precious Word, not the whim of some sys- tem. If we are to be *assured* of correct doctrine, we must do it God's way. This chapter will discuss the general

256

ideas and techniques necessary to study out a major concept in God's Word. It will not provide much detail and may generate several questions. But, it is valuable to have some idea of the direction one is going before the journey actually starts.

GIVE GOOD HEED

Ecclesiastes 12:9-10 has given us the general mechanic for any exegesis of Scripture. We are told that the "wise preacher" followed three simple steps in his search for truth. He first gave very close attention to the words and the message of the truth, then he penetrated and examined the truth as thoroughly as possible, and finally he composed and organized the various parts of that truth into "powerful sayings." We followed that mechanic in our search of II Timothy 4:2 and found that it was more than adequate to reveal the truth of that passage. Now we must use the same mechanic in a broader sense as we try to discover the truth of a Bible-wide concept.

Perform A Word Analysis The first phase, the "give good heed" phase, must be broken down into two major steps: word analysis and verse research. This initial step is not much different than the procedure that was involved in the simple word-study process. In fact, the same skills are used to determine the definitions of the words. The only difference is that there are now many words with similar meaning.

EVERY WORD MUST BE EXAMINED. Whenever a study is being made of a general concept, each word that has been used by the Holy Spirit to convey a shade of meaning which is relevant to that concept must be understood and related to the other parallel words. We cannot take the chance of missing any piece of information.

DETERMINE THE WORD GROUPS within the Hebrew or Greek words. When we were researching the various words earlier, we noted that some words are source words from which others are derived. Our job then was to find the other words which were linguistically equal to the source word, so that we might recognize those other forms in the concordance. We must do essentially the reverse now. Since we will be initially observing many different word forms, we must combine the various words into the parent groupings. We wish to reduce the number of words to the *kinds* of words rather than increase the awareness of word *forms.*

COMPARE THE HEBREW AND GREEK WORDS for parallel terms. Even though the Old and New Testaments are written in two vastly different languages, they were both written under the infallible guidance of the Holy Spirit. Therefore, there will be observable word parallels that must be distinguished for proper relationships between the verse content. Just as we used only those verses that contained the same word group within a Testament, we must now determine those word groups that can be paralleled between the Testaments.

SUMMARIZE THE WORD GROUP DISTINCTIONS. The same process is involved here as was involved in the simple word study. Each word must be analyzed for its word history and radical meaning in order to arrive at the best definition possible. However, now that there are many similar word groups, our analysis must be made of the relationship between those word groups. There will be some similarities between those word groups since we are dealing with a common subject area, but there will also be some differences. Both the similarities and differences must be noted and summarized adequately.

Complete The Verse Research In The Concordance

This second major step in the "Give Good Heed" phase is itself broken down into two stages: the *precept* stage and the *line* stage. One of the biblical criteria given to us was the requirement of the inductive approach. That is carefully outlined in the building process of Isaiah 28:9-10 beginning with the discovery of the "precepts."

THE PRECEPT STAGE is the initial research stage. The Hebrew word for "precept" simply means commandment. Therefore, we should be searching the concordance listings for those verse excerpts that seem to express a direct command about the subject under study. This initial step merely involves the recording of the verses on a worksheet. It does not involve verse analysis.

THE LINE STAGE is a little more involved, but not any more complex than anything experienced heretofore. The Hebrew word for "line" describes a measuring device similar to our ruler that was used to mark smaller increments. This stage of concordance research is interested in those other verses that are not "precepts." That is, we must note and record all information in the Scripture that is not a direct command, but is a quality, or a characteristic about one concept. However, it is the nature of a "line" to be repetitive. "Precepts" are made up of "lines," and many precepts will have some of the same "lines" in them. If the "precepts" were to be illustrated as feet, yards, miles, etc., and the "lines" illustrated as inches, half-inches, quarter-inches, etc., then one could see the basic relationship between these two concepts more easily. The job of the student in this instance is to find those "lines" that have *new* information about some of the "precepts." It is sometimes valuable to keep a record about the number of times a particular "line" is repeated, but it is not at all necessary to continually record the same "line," even though it is repeated in another reference. Once again, the objective in this step is merely to record the verse references that may apply, not to perform a verse analysis.

SEEK OUT

Once the first phase of this study is completed, it is necessary to perform the same kind of work on each verse as was done in the thought-study process. However, it is not necessary to go into the depth of analysis for each verse that was done then. The objective of this stage is to determine the key teaching of each *precept* and *line* so that they may be properly categorized and organized later on into the "proverbs" of a final outline.

Work Through The Precepts

Since there is so much information to be correlated in a study of this nature, and since the *lines* are mostly related to points within the *precepts*, it is necessary to conduct a two-stage approach in this *seek out* phase. The *precepts* will contain the major principles and building blocks for the concept outline and must be developed before the *lines*. It will be necessary to work through the entire selection of *precepts* before going on to the *lines*.

Read Each Verse In Its Context

We must follow the same approach in this study as was found necessary in the earlier study. Although the concordance is an invaluable time-saver, it can never take the place of the contextual setting of the Bible itself. Every verse that has been listed as a "precept" or "line" must read in its context for proper identification.

Determine The Key Elements

Verse or passage analysis merely requires that we determine the thesis or main theme of each parallel verse used. But in this level of study, it is necessary to record much more information about each verse since we are dealing with many sections of Scripture using several similar words.

DETERMINE THE KEY THESIS of each verse and record it in as brief a form as possible. This is precisely the same as the work done earlier and is done for the same purpose. It should be noted that the multiplicity of verses involved will make this step more time consuming and to some degree more demanding. It is not more complex, however.

DETERMINE THE CONTEXTUAL THEME of each verse and record. This procedure is new to this type of study. Although it was necessary to determine context in the earlier study, it was not necessary to record the distinctions. In this type of study, each section of Scripture will affect the use and the application of the various verses to some degree. It is therefore, imperative that

260

the contextual thought be recorded along with the key thesis of the specific verse so that the student may more carefully analyze the material later.

DETERMINE THE KEY WORDS of each verse. Some words will need to be verified by a word study. As has already been emphasized, every student of the Bible must define the meanings of key words in the Scripture by recourse to the original languages. The more one studies, the more words are known from previous studies. But if a word is key to understanding a verse, the student must verify that word through a word study.

DETERMINE ANY UNKNOWN CONCEPTS. It is not uncommon to uncover parallel concepts that must be explored before proper organization can be made of the research data. When such an unknown concept or subject appears in the verses, a record should be made of that point in order that it may be examined later.

Categorize The Verses

This procedure is the same as the earlier study process. It will be necessary to consider additional data in making those category decisions, but the procedure and techniques are the same. It may become necessary to verify some words in the various verses in order to clarify verse meanings, and it may become necessary to perform a parallel study similar to this whole procedure before some ideas can be verified. One point that must always be observed is that we are never at liberty to assume some point of doctrine. If a verse is written with language or is structured in such a manner that the meaning is not clear, then the student must either verify the message or not use the verse.

Pinpoint The Relationships

Just as we followed up the categorizing of verses in the thought study procedure with careful analysis of the category relationships, so we will do now. The procedure is the same.

Make Outline Of Precepts

This step is in addition to the way the thought study process was conducted. The addition is necessary since we will be repeating our categorizing and pinpointing steps for the "lines" of our study in a separate stage. This first run through the "precepts" will produce a good perspective from which to view the "lines" that follow. It is necessary that we organize our category relationships into an initial sentence outline that will provide a coherent base for integrating the "lines" into the final outline. It is not necessary to make as detailed an outline as is done for the final procedure in thought studies, but it is necessary to record the impressions made by the organization of the "precepts."

Work Through The "Lines" This job is generally the same as the "precept" stage with the exception of having to correlate the "lines" to the various "precepts." The initial steps are all the same:

1. Read each verse in its context.
2. Determine the key elements.
   a. Record the key thesis.
   b. Record the contextual thought.
   c. Record the key words.
   d. Record the unknown subjects.
3. Categorize the verses.
4. Pinpoint the relationship.

Make Outline Of Lines This procedure is essentially the same as was done for the "precepts." However, it is now necessary to integrate the sub-points of the "lines" into the major points of the "precepts." The outline need not be very detailed, but it must reflect those overall impressions that are gained during the categorizing process. One consistent problem with this depth of study is that it is very difficult to find time to do the study at one sitting. More than likely, the student will find that this kind of work will involve several sessions, sometimes over a period of weeks. Therefore, it is absolutely necessary that an initial outline be made at the completion of the categorizing stage for both the "precepts" and the "lines." That outline need only summarize the major "flow" of the thoughts, but it must be readable and sufficiently clear to refresh the memory when study is resumed.

SET IN ORDER MANY PROVERBS

The final phase of our study is the most time consuming and demanding of all. In the thought study process, the final outline was mostly a mechanical structuring of the categorizing and pinpointing work. However, we were dealing with only one thought then, whose emphasis was specifically limited to the context and message of the study verses. In the concept study, we are dealing with many passages, many contexts, and many messages. Our study is confined to a single subject area, but that subject will normally be broad enough to encompass a wide variety of thoughts. Therefore, the "proverbs" which must be "set in order" will have to do two things: distinguish between thought areas and relate each of those thought areas to the study concept. That will require more careful attention to the complex interrelations than was necessary in the simpler thought study.

Review All Categories The first approach must be to review each category and relationships established in the categorizing step. We made an initial outline expressing the obvious points and relationships, but now we must try to observe the finer points of the category areas. One main objective in this step is to see if any of the "lines" are more properly placed as "precepts" or vice-versa. Frequently, those verses which appear to be minor points in the concordance will contain major principles in their contextual setting. Much of that will come out during the work of "seeking out," but there is a good portion of such information that can only be properly viewed when all the verse categories are examined as an overall concept.

Separate The Thought Areas As the review of the categories progresses, we must distinguish those thought areas that are significantly different enough to be treated separately. It is not uncommon for a broad subject to contain many thought areas that should be examined with a separate outlining process. The objective of this step is merely to separate or distinguish the major thought areas from the supportive information.

Develop One Thought Area At A Time

Since we are normally dealing with a broad concept that will contain more than one thought area, it is best to develop the outline for only one thought area at a time. The task is difficult enough without requiring mental sorting and correlation of multiple areas before each area has been properly organized. The student will proceed to outline each thought area in just the same manner as for any thought study, the one difference being that there are two work areas from which to draw information: the "precepts" and the "lines."

Relate All Thought Areas To Each Other

Once each thought has been developed into a well-structured outline, it is necessary to tie all of the thoughts together into a coherent teaching that relates the entire concept. This kind of work takes special sensitivity on the part of the student and must be done carefully. Any time a Bible student branches out beyond the confines of one passage of Scripture, he or she must be especially sensitive to the leading of the Holy Spirit for that "feel" for the teaching. We discussed that in some depth when we were finalizing the outline for the thought study process. And, then as now, it still seems unusual to talk about "feeling" something when we are trying to be as objective as possible. However, that is the one difference between mere scientific research and Biblical research. We are searching the "Word of God, which liveth and abideth forever" (I Peter 1:23). That Word is not a mere collection of mental musings and stories. It is a living Spirit (John 6:63). We must, therefore, train ourselves to become sensitive to the directive and teaching power of the Holy Spirit.

But . . . and this is a big "but," that sensitivity to and "feeling" for the "life" of the Word of God will only be correct *after* we have "done that which was our duty to do" (Luke 17:10). We must follow the objective and inductive approach demanded by Isaiah 28:9-10 and Ecclesiastes 12:9-10 *before* we can expect the Holy Spirit to enlighten us. When we have examined the words, researched throughout the Scriptures, penetrated the teachings of the Scriptures, and organized and categorized the information, then we can expect the subjective help of the Lord in finalizing and relating the information.

Determine How To Use The Study

Just as was necessary in every other kind of Bible study, so we must now determine what areas can be benefited by an application of the information within the study. One difference that this kind of study offers is the wide spectrum of thought. It is entirely likely that the student will find multiple applications for the work and may, indeed, find source material for many, many areas. There are, of course, four basic ways to approach a search for applications. They are:

1. Always apply personally.
2. Always apply professionally.
3. Always apply to your local church.
4. Always apply to teaching situations.

File The Study

Obviously, this much work demands preservation. It is foolish not to develop some system of recall, whereby the information may be easily recovered and reviewed at a later time. Some studies can be filed topically, some can be filed Biblically, and some may be filed theologically. With the depth of study performed at this level, the student may find it beneficial to cross-file the information in two or more locations. Or, it may be worthwhile to file a portion of the study topically and a portion Biblically. Whatever the case, file the work!

SUMMARY

This chapter has provided only an overview of the basic technique for the study of a concept. It has not attempted to develop the specifics, nor has it attempted to amplify the unusual problems that may be encountered. It is well at this point to review the main points of this study.

I. Give Good Heed.
    A. Perform a word analysis.
       1. Examine every word on the subject.
       2. Determine the word groups.
       3. Compare the Hebrew and Greek word parallels.
       4. Summarize the word group distinctives and similarities.
    B. Perform a verse research.
       1. Locate the "precepts" in the concordance.
          a. Look for direct commands.
          b. Look for information that is directly related to the concept.
       2. Locate the "lines" in the concordance.
          a. Look for character or quality descriptions.
          b. Look for information that is supportive of the "precepts."

II. Seek Out.
    A. Work through the "precepts" first.
       1. Read each verse in its context.
       2. Determine the key elements of each verse.
          a. Record the main thesis.
          b. Record the contextual theme.
          c. Record the key words.
          d. Record the unknown concepts.
       3. Categorize the verses.
       4. Pinpoint the relationships.
       5. Make an initial outline.

B. Work through the "lines" next.
  1. Read each verse in its context.
  2. Determine the key elements in each verse.
     a. Record the main thesis.
     b. Record the contextual theme.
     c. Record the key words.
     d. Record the unknown concepts.
  3. Categorize the verses.
  4. Pinpoint the relationships.
  5. Make an initial outline.
III. Set In Order Many Proverbs.
  A. Review all the categories.
  B. Separate the individual thought areas.
  C. Develop one thought area at a time.
  D. Relate all thought areas to each other.
  E. Determine how to use the study.
  F. File the study.

That outline should congeal the overall perspective and be beneficial for quick review. Now we must examine more specifically the actual preparation of a concept from the Scriptures. Are you willing to learn? Read the next chapter.

18

WORD ANALYSIS

It will not be possible in this book to give the same depth of detail to the study of a concept as was given to the examination of the thought study. The amount of data covered would require more space than the previous study, and this kind of study contains too many variables. However, since we are dealing with very few *new* skills, it will not be necessary to analyze each procedure so carefully. Those areas that are different will be discussed adequately, and those procedures that require new skills will be given detailed treatment.

One note of caution should be sounded at the start of this portion. No Bible student should attempt a study of this depth until he or she has become familiar and proficient with the procedures outlined heretofore. Since a conceptual study requires multiple word and thought studies, it would be somewhat presumptuous to tackle a conceptual study until those skills were comfortably mastered. Much of the instruction in this portion of the book will assume that mastery, and the instruction will also assume possession of a Strong's concordance. Please get one before studying this portion of the book. You will be unable to gain much benefit from the instruction otherwise.

Make A Worksheet

As we have already discovered, organization of research data is imperative. It is not wasted effort to make a worksheet; rather, it is invaluable. We must not only record our working procedure, but we must also record our working progress in such a manner that is suitable for evaluation.

A word analysis at this level requires four things:

1. The word number.
2. The word spelling.
3. The word definition.
4. The other English translations.

Therefore, the worksheet should look like this:

Word	Word Spelling	Definition	Other English Translations

The spelling of the word is not necessary except for those students who wish to build their knowledge of key Hebrew and Greek words. If the student gets in the habit of spelling out and pronouncing the words during the various studies, a surprising familiarity with the languages will rapidly develop. Besides that, it is always beneficial to include the proper word spellings on the final outline when summarizing the conceptual perspective.

Examine Every Word On The Subject

This initial "heeding" is quite mechanical in one respect—and deceptively difficult in another. On the one hand, the actual examination of the various words involves merely multiple word studies using the Hebrew and Greek dictionaries. But on the other hand, the student must give some careful consideration to what words to examine. When the concept to be studied is relatively simple, then there will be few words involved. However, when the concept involves a complex question, or when it involves a theological dilemma, there may be difficulty in knowing where to begin.

START WITH THE MOST OBVIOUS WORD. Every question, every subject, every problem has to be expressed in words. Since the concordance is structured around the English words, the most logical beginning to any conceptual study is that word or words which are key expressions of the concept. Once the study gets under way, the Bible itself will begin to supply additional thoughts that are necessary for proper understanding and evaluation of the concept.

We shall concern ourselves in this book with a study of the concept of love. That concept is quite broad and pervades almost every doctrine of the Scriptures. It is basic to the understanding of salvation and is the force that draws all men toward the Savior. Therefore, it is vital that we understand it well. A surface understanding is not adequate. Nor is an emotional response adequate. We must *know* what love *is*. We must know how to distinguish between different kinds of love. Anything short of such knowledge is incomplete and can lead to grievous error.

Since the skills involved in this initial step have already been covered earlier in this book, it will not be necessary to repeat the detailed progression of the work. However, a quick review of the word study process is worth reading.

1. Locate the key concept word in the main concordance.
2. List all the word numbers that appear under the the key concept word.
3. Locate each study word by its numerical code in the appropriate language dictionary.
4. Trace out all the information about each word.
5. Analyze and summarize the definition.
6. Record each leading English word that translates the Hebrew or Greek study word.

These six steps are to be repeated for each and every word in the concept study. As the study progresses, the Bible itself will supply other key words which must also be analyzed by the same process. Here is the way the Word Analysis Worksheet would look after doing this work for "love."

OLD TESTAMENT WORDS			
Word	Word Spelling	Definition	Other English Translations
157	'ahab	to have affec-tion-**root**	like, friend
160	'ahabah	affection (157)	
2836	chashaq	to cling, join **root**	delight, desire, long
7355	racham	to fondle, compassionate **root**	compassion, mercy, pity
1730	dod	to boil **root**	beloved, brother, uncle
7474	rayah	female associate (7453)	
5691	agabah	amorousness (5789)	
5690	egeb	love-amative (5689)	
4261	machmad	delightful (2530)	beloved, desire, goodly, pleasant
7453	reya	an associate (7462)	

3039	yediyd	loved (1730)	amiable, beloved
159	'ohab	affection (157)	
2896	towb	good (2695)	widely used adjective
5689	'agab	to breathe after- **root**	date

NEW TESTAMENT WORDS

Word	Word Spelling	Definition	Other English Translations
25	agapaō	to love in a moral sense- **root**	beloved
5368	phileō	fond of (5384)	
26	agapē	affection or benevolence (25)	charity, dear
2309	thelō	to determine, choose	please, desire disposed
5360	philadelphia	fraternal affection (5361)	
5365	philarguria	avarice (5366)	
5362	philandros	fond of man (5384)	(5384 - philos)
5388	philoteknos	fond of children (5334)	fond, friendly: - friend
5363	philanthrōpia	fondness of mankind (5364)	
5361	philadelphos	fond of brethren (5384)	
5367	philautos	fond of self (5384)	
5369	philedonos	fond of pleasure (5384)	
5377	philotheos	fond of God (5384)	
5383	philoproteuō	fond of being first (5384)	

WORKSHEET EXPLANATION

All the word numbers appear in the order of their occurrence in the Strong's listings. The Old Testament words should be separate from the New Testament words on the worksheet for ease of research and recording. The word listing for "love" also required an examination of "loved; loves; love's; lovest; loveth; loving." The English word "lovingkindness" followed immediately in the same section and seems to be a parallel term to this study. For purposes of worksheet organization, the student would list all Old Testament words under each word heading before listing all New Testament words. The root words are recorded on the worksheet by simple notation, and the derivatives of any given root word are noted by recording the word number in parenthesis after the definition.

SEARCH THE CONCORDANCE FOR THE OTHER ENGLISH WORDS. In the first word analysis, we recorded the other English translations for all the various Hebrew and Greek words that had been translated by "love" and its various forms. Now we must extend the word analysis to discover any other Hebrew or Greek words that may be used by the Holy Spirit to teach some of the aspects of love not suggested by the other words. To do this we must limit the word study to those words that express some parallel thought to our study concept. When we were studying a passage of Scripture, we constantly limited the verses chosen by the study thesis, so we must now choose only those words that are an obvious parallel to our study concept.

For instance, our worksheet shows that the Hebrew word *ahab*, number 157, is also translated by the English word "like." That word is an appropriate *English* parallel to "love" in certain ways. But, we must find other *Hebrew* and *Greek* words that express that same shade of meaning. To do that we must look up "like" in the main concordance and locate the various Hebrew and Greek numerical codes, following that procedure with a dictionary study for the definition. However, "like," in English, can also mean "similar." "Similar" is not at all parallel to "love." We must not record those Hebrew and Greek words translated by "like" that mean "similar." Therefore, we must check the concordance contextual setting for every different word possibility to insure that the Hebrew or Greek words are indeed linguistically and conceptually parallel to "love." That check will prevent a conceptual "rabbit track" after some other, dissimilar study. When we do that work for all the words suggested by our initial worksheet, we find the following information:

OLD TESTAMENT WORDS			
Word	**Word Spelling**	**Definition**	**Translations**
3033	yediduwth	affection, darling	beloved
2530	chamad	to delight in **root**	beloved, desire, lust
3357	yaqqiyr	precious	dear
2654	chaphets	to incline to	delight, desire favor
7522	ratson	delight	delight, desire favor
6026	anag	to be soft	delight, delicate
8173	sha'a	to look, to fondle	delight, dandle, play
8191	sha-shua	enjoyment (8173)	delight, pleasure
8669	teshuwquh	a longing	desire
8378	ta'avah	a delight	desire, dainty, pleasant
2550	chamal	to spare	compassion, pity spare
8373	ta'ab	to desire	long
2968	ya'ab	to desire	long

NEW TESTAMENT WORDS			
Word	Word Spelling	Definition	Other English Translations
27	agapētos	beloved (25)	beloved, dear
1784	entimas	valued	dear, precious
5093	timiotatos	valuable	dear, precious
4913	sunedomei	feel satisfaction	delight
2107	eudakia	satisfaction, delight	desire
3713	oregomai	to stretch out for	desire, covet
5384	philos	a friend, friendly	----
2083	hetairos	comrade	friend, fellow
1653	eleeō	have compassion on	compassion, mercy
3627	oiktereō	to exercise pity	compassion
3356	metriopatheō	gentle	compassion
4834	sumpatheō	sympathy	compassion
1971	epipotheō	to yearn, crave	long, desire, lust

There are several factors hidden in the work process that must be amplified.

1. Each parallel English word must be considered for the possible non-parallel applications: i.e., "like" and "similar."

2. Each concordance listing must be scanned for the contextual setting to determine whether questionable Hebrew or Greek words are parallel to the concept study idea.

3. Each possible Hebrew or Greek word must be considered in light of the limitation of the study. That is, if the amplified definition of a given word in the dictionary reveals that the intent of the word is not directly parallel to the concept under study, the word must not be used.

4. Each English translation of any given word in the dictionary must be considered in light of the conceptual limitation. That is, a Hebrew or Greek word may be broad enough to be rendered by two different English words depending upon the use of those words in the Biblical context. In the case of

of the Hebrew word, *sha'a* (#8173), the word is rendered "delight" and "play." The first rendering may have significance to the study of the "love" concept. The second would not.

Obviously, this study is more complex than was experienced in the basic word and thought studies. That is why a student should not attempt this level until he or she is proficient in the use of the concordance. As one becomes familiar with the procedures, a genuine sensitivity to the process develops that will help guide the student in the work. However, there is much more of the human element involved throughout the study. Constant judgment must be made about various words or verses. Therefore, it is imperative that the student begin every study session with the conscious prayer for the Holy Spirit's guidance and maintain that communication with the Lord all during the working time.

Determine The Word Groups

This procedure is new to the concept study. During the word and thought studies, we made an effort to expand the study word to include those parallel forms which were derivatives of the study word. In this type of study, we are starting with the many parallel forms of many parallel words. Our job must now be to reduce those words to their parent groupings so that we may visualize the broad areas of the concept.

FIND THE ROOT WORDS. Initially, the place to start is the root words. If the worksheet was developed properly, this should not be difficult since the root words should have been marked on the worksheet.

FIND THE DERIVATIVES OF THE ROOT WORDS. This step may be more involved, but should be rather easy. Most of the derivatives will be very close numerically and can be spotted as well by similar spelling. Those words that are separated by several alphabetical headings should have been marked on the worksheet with the appropriate root word's numerical code.

277

FIND THE SYNONYMS. Most words have closely parallel words that are not derived from the same root word. The definitions will be very similar and will generally produce the same translation. Those words that are closely paralleled by definition should be included in the same word grouping.

Since there are so many words involved, it is usually best to make another worksheet for this step. The more organized and concise the material is, the more effective its use. After performing the above steps, the worksheets would look something like this:

WORD GROUPINGS: Old Testament			
Word	Word Spelling	Definition	Other English Translations
157	'ahab	to have affection - **root**	like, friend
610	ahabah	"	
159	'ohab	"	
3033	yediduwth	affection, darling	beloved
2530	chamad	to delight in - **root**	beloved, desire
5261	machmad		goodly, pleasant
7522	ratson		favor
8191	sha-shua	enjoyment	delight, pleasure
8378	talavah		dainty
1730	dod	to boil - **root**	beloved
3039	yeliyd	loved	amiable, beloved
2836	chashaq	to cling to - **root**	delight, desire, long
2968	ya-ab	to desire	long
8373	ta'ab	to desire	long
8669	teshuwquh	a longing	desire
2654	chaphets	to incline to	delight, desire, favor
5689	'agab	to breathe after - **root**	date
5690	egeb	love	
5691	agabah	amorousness	
3357	yaqqiyr	precious	dear
7355	racham	to fondle - **root**	compassion, mercy, pity
2550	chamal	to spare	spare, mercy, pity
2617	chacad	kindness	favor, kindness, mercy
7453	reya	an associate - **root**	amiable, beloved
7474	rayah	female associate	
2896	towb	not applicable	good
6026	anag	not applicable	soft

WORD GROUPINGS: New Testament

Word	Word Spelling	Definition	Other English Translations
25	agapaō	love in a moral sense - **root**	beloved
26	agapē	affection	charity, dear
27	agapetos	beloved	beloved, dear
1784	entimos	valued	dear, precious
5093	timioras	valuable	dear, precious
5384	philos	find, friendly - **root**	friend
5360	philadelphia	fraternal affection	brotherly love
5361	philadelphos	fond of brethren	
5362	philandros	fond of man	
5363	philanthrōpia	fond of mankind	
5365	philarguria	avarice	
5367	philautos	fond of self	
5368	phileō	to be fond of	
5369	philedonos	fond of pleasure	
5377	philotheos	fond of God	
5383	philoproteuō	fond of being first	
5388	philoteknos	fond of children	
2083	hetairos	comrade	friend, fellow
2309	thelō	to determine, choose	desire, disposed, intend
1653	eleeō	have compassion on	compassion, mercy
3627	oiltereō	to exercise pity	compassion
3356	metriopatheō	gentle	"
4834	sumpatheō	sympathy	"
4913	sunedomai	feel satisfaction	delight
2107	eudokia	satisfaction, delight	desire
3713	oregomai	to stretch out for	desire, covet
1971	epipotheō	to yearn, crave	long, desire, lust

The overall effect of this step has been to reduce the several disconnected word analysis sheets into two, more organized worksheets from which the entire study can begin. These worksheets will be referred to time and again during the remainder of the study process. That is the main reason for marking their organization so specifically. Information that is not visually usable is worth much less than well organized, clearly categorized data.

279

Compare The Interlingular Word Parallels

The two worksheets that have resulted from the multiple word studies must now be correlated into a comparative analysis of the intertestamental language parallels. This is done to help us relate passages in the Old Testament with linguistically parallel passages in the New Testament.

MAKE A NEW WORKSHEET. This worksheet will be designed to reflect the major word analysis worksheets and provide a quick-glance survey of all words. Since it does not have to be as detailed as the main word analysis sheets, it can follow the same basic format while leaving out repetitive information.

OLD TESTAMENT		NEW TESTAMENT	
Word	Summary Definition	Word	Summary Definition

FIND THE PARALLEL DEFINITIONS. Obviously, this is the first place to begin. Using the two worksheets, locate those words in the Old Testament and those words in the New Testament that have the same, or basically the same, definitions.

FIND THE PARALLEL TRANSLATIONS. Once we have located the parallel definitions, we can look for those words that have a less obvious parallel in the definition, but have been translated by parallel English words. Most often, these terms will be within the same word grouping on the word analysis worksheets.

FIND THE RELATIONSHIPS WITHIN THE GROUPINGS. It is frequently necessary to pinpoint a sub-grouping within a larger word group. This is most often true of those groups that are associated not only by word definition, but also by word translation. Sometimes a word falls into one category simply by virtue of the fact that it does not fit anywhere else. Whatever

280

may be the reason, some words will not be directly parallel to others within a group, but are obviously not at all parallel to another group. When this is so, identify those words as a sub-category, or sub-group. The new worksheet should look something like this:

OLD TESTAMENT		NEW TESTAMENT	
Word	**Summary Definition**	**Word**	**Summary Definition**
157 159 160 3033	affection	5384 25	fond of (5360-5369, 77, 83, 88, 2-83) love (25-27)
2530 4261 7522 8191 8378	delight enjoyment	4913 2107	delight/satisfaction
2836 2968 8373 8669 2654	desire/cling to long for incline to	3713 1971	to stretch out to yearn
7355 2550 2617	to fondle/compassion to spare kindness	1653 3627 3556 4834	compassion/mercy/pity sympathy
5689 5690 5691 3357	to breathe after precious	1784 5093	valuable
1730 3039	to boil		
7453 7474	an associate		

Summarize Word Group Distinctives

It is entirely possible to perform this step mentally, or to satisfy the requirements of this point during the summary word grouping process on the worksheet. However, more complex concepts will require a written analysis or outline of the word group distinctive and will require some careful thought. It is a good practice for every new student to write down the summary to assist in more accurate retention of the information. One of the simplest and most effective ways to summarize information is by way of a sentence outline. Such an outline of the previous worksheet would look like this·

I. Love may be expressed by affection.
(O.T. 157-160, 3033)
  A. It may be friendship or fondness.
    (N.T. 5384 & derivatives)
  B. It may be love in a moral or social sense.
    (N.T. 25-27)
  C. It may be mere close association.
    (O.T. 7453, 74)
II. Love may be expressed by delight.
(O.T. 2530 and derivatives)
  A. It may be satisfaction.
    (N.T. 4913, 2107)
  B. It may be enjoyment.
    (O.T. 8191)
III. Love may be expressed by desire.
(O.T. 2836 and derivatives)
  A. It may have the sense of clinging to.
    (O.T. 2836)
  B. It may have the sense of longing for.
    (O.T. 8669; N.T. 1771)
  C. It may have the sense of inclining to.
    (O.T. 2654; N.T. 3713)
IV. Love may be expressed by compassion.
(O.T. 7355; N.T. 1653)
  A. It may be mercy.
    (O.T. 2550; N.T. 3627, 3556)
  B. It may be kindness.
    (O.T. 2617)
  C. It may be sympathy.
    (N.T. 4834)

V. Love may be expressed by passion.
   A. It may be in the sense of breathing after.
      (O.T. 5689)
   B. It may be in the sense of boiling.
      (O.T. 1730)
VI. Love may be expressed by valued esteem.
    (O.T. 3357; N.T. 1789, 5093)

This outlining procedure has helped to reveal an improper relationship in the word grouping worksheet. We had previously categorized word numbers 3357 (Old Testament) and 1784, 5093 (New Testament) under the root word 5689 "to breathe after." The two Old Testament words, 1730 and 3030, had been left in a separate category. In checking back on the original worksheets, it is easy to see that these words were grouped through a process of elimination. That is, they were placed in their respective categories mainly because we did not know what else to do with them.

That is not at all unusual, especially since we have done no Scriptural exegesis yet, and we are merely trying to sort out the linguistic parallels. Whenever such abstract work is being done, it is likely that some initial confusion will result. That underscores the value of trying to construct a sentence outline from the information on the word groupings. If such a misplaced parallel did creep into the worksheets, it is probable that the outlining process will reveal and help correct it. When such discoveries are made, the worksheets must be corrected.

Now that the word analysis is complete, we may begin to search the concordance for the "precepts" and "lines." The work we have just done will be valuable preparation for such research by helping to fix in our mind's eye a sensitivity to the broad areas of this concept study. If you are ready to begin, read the next chapter with your concordance at the ready.

19

VERSE RESEARCH

Although the word analysis phase has helped to establish some abstract "precepts," it does not provide the actual data for the Biblical structure. The word analysis gives general perspective; the verse research locates the specific pieces.

Prepare The Main Data Worksheets

As always, the data must be collected in an organized and usable manner. This initial process does not call for any more recorded information than multiple verse references collected from the concordance listings. However, each verse will be analyzed during the next major phase of this study, so we should organize the worksheet to record that work as well. During our discussion of the "seek out" phase, we discovered that we had to know the thesis, contextual theme, key words, and unknown concepts for each "precept" or "line." Therefore, our worksheet should have six columns.

MAIN DATA WORKSHEET					
Verse Reference	No.	Thesis	Contextual Theme	Key Words	Unknown Concepts

Locate The Precepts

We have already discussed the requirement laid down by Isaiah 28:9-10 and have committed our research approach to that requirement. In a study of any length, it will be necessary to approach this stage in several steps.

1. Read through the concordance listings and record only those verse references that appear to be direct commands for the study concept.
2. Read through the main concept word headings first.
3. Read through the parallel English words next.
4. Maintain a distinction between Old and New Testament references.
5. Start another worksheet for each testament.

Please do not be tempted to combine these steps until you have become very proficient in labeling the distinctives. The information in the concordance listings is too sparse to verify the specifics adequately. Therefore, it can only increase the likelihood of error to "save time" through a rapid combination effort. Even the older and more competent Bible students find that speed is never justified by its accuracy. Be willing to spend whatever time is necessary to do the job correctly, and the Lord will reward you beyond your expectations.

The following worksheets contain the "precepts" for our study on "love."

MAIN DATA WORKSHEET: PRECEPTS

Old Testament: Commands

Verse Reference	No.	Thesis	Contextual Theme	Key Words	Unknown Concepts
Lev. 19:18	157				
Deut. 6:5	"				
Deut. 10:19	"				
Deut. 11:1	"				
Deut. 11:13	"				
Deut. 11:22	"				
Deut. 19:9	"				
Deut. 30:6	"				
Jos. 23:11	"				
Ps. 31:23	"				
Is. 56:6	"				
Am. 5:15	"				
Zech. 8:17	"				
Zech. 8:19	"				
Ps. 37:4	6026				
Is. 55:2	6026				
Deut. 5:21	2530				
Deut. 7:25	"				
Prov. 3:3	2617				

MAIN DATA WORKSHEET: PRECEPTS

New Testament: Commands

Verse Reference	No.	Thesis	Contextual Theme	Key Words	Unknown Concepts
Mat. 5:43	25				
Mat. 5:44	"				
Mat. 19:19	"				
Mat. 22:37	"				
Mat. 22:39	"				

Mk. 12:30	"				
Mk. 12:31	"				
Mk. 12:33	"				
Lk. 6:27	"				
Lk. 6:35	"				
Lk. 10:27	"				
Jn. 13:34	"				
Jn. 15:9	26				
Jn. 15:12	26				
Jn. 15:17	"				
Rom. 12:9	"				
Rom. 13:8	25				
Gal. 5:13	26				
Gal. 5:14	"				
Eph. 4:2	"				
Eph. 4:15	"				
Eph. 5:2	"				
Eph. 5:25	25				
Phil. 2:2	26				
Col. 3:19	25				
I Th. 3:12	26				
Heb. 10:24	"				
Heb. 13:1	5360				
Jas. 2:8	25				
I Pet. 2:17	"				
I Pet. 3:8	5361				
I Jn. 2:15	25				
I Jn. 3:11	"				
I Jn. 3:23	25				
I Jn. 4:7	26				
I Jn. 4:11	25				
II Jn. 5	"				
Jude 21	26				
Rom. 12:10	5387				
Col. 3:2	5426				

Col. 3:14	26				
II Tim. 2:22	"				
I Pet. 4:8	"				
I Cor. 14:1	2206				
I Pet. 2:2	1971				
Gal. 5:26	2755				
Jude 22	1653				

These three worksheets represent approximately one hour's work. The procedure is not difficult, but it is exacting. A student must be mature enough in the Lord to be willing to go through the steps patiently. There are no shortcuts. Three observations need to be made about this kind of verse research:

1. The listings in the concordance are so terse that it is inevitable that the student will misread or misapply a few references. This will be corrected in the "seek out" stage.

2. Since there are so many references in a major concept study, it is difficult to decide what references to record. The limiting factor is the scope of the concept itself. The word analysis study will have formulated a perspective for the concept, and the student must continually test the concordance excerpt statement by that perspective. That is, "Does this statement directly relate to the commands to love, or is it merely a statement about loving something else?

3. Normally, the student will find some 5% or 10% of the verses will be given as a direct command about the subject. In this case, it was necessary to check some 1,000 verse listings under ten major word headings. Out of that work we have found 63 references that can be labeled "precept commands."

We now must go back over the same verse listings and look for the character/quality verses references.

**Locate
The Lines**
Technically, every other verse on the subject of love is a "line."

However, we are not going to profit by listing all other references and then trying to sort them out. Our job must be more systematic than that. Remember, the Scripture tells us to "give good heed" in our initial approach to doctrine. Therefore, we must make the same critical evaluation of the concordance listings as we had done for the "precepts." There are five factors to remember during this step.

1. Always test the listing by the scope of the concept. That is, do not record any reference that does not give some direct information relating to the concept under study.

2. Do not record repetitive information. That is, those verses that repeat a phrase or thought of a verse recorded earlier should not be recorded.

3. Look for new information other than that which has already been covered by the "precepts." It is not possible at this stage to be very accurate with this factor because the "precepts" have not been amplified yet. However, there will have been several repetitive points in the "precepts" that will remain in the memory during this procedure. Do not record those "line" verses that merely repeat a "precept" thought.

4. Look for information that will amplify or support the "precept" data. Some verses will provide reasons, others will give answers, and still others will introduce interesting information about a major "precept." The student should be sensitive to those kinds of "line" verses.

5. Look for those verses that describe a quality or a characteristic. Sometimes a verse will be worded so that it is a clear definition of some aspect of the study concept. These are the kinds of "lines" that will assist us in "measuring" the "precepts" given to us by the Holy Spirit.

MAIN DATA WORKSHEET: LINES

Old Testament: Character/Quality

Verse Reference	No.	Thesis	Contextual Theme	Key Words	Unknown Concepts
Lev. 19:34	157				
Duet. 10:12	"				
Deut. 13:3	"				
Judg. 5:31	"				
II Sam 1:26	160				
IIChr. 19:2	157				
Ps. 4:2	"				
Ps. 5:11	157				
Ps. 40:16	"				
Ps. 97:10	"				
Ps. 119:97	"				
Ps. 122:6	"				
Prov. 8:36	"				
Prov. 10:12	160				
Prov. 15:17	"				
Prov. 17:9	"				
Dan. 8:6	"				
Ecc. 3:8	157				
Mic. 6:8	160				
Prov. 12:1	157				
Prov. 15:9	"				
Prov. 17:17	"				
Ps. 40:8	2654				
Ps 1:2	2656				
Ps. 119:16	8173				
Ps. 112:1	2654				
Prov. 11:33	8378				
Prov. 19:32	"				

MAIN DATA WORKSHEET: LINES

New Testament: Character/Quality

Verse Reference	No.	Thesis	Contextual Theme	Key Words	Unknown Concepts
Mt. 5:46	25				
Mt. 10:37	5368				
Mt. 24:12	26				
Lk. 7:47	25				
Jn. 8:42	25				
Jn. 13:35	26				
Jn. 14:15	25				
Jn. 14:23	"				

Jn. 15:10	26				
Jn. 15:13	26				
Rom. 13:10	"				
I Cor. 8:3	25				
II Cor. 5:14	26				
II Cor. 6:6	"				
Gal. 5:6	"				
Gal. 5:13	"				
Eph. 2:4	"				
Eph. 3:17	26				
Eph. 4:2	"				
Eph. 4:15	"				
Eph. 5:28	25				
I Th. 5:8	26				
I Tim. 6:10	5365				
Heb. 10:24	26				
I Pet. 1:22	5360				
I Pet. 3:10	25				
I Jn. 2:5	26				
I Jn. 2:15	25				
I Jn. 3:16	26				
I Jn. 4:7	"				
I Jn. 4:10	"				
I Jn. 4:12	"				
I Jn. 4:16	"				
I Jn. 4:17	"				
I Jn. 4:18	"				
I Jn. 4:19	25				
I Jn. 4:20	"				
I Jn. 4:21	"				
I Jn. 5:2	"				
I Jn. 5:3	26				
II Jn. 6	"				
Rev. 2:4	"				
Jn. 3:19	25				
Jn. 12:43	"				
Jn. 14:28	"				
Jn. 15:9	"				
Jn. 15:12	"				
Rom. 8:37	"				
Mt. 10:37	5368				
Jn. 12:25	5368				
Jn. 14:21	25				
Jn. 16:27	5368				
Rom. 7:22	4913				
I Co. 8:1	26				
I Co. 13:1-8	"				
I Co. 13:13	"				
I Tim. 1:5	"				
I Pet. 4:8	"				
Rom. 10:1	2107				

With the completion of the character/quality research, we now have six worksheets containing some 156 references that should represent the major points of this study on love. There are several observations that would be worth noting here:

1. The time necessary to complete the procedure thus far, which is fairly representative of the average concept study length, was about two hours.

2. The 156 verses recorded are approximately 15% of the 1,000 verses which were listed in the concordance. Very few studies will produce a higher percentage.

3. The student will always feel the pressure to record more verses than necessary. There must be a constant check against the purpose of the study in order to prevent the accumulation of too much data. Every verse must indicate some direct information about the study of the concept. Those verses that merely use the word in connection with another subject are not likely to apply.

4. The six worksheets reveal the following patterns:

   a. Twice as many New Testament references as Old Testament.

   b. The Old Testament predominantly uses the Hebrew word, *ahab,* #157.

   c. The New Testament predominantly uses the Greek word, *agapeō,* #25.

   d. Those two words have now been verified as linguistic parallels and will obviously figure heavily in the study process.

Although all of the concordance research has been completed for this stage, it will be necessary to examine every verse in the Bible in its context. The concordance listings are too terse to insure an accurate reading of every passage content. And since we are dealing with the absolute truth of God's Word, we cannot take the chance that we would miss any point which would affect the understanding of any "precept" or "line." Therefore, after we have performed the "seek out" stage of our study process, we will have to read every one of the remaining 850 verses in their contextual setting to find whatever additional information that will embellish our understanding.

Right now, however, we must begin to analyze the verses we have on our worksheet. Get your Bible out and read chapter twenty.

20

ANALYZE
THE PRECEPTS

This chapter will outline the steps involved for the "penetration" of verses selected during the "give good heed" phase. Fortunately, the process, though lengthy, is repetitive and can be observed easily by the discussion of the abstract concepts. Therefore, we will examine the procedure in depth only as there are new or difficult steps. A review of the overall process will be helpful here.

1. Read each verse in its context.
2. Determine the key elements of each verse.
   a. Record the main thesis.
   b. Record the contextual theme, if necessary.
   c. Record the key words, if necessary.
   d. Record the unknown concepts, if necessary.
3. Categorize the verses.
4. Pinpoint the relationships.
5. Make an initial outline.

We have already gone over the various reasons why it is necessary to read every key verse in the specific contextual setting, so it would be superfluous to repeat those reasons here. We have also discussed the reasons for recording the four areas of specific data from each verse. However, it will be worthwhile to examine some of the specific mechanics and skills involved in these four areas before we actually begin the procedure.

Record The Main Thesis

This information will be critical when we return to the worksheets to categorize the verses. It is necessary to develop the skill of brevity for all these steps, since the multiplicity of verses will present too much information if the student is wordy. The thesis should be stated in one word, if possible certainly no more than a short phrase. These words and phrases will be used later for categorizing the verses. The student should pick out the key word or key point of the verse and record it on the worksheet.

Record The Contextual Theme

This information is the key to sorting out the various sub-points in our later outlining. It should be used in much the same way as the short summary of each verse was used during the thought study. The objective here is to record the major thrust of each verse as it is presented within its context. Normally, that thrust is easily seen and can be recorded in a short phrase. Sometimes, it is necessary to read several verses surrounding the passage and summarize the intent of the writer. Occasionally, the context will limit the verses to a specific person, nation, or event. In that case, we must decide if the verse is too narrow in its application to be considered within the broad intent of the concept under study. Unfortunately, the limitation of passages to certain people or time frames has been made problematic through the "interpretations" of different theological schools of thought. If such an interpretation is doubtful, that is, if there is a question about the limitation of a passage, withhold the use of that passage until all the data from the rest of the study has been collected. Quite frequently, the Scriptures will organize the data more correctly than a "system" of theology.

To summarize, the following steps should be observed when analyzing the contextual theme:

1. Record the major theme of the immediate context in as brief a notation as possible.
2. Summarize the surrounding contextual theme if it is necessary for proper understanding of the verse.
3. Eliminate those passages whose context seem to limit the verse to a specific application, unless other data warrants its inclusion.
4. Only record those contextual themes that are necessary for proper understanding or correct limitation of the application.

Record The Key Words

This information is necessary to alert the student to those words which must be defined before accurate understanding of the verse can be had. It is *not* necessary for the student to record every key word in a verse unless the words are all unfamiliar. It *is* necessary to record those word or words which are critical to the verse meaning, if those words are not known. The more proficient the student becomes in Bible study, the fewer words will be required for this factor. However, when there is doubt, or when the meaning of the verse hinges upon the proper understanding of a word, the word should be recorded on the worksheet.

Remember The Purpose

Keep in mind that the concept study is limited to the study of a specific concept. A constant limitation must be made on the information recorded. No information may be used that does not directly bear on the study concept. Just as we found ourselves "weeding out" information in the thought study process through the "filter" of the main thesis, so we must now "weed out" any information that does not pass through the "filter" of the study concept. We must constantly ask ourselves if the information amplifies, clarifies, or enhances the understanding of the study concept. If it does not, do not record it.

Eliminate Any Verse Which Does Not Apply

Every concept will have overlapping relationships with other concepts. It is impossible to eliminate some verses from the worksheet during the initial concordance research, but as we actually read the verses in their contextual setting, we will be able to eliminate verses whose subject is not directly tied to our study concept. Those verses that have a negative emphasis may not apply, since the negative may be directed to another object. Those verses that have a limited emphasis may not apply, since the emphasis may not be directed to the overall concept. Careful discernment is required here, and the student must develop this skill through constant practice. If there is doubt about the application of any passage, include the passage and depend on the remaining procedure to verify or discard that factor.

When the preceding steps are done for a study on those verses already recorded on our worksheets, the result would look something like this:

MAIN DATA WORKSHEET: PRECEPTS

Old Testament: Commands

Verse Reference	No.	Thesis	Contextual Theme	Key Words	Unknown Concepts
Lev. 19:18	157	neighbor			
Deut. 6:5	"	God	all heart, soul, etc.	might	
Deut. 10:12	"	God	"		
Deut. 10:19	"	stranger			
Deut. 11:1	"	God	keep commandments		
Deut. 11:13	"	God	promise for care		
Deut. 11:22	"	God	promise for protection		
Deut. 19:9	"	God			

Deut. 30:6	"	God			
Jos. 23:11	"	God	warning		
Ps. 31:23	"	God	preservation		
Is. 56:6	"	God	reward		
Am. 5:15	"	----	----		
Zech. 8:17	"	----	----		
Zech. 8:19	"	----	----		
Ps. 37:4	6026	God	provision		
Is. 55:2	6026	----	----		
Deut. 5:21	2530	----	----		
Deut. 7:25	"	----	----		
Prov. 3:3	2617	not	"mercy"& truth		

MAIN DATA WORKSHEET: PRECEPTS

New Testament: Commands

Verse Reference	No.	Thesis	Contextual Theme	Key Words	Unknown Concepts
Mat. 5:43	25	neighbor			
Mat. 5:44	"	enemies		bless, curse, etc.	
Mat. 19:19	"	neighbor			
Mat. 22:37	"	God	1st & greatest commandment	first, great	
Mat. 22:39	"	neighbor	2nd command.	second	
Mk. 12:30	"	God			
Mk. 12:31	"	neighbor			
Mk. 12:33	"	God		understanding	
Lk. 6:27	"	enemies			
Lk. 6:35	"	enemies	do good, lend		
Lk. 10:27	"	God/ neighbor			
Jn. 13:34	"	one another	like Christ	disciples (36)	
Jn. 15:9	26	continue			
Jn. 15:12	26	one another	like Christ		
Jn. 15:17	"	one another			
Rom. 12:9	"	w/o dissim.		dissimulation	
Rom. 13:8	25	one another	fulfilled law	fulfilled	
Gal. 5:13	26	----	----		
Gal. 5:14	"	neighbor	----		

Eph. 4:2	"	----	----		
Eph. 4:15	"	----	----		
Eph. 5:2	"	walk in	like Christ	walk	walk
Eph. 5:25	25	wives	like Christ		
Phil. 2:2	26	same love		same	
Col. 3:19	25	wives	not bitter	bitter	
I Th. 3:12	26	one another	the Lord makes	increase, abound	
Heb. 10:24	"	provoke not		consider	
Heb. 13:1	5360	continue	brotherly love		
Jas. 2:8	25	neighbor	royal law	royal	
I Pet. 2:17	"	brotherhood			
I Pet. 3:8	5361	as brethren			
I Jn. 2:15	25	not world			
I Jn. 3:11	"	one another			
I Jn. 3:23	25	one another			
I Jn. 4:7	26	one another			
I Jn. 4:11	25	one another			
II Jn. 5	"	one another			
Jude 21	26	keep in	love of God	keep	
Rom. 12:10	5387	one another		affectioned	
Col. 3:2	5426	set on above			
Col. 3:14	26	put on	bond of perfectness	put on (12)	
II Tim. 2:22	"	follow	with them that call	follow	
I Pet. 4:8	"	have	among yourselves	fervent	
I Cor. 14:1	2206	follow			
I Pet. 2:2	1971	milk of Word	"desire"		
Gal. 5:26	2755	----	----		
Jude 22	1653	----	----		

Categorize The Verses

This step is quite similar to the same operation in the thought study procedure. Our objective is the same: to organize the verses under main category headings that will enable us to view the information more systematically. There are a few peculiarities to the concept study, however, and it will be worthwhile to discuss them here.

MAKE A NEW WORKSHEET. This is not optional with the concept study because there is too much information to keep visually sorted without a new worksheet. Besides that, every concept study will generate several main data worksheets which are somewhat cumbersome to use continually. The category worksheet, if developed properly, will condense the main data worksheets considerably. The worksheet should be divided into two halves that will allow enough space for verse references and verse contextual information to be recorded on each half. It might look like this.

CATEGORY WORKSHEET: PRECEPTS	
XXX:XX ------ XXX:XX ------	XXX:XX ------

LIST THE CATEGORIES VERTICALLY. The purpose of any worksheet is to facilitate the organization and understanding of information. Since we are dealing with a multiplicity of verse references, each of which has specific information to be categorized, we should list each verse vertically, under the main heading of the category to which it is related. That will help us keep a visual separation, thereby helping us to pinpoint the relationships within each category later.

USE THE "THESIS" COLUMN AS A GUIDE. On the main data worksheet is recorded the main thesis of each verse. If that job has been done correctly, the "thesis" will be stated in one or two words. That "thesis" will be the key to establishing categories for the concept study. During the thought study, we worked a little differently in that we "invented" the categories from the combination of several "theses." In the concept study, we will use each "thesis" as a category, unless it is evident that the "thesis" is expressed by only one verse. At this early stage of organization, it is usually best to put all of the one-verse theses into a "miscellaneous" category which can be broken down later.

CONDENSE AND RECORD THE CONTEXTUAL THEME. This step is somewhat repetitive, but it is necessary if we are to condense the several main data worksheets into one or two usable category worksheets. However, this step need not be merely mechanical. Each contextual theme may itself be condensed into one or two word summaries that can be used to pinpoint the relationship of the verses later.

CATEGORY WORKSHEET: PRECEPTS

God		One another	
Deut. 6:5	heart, etc.	Jn. 13:34	like Christ
Deut. 10:12	heart, etc.	Jn. 15:12	like Christ
Deut. 11:1	keep comm.	Jn. 15:17	command
Deut. 11:13	promise	Rom. 13:8	fulfill law
Deut. 11:22	promise	I Th. 3:13	Lord makes
Deut. 19:9	walk in ways	I Jn. 3:11	message from beg.
Deut. 30:6	heart, etc.		
Jos. 23:11	warning	I Jn. 3:23	command
Ps. 31:23	promise	I Jn. 4:7	source is God
Isa. 55:6	promise	I Jn. 4:11	like Christ
Ps. 37:4	promise	II Jn. 5	message from beg.
Mat. 22:37	1st comm. heart	Rom. 12:10	kindly affectioned
Mk. 12:30	heart, etc.	I Pet. 2:17	love brotherhood
Mk. 12:33	heart, etc.	I Pet. 3:8	love as brethren
Lk. 10:27	heart, etc.	Heb. 13:1	continue in
Neighbor		**Miscellaneous**	
Lev. 19:18	as thyself	Jn. 15:9	continue in
Mt. 5:43	contrast w/ enemies	Det. 10:19	strangers
		Rom. 12:9	w/o dissimulation
Mat. 22:39	2nd command		
Mk. 12:31	2nd command	Eph. 5:2	walk in
Lk. 10:27	2nd command	Eph. 5:25	love wives
Gal. 5:14	fulfill law	Col. 3:19	"
Jas. 2:8	royal law	Heb. 10:24	provoke unto
Enemies		I Jn. 2:15	love not world
Mat. 5:44	bless/good/pray	Jude 21	keep in
		Col. 3:2	set on above
Lk. 6:27	love/do good	Col. 3:14	put on
Lk. 6:35	lend/reward		

302

Miscellaneous				
I Cor. 14:1	follow		Phil. 2:2	have some love
I Pet. 2:2	love milk of		II Tim. 2:22	follow with
	word		I Pet. 4:8	have fervent

Pinpoint The Relationships

This important step is almost identical to the process already so familiar in the thought study. The objective is the same: to establish the priorities of the logical order of the various points within a category. The slight difference is in the depth to which the relationships are pinpointed. When analyzing a single passage, the student must be quite precise in establishing the positions of priority or reason within the context of the passage. When organizing the general pattern of relationships within the precepts of a study concept, however, the student must only create a tentative pattern from which to examine later data. It would be unsound to demand certain relationships before all the data is available. It would be equally unsound to refrain from setting some tentative category relationship for its understanding. Therefore, as we follow the Biblical injunction to build "precept upon precept," we will try to develop an understandable composite of the "precepts" from which to view the "line upon line." That will come next.

RELATE EACH CATEGORY HEADING FIRST. Obviously, the first relationships to be established are those between the category headings. This is a relatively simple procedure and should take no more than a few minutes. As the category relationships are being determined, a number should be written next to the category headings to facilitate the outlining process which follows. It is beneficial to circle that number to help locate the position easily.

RELATE THE CONTEXTUAL THEMES NEXT. Once the category relationships have been established, the various contextual themes must be grouped into sub-categories. In order to prevent making another worksheet, a simple identification of sub-category relationships by alphabetical sorting is adequate. The student should work through one major category heading at a time, making sure that the sub-category contextual themes are being held to application within their own major category heading.

It is not necessary to examine each verse within a contextual theme sub-category yet. This initial work is only tentative and may well change as the study progresses. After both the "precepts" and "lines" have been organized and correlated, it will be necessary to bring each verse into sharp focus. Until then, it is only necessary to carry the relationships as far as the contextual sub-groupings.

When all the preceding work is performed, the category worksheet will look something like this:

CATEGORY WORKSHEET: PRECEPTS

God ①

Deut. 6:5	heart, etc. ⎫ ⓐ
Deut. 10:12	heart, etc. ⎭
Deut. 11:1	keep comm. ⓑ
Deut. 11:13	promise ⎫ ⓒ
Deut. 11:22	promise ⎭
Deut. 19:9	walk in ways ⓑ
Deut. 30:6	heart, etc. ⓐ
Jos. 23:11	warning ⓓ
Ps. 31:23	promise ⎫
Isa. 55:6	promise ⎬ ⓒ
Ps. 37:4	promise ⎭
Mat. 22:37	1st comm. ⓐ heart
Mk. 12:30	heart, etc. ⎫
Mk. 12:33	heart, etc. ⎬ ⓐ
Lk. 10:27	heart, etc. ⎭

Neighbor ②

Lev. 19:18	as thyself ⓐ
Mt. 5:43	contrast w/ enemies ⓑ
Mat. 22:39	2nd command ⎫
Mk. 12:31	2nd command ⎬ ⓐ
Lk. 10:27	2nd command ⎭

One another ③

Jn. 13:34	like Christ ⎫ ⓑ
Jn. 15:12	like Christ ⎭
Jn. 15:17	command ⓐ
Rom. 13:8	fulfill law ⓒ
I Th. 3:12	Lord makes ⓒ
I Jn. 3:11	message from beg. ⓐ
I Jn. 3:23	command ⓐ
I Jn. 4:7	source is God ⓒ
I Jn. 4:11	like Christ ⓑ
II Jn. 5	message from beg. ⓐ
Rom. 12:10	kindly affectioned ⓐ
I Pet. 2:17	love brotherhood ⎫ ⓐ
I Pet. 3:8	love as brethren ⎭
Heb. 13:1	continue in ⓐ

Miscellaneous ④

Jn. 15:9	continue in ⓐ
Det. 10:19	strangers ⓑ
Rom. 12:9	w/o dissimulation ⓒ
Eph. 5:2	walk in ⓐ

		Eph. 5:25	love wives } ⓑ
Gal. 5:14	fulfill law ⓒ	Col. 3:19	"
Jas. 2:8	royal law ⓓ	Heb. 10:24	provoke unto ⓐ
Enemies ②ⓐ		I Jn. 2:15	love not world ⓑ
Mat. 5:44	bless/good/ pray	Jude 21	keep in ⓐ
		Col. 3:2	set on above ⓑ
Lk. 6:27	love/do good	Col. 3:14	put on ⓐ
Lk. 6:35	lend/reward	Phil. 2:2	have some love ⓒ
Miscellaneous ④		II Tim. 2:22	follow with ⓐ
I Cor. 14:1	follow ⓐ	I Pet. 4:8	have fervent ⓒ
I Pet. 2:2	love milk of word ⓑ		

Make An Initial Outline

Once the relationships are tentatively established, it is always worthwhile to think through the reasoning process that helped establish the relationships and to record those thoughts in the form of an initial outline. There are several reasons why this step is not optional. To begin with, the "precepts" are given to us by the Lord as the initial building blocks of knowledge. We would be rather presumptuous if we did not lay the foundation before we tried to build the superstructure.

Secondarily, the mechanical discipline of composing and recording sentence outlines forces our conscious brain to think more clearly than otherwise, thereby helping us to analyze the material more carefully and assisting our memory in the retention of the material. Also, the multiplicity of information makes a greater demand on our sensitivity to the subjective assistance of the Holy Spirit. His help comes most strongly while we are actually dealing with the Scriptures themselves. The farther we get away from the words of Scripture, the more we put our own thoughts and training into focus. Therefore, we should try to record the relationships—the outline of the various thoughts, while the impressions of the Holy Spirit are still fresh on our mind. If we must interrupt our study, and the chances are excellent that we will have to, then the recorded outline will be sufficient to renew our thinking to the point of departure.

In our study on love, the worksheet for the precept categories presents a rather concise structure for our further study. The first two category priorities are set by the words of the Lord Jesus Christ Himself when He said that the first commandment was to love God, and the second was to love your neighbor. The third priority seems to be the many verses dealing with the love that the Christian brethren are to have toward each other. That is because there is so much discussion and repetition of the commandment. Those three commands to love one's enemies are really connected to the second commandment as a facet of that concept, so they would be noted as a sub-category rather than a main point. And the various "one-liners," verses which do not seem to fit easily into one of the other categories, can be placed into a "miscellaneous" section initially. The outline of precepts should look something like this:

THE PRECEPTS OF LOVE

I. The first commandment is to love God.
    A. That love is to be with the total being. Deut. 6:5; 10:12; 30:6; Mt. 22:37; Mk. 12:30, 33; Lk. 10:27
    B. That love is to express itself in obedience. Deut. 11:1; 19:9
    C. That love has many promises given for its obedience. Deut. 11:13, 22; Psa. 31:23; 37:4; Is. 56:6
    D. That love has a warning given against its neglect. Jos. 23:11

II. The second commandment is to love your neighbor.
    A. That love is to be with the same quality as you love yourself. Lev. 19:18; Mt. 22:39; Mk. 12:31; Lk. 10:27
    B. That love is to be given even to your enemies. Mt. 5:43-44; Lk. 6:27, 35

C. That love is said to fulfill the law. Gal. 5:14
D. That love is said to be the royal law.
   Jas. 2:8
III. There is a commandment to love the brethren.
   A. It is the message from the beginning.
      Jn. 15:17; I Jn. 3:11,23; II Jn. 5;
      I Pet. 2:17; 3:8; Rom. 12:10
   B. It is reflected by Christ. Jn. 13:34; 15:12;
      I Jn. 4:11
   C. It has its source with God. I Th. 3:12;
      I Jn. 4:7
   D. It fulfills the law. Rom. 13:8
IV. There are many general commandments to
    love.
   A. Some commands demand our continuance
      in love. Jn. 15:9; I Cor. 14:1; Eph. 5:2;
      Heb. 10:24; Jude 21; Col. 3:14;
      II Tim. 2:22
   B. Some commands tell us what to love.
      Deut. 10:19; Eph. 5:25; I Pet. 2:2;
      I Jn. 2:15; Col. 3:2
   C. Some commands tell us how to love.
      Rom. 12:9; Phil. 2:2; I Pet. 4:8

That outline will need refining, but it does provide an excellent base from which we can build the picture that the Scriptures will draw for us. That picture will only be complete after we have gone through the "lines" of this study. The next chapter covers that procedure.

21

ANALYZE
THE LINES

This step is nearly identical with the procedure followed for the analyzation of the precepts. The only difference occurs during the outlining procedure which will be discussed in more detail. Another look at the overall procedure will be good for review.

1. Read each verse in its context.
2. Determine the key elements in each verse.
   a. Record the main thesis.
   b. Record the contextual theme, if necessary.
   c. Record the key words, if necessary.
   d. Record the unknown concepts, if necessary.
3. Remember the purpose of the study.
4. Eliminate any verse that does not apply.
5. Categorize the verses.
6. Pinpoint the relationships.
7. Make an initial outline.

Each of these points has been amplified in the previous chapter. If necessary, check back to the appropriate section for further review.

The first four steps of this process should be considered as one continuous procedure. The main data worksheets will be the core of all the concept study and should be developed carefully. Every verse which was selected from the concordance must be examined using the criteria of steps 1 through 4. When that work is done for the "lines" of this study, the worksheet would look something like this:

MAIN DATA WORKSHEET: LINES					
Old Testament: Character/Quality					
Verse Reference	No.	Thesis	Contextual Theme	Key Words	Unknown Concepts
Lev. 19:34	157	stranger			
Dt. 10:12	"	God	requirement		
Dt. 13:13	"	----	--------		
Jud. 5:31	"	as the sun	Song of Deb.		
I Sam. 1:26	160	----	----		
II Ch. 19:2	157	----	----		
Ps. 4:2	157	----	----		
Ps. 5:11	157	----	----		
Ps. 40:16	157	love salv.		magnified	
Ps. 97:10	"	hate evil			
119:97	"	love law			
122:6	"	----	----		
Prov. 8:36	"	----	----		
Prov. 10:12	160	covers sin			
Prov. 15:17	"	better than			
Prov. 17:9	"	covers sin		seeketh	
Dan. 8:6	"	----	--------		
Ecc. 3:8	157	a time to	has a season		
Mic. 6:8	160				
Prov. 12:1	157	----	----		
Prov. 15:9	"	----	----		
Prov. 17:17	"	friend			
Ps. 40:8	2654	do will			
Ps. 1:2	2656	delight in law			
Ps. 119:16	8173	in statutes		statutes	
Ps. 112:1	2654	in comm.		command.	
Prov. 11:13	8378	only good		good	

MAIN DATA WORKSHEET: LINES

New Testament: Character/Quality

Verse Reference	No.	Thesis	Contextual Theme	Key Words	Unknown Concepts
Mt. 5:46	25	love enemies			
Mt. 10:37	5368	worthy love		worthy	
Mt. 24:12	26	----	----		
Lk. 7:47	25	% love			
Jn. 8:42	25	----	----		
Jn. 13:35	26	known love	disciples		
Jn. 14:15	25	keep comm.	love God		
Jn. 14:23	"	keep words	"		
Jn. 15:10	26	abiding love	keep comm.	abide	
Jn. 15:13	"	greatest love			
Rom. 13:10	"	works no ill		ill	
Rom. 13:10	26	fulfills law		fulfilling	
I Cor. 8:3	25	----	----	constraineth	
II Cor. 5:14	26	constrain. love			
II Cor. 6:6	"	unfeigned love		unfeigned	
Gal. 5:6	"	----	----		
Gal. 5:13	"	----	----		
Eph. 2:4	"	----	----	rooted, grounded	
Eph. 3:17	"	grounded love			
Eph. 4:2	"	----	----		
Eph. 4:15	"	----	----		
Eph. 5:28	25	----	----		
I Th. 5:8	26	----	----	root	
I Tim. 6:10	5365	money love			
I Pet. 1:22	5360	unfeigned love			
I Pet. 3:10	25	love of life			
I Jn. 2:5	26	perfected love	keeps word		
I Jn. 2:15	25	----	----		

I Jn. 3:16	26	love's example	Christ's death		
I Jn. 4:7	"	love's source	God		
I Jn. 4:10	"	love's example			
I Jn. 4:12	26	perfected love	love one another		
I Jn. 4:16	"	God is love			
I Jn. 4:17	"	perfected love	Christ's life		
I Jn. 4:18	"	fearless love			
I Jn. 4:19	25	love's reason			
I Jn. 4:20	"	false love			
I Jn. 4:21	"	love brother			
I Jn. 5:2	"	love's obedience	assurance		
I Jn. 5:3	26	love's definition	obedience	grievous	
II Jn. 6	26	love's obedience			
Rev. 2:4	26	first love	ch. at Ephes.	first, left	
Jn. 3:19	25	love of darkness	salvation	"light"	light
Jn. 12:43	"	love of praise			
Jn. 14:28	"	----	----		
Jn. 15:9	"	Father's love			
Rom. 8:37	"	----	----		
Jn. 12:25	5368	love of life		lose, keep	
Jn. 14:21	25	keep comm.		lose, keep	
Jn. 16:27	5368	----	----		
Rom. 9:22	4913	delight in law		inward man	
I Cor. 8:1	26	love edifies		edifieth	edifica.
I Cor. 13:1-8	"	love's character		4-8 all words	
I Ti. 1:5	"	love's source	doctrine	end	
Rom. 10:1	2107	heart's love	salvation		

**Categorize
The Verses**
After the main data worksheets
have been completely filled out, it
is necessary to sort through the
various kinds of "lines" and place them in a more organized and usable fashion. We have already discussed
the necessity for a new worksheet and have gone through
the several mechanical procedures involved. There is no
difference in this work. If necessary, refer back to the
appropriate section in the last chapter for a review. Here
are the steps:

1. Make a new worksheet with two main halves.
2. List the categories vertically and record each verse
   reference.
3. Use the "thesis" column as the main category guide.
4. Condense and record the contextual theme of each
   verse.

When all that work is done for the "lines" of this study,
the category worksheet should look like this:

CATEGORY WORKSHEET: LINES			
Love of law		**Kinds of love**	
Ps. 119:97	law	Jud. 5:31	as the sun — Deborah
Ps. 1:2	delight in	Mt. 10:37	worthy
Ps. 119:16	statutes	Lk. 7:47	percentage
Ps. 40:8	do will	Jn. 13:35	known/effect
Ps. 112:1	commandments	Jn. 15:10	abiding
Jn. 14:15	commandments	Jn. 15:13	greatest
Jn. 14:21	commandments	II Cor. 5:14	constraining
Jn. 14:23	words	II Cor. 6:6	unfeigned
I Jn. 5:2	obedience/assurance	Eph. 3:17	grounded
I Jn. 5:3	obedience/definition	I Tim. 6:10	money
II Jn. 6	obedience	I Pet. 1:22	unfeigned
Rom. 7:22	delight in	I Jn. 2:5	perfected
Love of people		I Jn. 4:12	perfected
Prov. 17:17	friend	I Jn. 4:17	perfected
Lev. 19:34	stranger	I Jn. 4:18	fearless
Mt. 5:46	enemies	I Jn. 4:20	false
I Jn. 4:21	brother	Rev. 2:4	first love
Jn. 15:9	Father's	I Cor. 13:13	abiding

Love of salvation		Characteristics	
Ps. 40:16	magnified	I Cor. 13:1-8	description
Dt. 10:12	God	I Cor. 8:1	edifies
Rom. 10:1	heart's love	I Pet. 3:10	love life
Jn. 3:19	contrast darkness	Jn. 12:25	"
Characteristics		**Miscellaneous**	
Ps. 97:10	hate evil	I Jn. 3:16	example
Prov. 10:12	covers sin	I Jn. 4:10	example
Prov. 15:17	better than gold	I Jn. 4:7	source/God
Prov. 17:9	covers sin	I Jn. 4:19	reason
Ecc. 3:8	has a season	I Jn. 4:16	God is love
Prov. 11:23	only good	I Tim. 1:5	source/doctrine
Rom. 13:10	works no ill	Jn. 12:43	love of praise
Rom. 13:10	fulfills law		

Pinpoint The Relationships

The development of these categories did not parallel the categories of the "precepts," but they are not supposed to. These "lines" are qualities or characteristics of the abstract concept, love. It would be difficult to relate these points to commands—unless the commands are seen as the general framework in which to apply the various qualities or characteristics. The principles established by the lines will have an identification of their own, yet will be best understood in light of the major principles of the precepts. In this concept study, the major precept category of loving God will be amplified by the characteristic of the line category, "love of law" and "love of salvation." The line categories themselves have enough independence to be treated as a topical doctrine, but have their best effect when placed in relation to the major command to which they relate.

Also, it is the nature of a "line" to be a measuring device for many "precepts." That is, some of the general "lines" will apply throughout the commands as descriptive or qualitative data which will make the commands more understandable. In our study here, the line categories of "characteristics" and "kinds of love" will be broad enough to cross into several "precepts." Immediately, we must merely pinpoint the various relationships within the "lines" and then correlate the "line" categories to the "precepts." The procedure is the same as was discussed in the last chapter. These are only two steps to take:

1. Relate each category heading first.
2. Relate the contextual themes next.

CATEGORY WORKSHEETS: LINES

Love of law (1)

Ps. 119:97	law (a)
Ps. 1:2	delight in (c)
Ps. 119:16	statutes (a)
Ps. 40:8	do will (b)
Ps. 112:1	commandments
Jn. 14:15	commandments } (a)
Jn. 14:21	commandments
Jn. 14:23	words
II Jn. 5:2 (b)	obedience/ assurance (b)
II Jn. 5:3 (b) {	obedience / definition
II Jn. 6	obedience
Rom. 7:22	delight in (c)

Love of people (3)

Prov. 17:17	friend
Lev. 19:34	stranger
Mt. 5:46	enemies
I Jn. 4:21	brother's
Jn. 15:9	Father's

Love of salvation (2)

Ps. 40:16	magnified
Dt. 10:12	God
Rom. 10:1	heart's love
Jn. 3:19	contrast darkness

Miscellaneous (6)

I Jn. 3:16	example
I Jn. 4:10	example }
I Jn. 4:7	source/God (a)
I Jn. 4:19	reason (b)
I Jn. 4:16	God is love
I Tim. 1:5	source/doctrine (a)
Jn. 12:43	love of praise

Kinds of love (4)

Jud. 5:31	as the son-Deborah
Mt. 10:37	worthy
Lk. 7:47	percentage
Jn. 13:35	known/effect
Jn. 15:10	abiding
Jn. 15:13	greatest
II Cor. 5:14	constraining
II Cor. 6:6	unfeigned
Eph. 3:17	grounded
I Tim. 6:10	money
I Pet. 1:22	unfeigned
I Jn. 2:5	perfected
I Jn. 4:12	perfected }
I Jn. 4:17	perfected
I Jn. 4:18	fearless
I Jn. 4:20	false
Rev. 2:4	first love
I Cor. 13:13	abiding

Characteristics (5)

Ps. 97:10	hate evil
Prov. 10:12	covers sins
Prov. 15:17	better than gold
Prov. 17:9	covers sin
Ecc. 3:8	has a season
Prov. 11:23	only good
Rom. 13:10	works no ill
Rom. 13:10	fulfills law
I Cor. 13:1-8	description
I Cor. 8:1	edifies
I Pet. 3:10	love life
Jn. 12:25	love life

Every concept study will develop its own peculiarities. This study seems to have an "aloofness" to the bulk of the *lines* recorded on the worksheet. That is, it seems to be difficult to organize the sections into a series of relationships. When this happens, and it is not that infrequent, it is likely that the *lines* have such strength in their own right that they will have to be treated as major points in the overall structure of the concept. The "precepts" have already been organized and will serve as a base for working with some of the "lines." However, two major categories of the *lines,* the "characteristics" category and the "kinds of love" category, seem to be so strong that they will warrant a separate treatment.

Although we have checked each verse in its own contextual setting during the analyzation stage for the main data worksheet, we have been condensing and summarizing the verses together in an effort to reduce the volume of unrelated pieces of information. That is necessary, but it also raises the possibility of verse misplacement. That is, some verses may be "nudged" into a category, or some verses may be "summarized" too tersely, with the result that the verse becomes recorded in a category to which it does not belong. There is no way to prevent that happening. But the student must be sure that each verse is re-read, in its contextual setting, before it is cited in the final outline. We may never treat the Word of God as a mere research project. We *must* take the worshipful approach of constant care as we try to unfold the information so carefully recorded by the Holy Spirit. The more one studies the Word, the more awe one gains for its accuracy and relevancy. The more awe one gains, the more care and confidence one has in the study of God's Word.

Make An Initial Outline

This is the portion of the "lines" analytical work that is more difficult than the corresponding portion of the "precept" work. To begin with, we have already noted that at least two of the line categories are strong enough to be treated as parallel major points. We must therefore treat them independently from the remaining categories. Then, the other categories must be related to the precepts if possible. That will require an integration to the appropriate "precept" in such a fashion that we will be able to recognize that relationship when we come to the final outline stage.

The best way to approach this work is as follows:
1. Outline the independent points first.
2. Identify the precept which best seems to relate to another given category.
3. Outline that given category as though it were subjugated to the precept.
4. Record any peculiar observations about the categories.

When the work is done, the information on the character and quality of love would look like this:

Kinds of love
   A.   There is abiding love. Jn. 15:10; I Cor. 13:13
   B.   There is unfeigned love. II Cor. 6:6; I Pet. 1:22
   C.   There is perfected love. I Jn. 2:5; 4:12, 17
   D.   There are comparisons to love.
       1. As the sun. Judges 5:31
       2. To a percentage. Lk. 7:47
       3. As the greatest. Jn. 15:13
       4. To the first love. Rev. 2:4
       5. To false love. I Jn. 4:20
   E.   There are the effects of love.
       1. It makes known. Jn. 13:35
       2. It makes fearless. I Jn. 4:18
       3. It makes worthy. Mt. 10:37

Characteristics of love
   A.   Love reacts to evil.
       1. It hates evil. Ps. 97:10
       2. It covers sin. Prov. 10:12; 17:9
   B.   Love follows good.
       1. It seeks only good. Prov. 11:23
       2. It works no ill. Rom. 13:10
       3. It edifies. I Cor. 8:1
       4. It loves life. I Pet. 3:10; Jn. 12:25
   C.   Love fulfills the law — Rom. 13:10
       1. The description is given. I Cor. 13:1-8

I. Love God (B. express in obedience)
   A. We are to love God's commandments.
      Ps. 119:16, 97; 112:1; Jn. 14:15, 21
   B. We are to love God's words. Jn. 14:23
   C. We are to delight in God's law.
      Ps. 1:2; Rom. 7:22
   D. We are to obey God's Word.
      1. For His will. Ps. 40:8
      2. For our assurance. I Jn. 5:2
      3. For the observance of love. I Jn. 5:3
II. Love neighbor
   A. (A. love as self)
      1. Like the friend. Prov. 17:17
      2. Like the brother. I Jn. 4.21
      3. Like the Father. Jn. 15:9
   B. (B. love the enemy)
      1. Even the stranger. Lev. 19:34
      2. Even the enemies. Mt. 5:46
   Love of Salvation
   A. Because it is in our heart. Rom. 10:1
   B. Because it magnified God. Ps. 40:16
   C. Because it is the opposite of darkness. Jn. 3:19

We now have two outline sheets that briefly summarize the "lines" of love. Those two sheets, along with the outline sheet of the precepts, must now be integrated into a complex structuring of the Bible's teaching on love. That is the subject of the next chapter.

22

DEVELOP THE PROVERBS

This stage of our work brings to fruition all of the carefully dissected information of the earlier labor. There have been flashes of insight all during the study, but as is always the case, the "light" of the truth will not — indeed, cannot shine in its full brightness until all of the data are "set in order." As we have already discovered, that admonition by Solomon in the book of Proverbs is a strong injunction to compose, or to equalize, or to correctly align a multitude of powerful sayings, all of which are based on and correlated to the Word of Truth. That must be our constant objective.

Review All Categories In the concept study, there are many different angles from which to view the truth of the study. It is therefore imperative that every student be exceptionally careful to maintain a perspective of the "big picture." That is, we must never isolate any portion of the study in such a way that it comes independent of the others. There will be some thoughts that carry such strength in their own right that we will be wise to outline and develop their content separately from other thoughts. But we must always maintain the conscious awareness of the common bond that each portion of the study has to the overall concept.

The most effective way to insure that cohesion in this kind of study is to begin the final outlining process with a careful review of all the categories. By reviewing the entire study, the student is able to pick up some connections and/or distinctions that were not apparent during earlier work. Normally, this review can be conducted mentally without the necessity of any additional notation. However, if the study is lengthy, or seems to be complex in its relationships, it is wise to make pertinent notations on an additional sheet of paper. And until a student becomes comfortable with this step, it is wise to re-outline the entire study, using only the thoughts of the study, not the Scripture references. Such an outline would look something like this:

I. There must be love for God.
   A.   That is a total love of God.
      1. It is abiding.
      2. It is unfeigned.
      3. It is perfected.
      4. It is the first love.
   B.   That is a love of obedience to God.
      1. It loves His commandments.
      2. It loves His words.
      3. It loves to obey His words.
II. There must be a love for your neighbor.
   A.   That is the same love as you love yourself.
      1. It is like a friend.
      2. It covers sins.
   B.   That is a love that extends even to enemies and strangers.

C. That is a love that fulfills the law.

D. That is a love that is called the royal law.

III. There must be a love for the Christian brotherhood.

    A. It is commanded even from the beginning.

    B. It is exampled by the Lord Himself.

    C. It has its source in God Himself.

    D. It fulfills the law.

IV. There must be a continuance in love.

V. There must be an understanding of the characteristics of love.

    A. It hates evil.

    B. It follows good.

    C. It has direct personal selflessness.

    D. It fulfills the law.

VI. There must be an awareness of the effects of love.

    A. It makes known as disciples.

    B. It makes fearless.

    C. It makes worthy.

    D. It perfects.

VII. There must be a knowledge of other commands to love.

    A. Husbands are to love their wives.

    B. We are to love the things above.

    C. We are not to love the world.

    D. We are to love the milk of the Word.

    E. We are to love unity.

This composite outline has helped solidify a few "vague" relationships that were sensed earlier. Some of the "lines" were better related as "precepts" since they were common to all commands. A few of the precepts were left alone under their various headings for further clarification in the actual outlining. However, the result has been a clearer "picture" from which to work. This outline is *not* the final authority, nor will it be the same when the process is finished. But, it does give us a firmer track on which to run through the detailed study. It is always valuable to go through that sub-step when the study is as involved as this study on love.

Separate The Individual Thought Areas This is almost a redundant step since the thought areas will have been distinguished by the composite outline. However, it is always best to set the research goals objectively, thereby eliminating much confusion during the actual progress. The main objective of this step is to identify the confines of one complete thought. Normally, that will express itself in each individual "precept," but may extend down into some of the sub-points when those points are critical to the understanding of the "precept." If a composite outline has been recorded on paper, this step is virtually complete. If only a mental review has been made, then the student should write down the main thought areas so that the development of the final outline will proceed correctly.

Develop One Thought Area At A Time It seems obvious to require this procedure, so obvious that it tends be overlooked easily. We have been stressing the necessity of maintaining a constant awareness of the "big picture" and have failed to stress the importance of studying each thought-area as a unit to itself. Although we cannot develop each thought area to the depth of detail that we would have had it been approached as an individual thought study of a passage of Scripture, we must think deeply enough to answer the natural questions and amplify the basic message of the teaching. In order to do that, we must approach the outline of each thought area within its own structure. There are some basic rules that must be followed.

1. Use the composite outline as a guide only. That work, while invaluable as a guide, must be subjugated to the Scriptures themselves. Always check throughout the remaining points for any possible relevant factor contained in other areas.

322

2. Check every Scripture reference in its context before recording on the outline. There is no excuse for short-cuts here. Each reference must be checked. If the actual wording of the text does not allow for inclusion in that thought area of the outline, note the correct application on the composite outline sheet and proceed to the next point.
3. Check every Scripture reference with the main data worksheet. Be sure to examine every questionable key word or unknown concept before deciding how to use the reference in the outline. Do not assume knowledge. Make sure that you understand and know the truth of the passage.
4. Amplify each point sufficiently to eliminate any doubt of the application to the study concept. Each point must apply to the concept under study. Therefore, each point must be made clear enough so that the reader of the outline or the hearer of the presentation will not lack an understanding of the application. This may necessitate some additional concordance research to find Biblical support or clarification.
5. Make each point in complete sentence form. The reasons for this procedure were discussed adequately in chapter fourteen. The procedure is the same as for previous outlines.

When those steps are followed for each thought area in this study on "love," these resulting outlines develop.

THE STUDY OF LOVE

I. The most important love is a love for God.
  A. That love must involve the total being.
    1. It involves the heart, soul, and might. Deut. 6:5; Luke 10:27
    2. It also involves the mind and understanding. Matt. 22:37; Mk. 12:33

3. It is commanded many times. Deut. 6:5;
   10:12; 11:1; 13:22; 19:9; 30:6; Jos. 23:11;
   Ps. 31:23; 37:41; Is. 56:6; Mt. 22:37;
   Mk. 12:30, 33; Luke 10:27

B. That love must involve obedience to God.
   John 15:10

   1. It must involve a conscious obedience
      to every portion of God's instruction.
      Deut. 11:1; Jn. 14:21

   2. It must involve a love for the Words of
      God. Jn. 14:23

      a. We must delight in them. Ps. 1:2;
         112:1; 119:16, 97

      b. We must be assured by them.
         I Jn. 2:5; 5:2

      c. We must do them without hypocrisy.
         II Cor. 6:6

   3. It must involve a desire to do God's
      will. Ps. 40:8

   4. It must involve a delight in obedience.
      I Jn. 5:3

C. That love, when given, must involve the
   blessings of God.

   1. It will bring physical prosperity.
      Deut. 11:13-15

   2. It will bring physical protection.
      Deut. 11:22-25

   3. It will bring the desires of the heart.
      Ps. 37:4

   4. It will bring confidence in service.
      Jd. 5:31

   5. It will bring joy in worship. Isa. 56:6-7

D. That love, when neglected, must involve
   the judgment of God.

   1. Neglect will produce God's cursing.
      Josh. 23:11-16; Deut. 11:26-28

   2. Neglect may cause a church to lose its
      church-hood. Rev. 2:4-5

II. The next most important love is a love for your neighbor.
    A. That love must be with the intensity and quality as love for one's own self. Mt. 22:39
        1. That involves not avenging or grudging. Lev. 19:18
        2. That involves the closeness of a friend. Prov. 17:17
    B. That love must also be directed to one's enemies. Mt. 5:43-44
        1. That involves blessing, good deeds, and prayer. Mt. 5:43-48
        2. That involves non-violent reaction to personal injury. Luke 6:27-36
    C. That love is directed even to the stranger. Lev. 19:34
        1. That involves an unknown visitor. Deut. 10:19
        2. That involves anyone in need. Luke 10:29-37
    D. That love is said to be the fulfilling of the law. Gal. 5:14
        1. That involves all the law toward others. Rom. 13:8-10
        2. That is said to be the royal law. Ja. 2:8
III. The New Testament emphasizes love for the Christian brotherhood.
    A. That emphasis was from the beginning. I Jn. 3:11
        1. That beginning was the start of Christ's ministry. I Jn. 3:23; Jn. 15:17
        2. That message is repeated by the Apostles. I Pet. 2:17; 3:8; Rom. 12:10
    B. That emphasis is reflected in the life of Christ. Jn. 13:34; 15:9, 12, 13
        1. That love has its source in God. I Jn. 4:7-11; 5:1; I Thess. 3:12
        2. That love works perfection in us. I Jn. 4:12; 20:21

C. That emphasis fulfills the law.
  1. It cannot work ill. Rom. 13:8-10
  2. It is unfeigned and fervent. I Pet. 1:22; 4:8

IV. The Scriptures provide an excellent description of love.

A. Love hates evil.   Ps. 97:10-12; 119:158-159

B. Love follows after righteousness. Prov. 11:23
  1. It covers over sins. Prov. 10:12; 17:9
  2. It edifies. I Cor. 8:1
  3. It speaks good. I Pet. 3:10-13

C. Love is selfless.   I Cor. 13:1-8
  1. It is long-spirited and fit for use. Mat. 11:28-30
  2. It is not temper prone or boastful. Acts 17:5
  3. It is not naturally swelled up. Col. 2:18
  4. It does not behave shamefully. Rev. 16:15
  5. It does not promote itself. I Cor. 10:24, 31-33
  6. It is not irritated easily. Mt. 5:38-43, 46
  7. It will not reach an evil conclusion. Phil. 4:8; Rom. 12:3
  8. It will rejoice in the truth. Ps. 119:97, 111, 127
  9. It will cover and protect things. Prov. 10:12; 17:9
  10. It will have confidence in things. I Jn. 3:18-23
  11. It will have hope and endure. Rom. 8:24-25; I Pet. 2:20

D. Love never drops away or falls.   I Cor. 13:8
  1. It never falls from steadfastness. II Pet. 3:17
  2. It never falls from the first love. Rev. 2:5

      3. It always continues. Jn. 15:10; I Cor. 13:13

   E. Love will produce effective Christian character. Jn. 13:35

      1. It will produce righteous boldness. I Jn. 4:18; II Tim. 1:7

      2. It will produce the proper life view. Mt. 10:37-39; Jn. 12:25

      3. It will produce recognition of forgiveness. Luke 7:47

      4. It will produce active help to others. I Jn. 2:17-19; 4:19-21

      5. It will produce a zeal for souls. Rom. 10:1; Ps. 40:16

V.   The Scriptures also give some special commands to love.

   A. The Christian person is to live a life of love.

      1. He is to continue in Christ's kind of love. Jn. 15:9

      2. He is to pursue love. I Cor. 14:1; II Tim. 2:22

      3. He is to walk in love like Christ does. Eph. 5:2

      4. He is to envelope himself in love. Col. 3:14

      5. He is to persuade others to love. Heb. 10:24

      6. He is to guard against leaving the love of God. Jude 21

      7. He is to consciously think about loving heavenly things. Col. 3:2

      8. He is to avoid having the things of the world. I Jn. 2:15-17

      9. He is to avoid hypocritical love. Rom. 12:9

   B. The Christian person is to love their mate.

      1. The husband is to love his wife. Eph. 5:25

2. The wife is to love her husband.
   Titus 2:4
C. The new Christian person is to love the
   milk of the Word. I Pet. 2:2
D. The Christian people are to love unity.
   Phil. 2:2; Eph. 4:1-16

The final outline has changed considerably from the initial composite outline we made at the completion of the "line" analyzation step. Those changes are the result of trying to develop a structure without fresh contextual support from the Scriptures themselves. However, that composite outline was invaluable in checking the various areas of data which needed to be correlated. During the entire final outlining process, the student will find that the presence of the Holy Spirit will be very real, and that the insights necessary to relate the material will seem to be much more readily available than before. That is because the working of God's Spirit is most poignant when we are directly involved with the words of Scripture. The more we read and study the Word of God, the more we are directed into truth by its Author.

Relate All The Thought Areas Together

This work is nearly done. If we have been sensitive to the organization which has developed throughout the entire study process, we will have structured the final outline so that the relationships between the major thought areas are easily seen. It may be worthwhile to restate the main areas in such a way that the interrelations are seen at a glance. Such a restatement might look like this:

The first priority for every person, saved or not, is to love God with their entire being. Since that is so, it follows that God's command to love your neighbor as oneself is the next priority. That command has a special application to the Christian in in the New Testament emphasis to love the brotherhood. All of these commands to love have their explanation in the many descriptions about the character of love found throughout the Scriptures.

Finally, there are a few special emphasis commands for Christian living given in the New Testament.

If the student will summarize the study in writing, the overall concept will be made clear, and the written record will prove invaluable when the study is reused at a later date.

Determine How To Use The Study

We have already discussed the basic areas to look for applications of any Bible study. They are:

1. Always apply personally.
2. Always apply professionally.
3. Always apply to your local church.
4. Always apply to teaching situations.

However, this depth of study produces such a volume of information that it is wise to examine the data with the view to developing separate applications. In this study on love, there are five major studies.

1. The study on the love of God.
2. The study on the love for your neighbor.
3. The study on the love for the brotherhood.
4. The study on the descriptions of love.
5. The study on the commands to love Christian living.

Each of these studies has applications in all of the four major application areas. And, each of these studies could be studied more deeply with individual thought studies on key passages. It is impossible to exhaust the depth of the Word of God (Rom. 11:33). This study, as exciting and revealing as it has been, has only scratched the surface of the Bible's teaching on love. Each verse cited, can be examined for its special treasure. Each idea can be explored for its teaching throughout the Scripture. In other words, we could spend many, many more hours opening up the Scriptures with the insight we have gained through this work. Let the Spirit guide you into those additional studies that He feels will be most beneficial for the ministry He has given you.

File The Study With this much information, it will be necessary to cross-file the study. That is, multiple copies of the study outline should be made, or a card index should be made that will allow the information to be filed so that it can be recalled when any number of related questions or thoughts demand it. Each of the five major study areas should be listed or filed separately. The entire study should be filed together, and some of the main sub-topics should be filed within their subject scope. Several major passage outlines could be filed under the Bible references, and a few of the points could be filed under theological categories. Whatever system, however simple or complex, this information should be stored in the most optimum manner for immediate recall when necessary. The main advantage of this kind of study is that it does not have to be redone—*if* it is permanently recorded and filed!

During the past several chapters, we have discussed the Biblical procedure for developing an accurate understanding of the main teaching of the Scriptures on a general concept. It was not possible to discuss many of the details since the procedure was so involved. However, it was possible to demonstrate the feasibility of such a study for anyone with enough patience and enough love of the truth to complete. The next chapter will provide an overview of the entire process so that you can review it more easily.

23

STRUCTURED BIBLE STUDY SUMMARY

The difficulty of this study lies in the fact that there are many variables. Each concept of the Scripture has its own uniqueness, and that demands a very careful and sensitive spirit on the part of the Bible student. Isaiah has told us that the Lord needed mature Christians to study His Word because the process was difficult. The writer of the Book of Hebrews notes that those who are "of full age" are the ones who have had "their senses exercised to discern good and evil" (Heb. 5:14). Therefore, we cannot expect to jump into the meat of the Word until we have been thoroughly nourished on the "sincere milk of the word" (I Pet. 2:2).

Purpose This study is *not* designed for systematic theologians who are trying to organize the Bible systematically. It *is* designed to assist the sincere, mature Bible student in discovering the overall teaching of the Scriptures on a given topic.

This study procedure will *not* be adequate for relating various topics together, except as those topics naturally parallel each other. A student is not at liberty to "invent" short cuts to this study methodology. He is, however, at liberty to combine some of the natural duplication in worksheets as he becomes more proficient with the work. God's Word must be handled carefully. We have been given instruction for its study from the pages of Scripture. We should follow them.

GIVE GOOD HEED

I. Perform a word analysis.
  A. Make a new worksheet providing four columns.
      1. Record the word number.
      2. Record the word spelling.
      3. Record the word definition.
      4. Record the other English translations.
  B. Examine every word related to the concept.
      1. Start with the most obvious word.
          a. Locate the key concept word in the main concordance.
          b. List all the word numbers that appear under that heading.
          c. Locate each study word by its numerical code in the appropriate language dictionary.
          d. Trace out all the information about each word.
          e. Analyze and summarize the definition.
          f. Record each leading English word that translates the Hebrew or Greek study word.
      2. Search the concordance for the other English words.
          a. Consider each other word for non-parallel applications.

      b. Scan each concordance listing to verify questionable word usage.

      c. Consider each other word in the light of the concept under study.

  C. Determine the word groups.

    1. Make a new worksheet.

    2. Find the root words.

    3. Find the derivatives. of the root words.

    4. Find the synonyms.

  D. Compare the interlingular word parallels.

    1. Make a new worksheet.

    2. Find the parallel definitions.

    3. Find the parallel translations.

    4. Find the relationships within the groupings.

  E. Summarize the word group distinctives.

II. Perform a verse research.

  A. Prepare the main data worksheet.

    1. Prepare a column for the verse reference.

    2. Prepare a column for the word number.

    3. Prepare a column for the verse thesis.

    4. Prepare a column for the contextual theme.

    5. Prepare a column for the key words.

    6. Prepare a column for the unknown concepts.

  B. Locate the precepts.

    1. Read through the concordance listings and locate the commands.

    2. Read through the main concept headings first.

    3. Read through the parallel English words next.

    4. Maintain a distinction between Old and New Testament references.

  C. Locate the lines.

    1. Follow the same basic research procedure in the concordance.

3. Look for characteristics or qualities of the precepts.
4. Do not record repetitive information.

SEEK OUT

I. Analyze the precepts.
  A. Record the main thesis.
  B. Record the contextual theme.
    1. Record the major theme of the immediate context.
    2. Record in as brief a fashion as possible.
    3. Summarize the surrounding context, if necessary.
    4. Eliminate the passage if too limited by context.
    5. Withhold passage if too vague theologically.
    6. Record only those themes that are necessary for proper understanding of the passage application.
  C. Record the key words if unknown.
  D. Record the unknown concepts if necessary for passage clarity.
  E. Constantly check the verses by the purpose of the study.
  F. Eliminate any verse that does not apply.

II. Categorize the precepts.
  A. Make a new worksheet.
    1. Prepare two columns.
    2. List the categories vertically.
  B. Use the "thesis" column on the main data worksheet as a guide.
  C. Condense and record the contextual theme next to the verse reference.

III. Pinpoint the relationships of the precepts.
  A. Relate each category heading first.
  B. Relate the contextual themes next.
IV. Make an initial outline of the precepts.

    A. Follow the procedures already established in the thought study.

    B. Make a complete sentence outline.

V. Analyze the lines.

    A. Proceed exactly as with the precept analyzation.

       1. Record the main thesis.

       2. Record the contextual theme.

       3. Record the key words, if necessary.

       4. Record any peculiar observations about the categories.

    B. Categorize the lines.

    C. Pinpoint the relationships of the lines.

    D. Make an initial outline of the lines.

       1. Integrate the lines with the precepts.

       2. Subjugate the lines to the appropriate precept.

       3. Establish separate major points for independent thoughts.

SET IN ORDER MANY PROVERBS

I. Review all the categories.

    A. Develop a composite outline of the precepts and lines.

    B. Use complete sentence outlining.

    C. Separate the individual thought-areas.

II. Develop one thought area at a time.

    A. Use the composite outline only as a guide.

    B. Check every Scripture reference in its context before recording on the final outline.

    C. Check every Scripture reference with the main data worksheet.

    D. Make any additional word studies and verse studies necessary.

    E. Amplify each point sufficiently to eliminate any doubt of the message.

    F. Make each point a complete sentence.

III. Relate each thought area to the whole concept.

    A. Review in the light of the overall teaching.

      B. Write a paragraph expressing the relationship of each main thought area to the whole concept.

  IV. Determine how to use the study.

      A. Always apply personally.

      B. Always apply professionally.

      C. Always apply to your local church.

      D. Always apply to teaching situations.

      E. Always search for additional study opportunities.

   V. File the study.

24

BIBLE COMMENTARIES

There are hundreds of Bible commentaries, perhaps thousands. There are major encyclopedia works that try to cover every verse, and there are single volume works that only skim along the surface. There are critical commentaries, and there are devotional commentaries. There are textual approaches, topical approaches, and theological approaches. Some are written by preachers, some by scholars, some by evangelists, some by scientists, some by psychologists, and some even by blatant infidels. It would be an agonizing task to catalog them, and that catalog would have only limited interest. If you were to ask ten studious men for their favorite commentary, you would likely get ten different answers. Therefore, it would be of questionable value to recommend any particular work.

However, there are some general guidelines to use for *any* commentary that will be of value to the serious Bible student. If these suggestions are followed, the information contained in commentaries will be enhanced for its positive value and protected against its error.

Study The Bible First

This important principle is not at all incidental. If a Bible student has not tried to discover the truths from the pages of Scripture, he will be completely at the mercy of the persuasive powers of the writer of the commentary. All books, except the Bible, are written by men. Every man is subject to error. Even though a Bible commentator is completely sincere, it is *likely* that he will make some error in judgment. Even if a writer is a careful student of the Word, it is *likely* that he will overlook or misjudge some points. If you have not made an effort to find out as much as you can about the Bible subject *before* you read the commentary, you will be *unable* to judge between truth and error effectively.

On the other hand, if you have performed a good study, using the Biblical study procedures outlined by Ecclesiastes 12:9 and Isaiah 28:9-10, then you will at least have a basis for judging the content of the commentary. Furthermore, you will be more keenly aware of the areas in which you need further insight. Having studied the area in the Scriptures, you are at least aware of the questions to ask. But, more importantly, you will have placed into your "heart" the words of God before you solicit the words of men. God's words are the only true absolute. They alone will provide the check by which to "discern good and evil."

Determine What Kind Of Study Is Needed

Once you have performed a Bible study, you will then be able to analyze what areas are still deficient. Perhaps, you sense a lack of understanding about the words used. It would then be advisable to consult a word study book like Vine's or Girdlestone's. Or, perhaps it would be more advantageous to consult a good linguistically oriented commentary that you have found to be helpful. Sometimes, the study of the Scriptures will reveal a need for background information on the history or culture of the passage. That would suggest the consulting of a Bible dictionary or atlas and, in some cases, a more detailed commentary on the archaeological discoveries relevant to the subject.

Whatever the case, random reading through commentaries is usually fruitless. God has given excellent insight to many men over the centuries, and we may profit from them. However, you must use the same injunctions for commentary research that you have followed for Bible research: "give good heed, seek out, set in order many proverbs." Be wise enough to select the kind of research tool to suit the need revealed by your own Biblical research.

Take Time To Record The Findings

The objective of every research project is to increase knowledge about the truth. If you do not record the findings in each project, you will have to repeat your work again. That is wasteful and discouraging. If you are following the suggestions to study the Bible before you consult a commentary, you will already have worksheets prepared on the subject you are studying. It is therefore of little additional effort to record the key points of insight gained by commentary consultation. Furthermore, it will be much more efficient to work from condensed findings later, than to have to return to the verbage of the commentary.

Always Check New Insights By The Bible

Get in the habit of checking everything written or said by man against the truth of the Scripture. The Apostle Paul commended the Christians at Berea because they were astute enough to check everything he had said by the Scriptures (Acts 17:11). We must do no less. The greatest value that the commentaries of men render to us is that they stimulate our brain to think in areas, or of possibilities about which we have not yet discovered. When the Lord has so gifted a writer to uncover an area of truth which has not been our privilege to see yet, He *still* expects us to check that truth against His Word. The chances are excellent that such a check will do two things: confirm the insight and thereby reinforce that truth in our hearts, and secondly, it may reveal more truth than either the commentator or the Bible student had discovered. Always check new insights from Bible commentators by the Bible itself.

A PERSONAL NOTE

It has been my pleasure to write this book for your help and God's glory. Every one of us has been given gifts by the Holy Spirit to use in the Lord's Kingdom for the good of His people. The Lord has graciously given me a love for His Word and a love to teach. With that love has come a growing awareness of the methodology of the Scriptures which has given my own ministry a rich pasture. My prayer is that these instructions will help you gain more true wisdom from God's Word, and in so doing you will "teach others also." May God bless you as you serve Him and seek to bring glory to His matchless Name.